. . . . *History Matters*

HISTORY

MATTERS

. . . . Contemporary Poetry

on the Margins of American Culture

IRA SADOFF

University of Iowa Press, *Iowa City*

UNIVERSITY OF IOWA PRESS, IOWA CITY 52242
Copyright © 2009 by the University of Iowa Press
www.uiowapress.org
Printed in the United States of America

DESIGN BY TERESA W. WINGFIELD

Significantly different versions of many of the essays in this book appeared in the *American Poetry Review*, *Georgia Review*, and *New England Review*.

The University of Iowa Press is a member of Green Press Initiative and is committed to preserving natural resources.

Printed on acid-free paper

Library of Congress Cataloging-in-Publication Data
Sadoff, Ira.
History matters: contemporary poetry on the margins of American culture / by Ira Sadoff.
　　p.　　cm.
Includes bibliographical references.
ISBN-13: 978-1-58729-797-7 (cloth)
ISBN-10: 1-58729-797-3 (cloth)
1. American poetry—20th century—History and criticism.　2. American poetry—21st century—History and criticism.　3. Literature and society—United States—History—20th century.　4. Postmodernism (Literature)—United States.　I. Title.
PS323.5.S23 2009　　　　　　　　　　　　　　　　2008041457
811'.540911—dc22

CONTENTS

Acknowledgments and Permissions

I AM MOST GRATEFUL to Holly Carver and Joe Parsons for their encouragement and hands-on attention to this project. I am grateful to James Weaver for his attentive, respectful eye in copyediting the manuscript. I am also grateful to the editors of the *American Poetry Review* for publishing early versions of some of these initial chapters and for giving me the freedom to express any number of controversial ideas. I am also grateful to my students at Colby College, who provided both inspiration and intellectual curiosity in many of our discussions of contemporary poetry. And of course I'm most grateful to my wife, Linda, who not only encouraged me but read endless revisions of most of these pieces without complaint, which is more than I can say for myself.

"April 3," by Cole Swensen, from *Such Rich Hour* (Iowa City: University of Iowa Press, 2001), used by permission of the publisher.

"Black Nikes," by Harryette Mullen, from *Sleeping with the Dictionary* (Berkeley: University of California Press, 2002), used by permission of the publisher.

"Brutal Lesson," by Arthur Vogelsang, from *Left Wing of a Bird* (Lexington, KY: Sarabande Books, 2003), used by permission of the publisher.

"Dear Ears, Mouth, Eyes, and Hindquarters," by Diane Williams, from *Colorado Review* (Summer 2001), used by permission of the author.

"Dispatches: Journals," by Olena Kalytiak Davis, *The Poetry Foundation*, http://www.poetryfoundation.org/dispatches/journals/2006.01.30.html, used by permission of the author.

"dogs and boys can treat you like trash, and dogs do love trash," by D. A. Powell, from *Cocktails* (St. Paul, MN: Graywolf Press, 2004), used by permission of the publisher.

"Late Ripeness" and "Hanging Gardens," by Czesław Miłosz, from *Second Space* (New York: Harper Collins, 2004), used by permission of the publisher.

"Like plumb birds along the shore," by Lyn Hejinian, from *My Life*, ©1980, 1987 by Lyn Hejinian. Reprinted with the permission of Green Integer Books, http://www.greeninteger.com.

"Meteorology," by James Galvin, from *Elements*, ©1988 by James Galvin. Reprinted with permission of Copper Canyon Press, http://www.coppercanyonpress.org.

"Natural Woman," by Judith Taylor, from *Curios* (Lexington, KY: Sarabande Books, 2000), used by permission of the publisher.

"No More Marriages," by Linda Gregg, from *Too Bright, to See* (St. Paul, MN: Graywolf Press, 1987), used by permission of the publisher.

"On Rachmaninoff's Birthday," by Frank O'Hara, from *The Complete Poems of Frank O'Hara* (Berkeley: University of California Press, 1995), used by permission of City Lights Publishers.

"Phantom Pains," by Dean Young, from *Design with X* (Middletown, CT: Wesleyan, 1988), used by permission of the publisher.

"September," by Joanne Kyger, from *As Ever: Selected Poems* (New York: Penguin, 2002), used by permission of the publisher.

"Stereo," by Anne Waldman, from *Marriage: A Sentence* (New York: Penguin, 2000), used by permission of the publisher.

"the unbosoming" and "the lais of long lost days . . . ," by Olena Kalytiak Davis, from *shattered sonnets, love cards, and other off and backhanded importunities* (New York: Bloomsbury, 2003), used by permission of the publisher.

"Wild Gardens Overlooked by Night Lights," by Barbara Guest, from *Fair Realism* (Los Angeles: Sun & Moon, 1989), reprinted with the permission of Green Integer Books, http://www.greeninteger.com.

. . . . *History Matters*

INTRODUCTION

Tomorrow would alter the sense of what had already been learned.
                                   —JOHN ASHBERY, "Soonest Mended"

THIS BOOK PROJECT BEGAN as an essay on jazz and poetry called "Inside/Out," drawing parallels between poetry and improvisatory music, specifically artists who both work inside the boundaries of "the tradition" and those who play "outside," without fixed signposts, what we sometimes call free jazz. In the essay I pursued correspondences between music and poetry because both arts provide aesthetic and philosophical models for how and why art moves us as readers and listeners, but they also provide strategies for artistic creation. Whether as artists we willfully choose an aesthetic or not, our aesthetic values are inevitably formed by the stimulation other contemporary artists provide us, by the history of the art, and by ideas and values that have interest and currency in the culture at large. That we live and write in history, which is the central conviction of this book, is both obvious and provocative: the so-called culture wars locate but also reduce and blur complex arguments about human nature, the nature of identity, the permeable relationships between the individual and the social world, the spiritual and material. These conflicts ultimately suggest disagreements about the function of art: to preserve culture or to interrogate it.

I maintain that our concerns, our discourse, and our sense of form are all subject to the pressures of the culture in which we live. In the twentieth and twenty-first centuries, scientific, psychological, and sociological theorizing gesture toward flux, relativity, and entropy, from Albert Einstein to Werner Heisenberg to recent studies about the mutability of personality. Philosophers like Jacques Derrida and Michel Foucault interrogate all systems of knowledge, including science itself, as ideological: knowledge, for them, serves as a regime of power. In this more complex social world, our understandings about what it means to be an individual, to maintain a stable identity, have also changed. What we desire turns out to be far from an interiorized or spiritualized experience that can be teased out or even momentarily deciphered.

Similacrum, as posited by Jean Baudrillard and Gilles Deleuze, is in some way the fulcrum of postmodernism: experience is not only subjective but also indirect; the forces that constitute the self are so multiply replicated, the word "self" is depleted of meaning. Identity is a convenient social fiction. These cultural pressures, these shifts in bodies of knowledge, influence the terms of poetic thinking and experience. We might consider love and beauty as universals, but the particulars of those experiences, increasingly in a globalized culture with speedy communication and an assault of sensory data, will obviously be drawn from and affected by our public as well as our private lives. So those words "love" and "beauty," just by example, have different significations for us than they did for John Donne and Andrew Marvell.

One philosophical question our age requires of us and our art, then, is how do we meet these changes? In the past two decades, the increased interest in religion and the attempt to emphasize correspondingly stable institutions—marriage, the myth of creation—in our culture have certainly provided conservative alternatives and resistance to secular and material engagement; the recurrence of interest in Buddhist sects and less-rigorous popular self-help books that rely on *being present* and *staying in the moment* points to our heightened discomfort in inhabiting our culture. These expressions of longing—this desire to bring peace, wholeness, and retreat from entropy and a great cultural emptiness—are not surprising. How could these concerns as well as others —feelings of helplessness, for example, feeling small and lost—not appear with greater frequency in our artistic work now?

All the poets discussed in *History Matters* engage in a conversation about the import of history and the forces of change. Either by acts of resistance, resignation, or reconciliation, they grapple with experiential and artistic change. While avant-garde artistry often develops out of resistance to a dominant culture, much adventurous and engaged writing simultaneously explores, extends, appropriates, and interrogates that literary and cultural milieu. In the present moment, much adventurous writing occurs on the margins of representation and the postmodern, those binaries we associate with the tradition and the avant-garde. Artists like Igor Stravinsky and Pablo Picasso constantly reinvented themselves, continually responding to their artistic, intellectual, and cultural environments, making use of but not being enslaved by new artistic movements like modernism, futurism, and surrealism; parenthetically, at a time when white artists made use of the sudden visibility of African culture in the early 1900s (African sculpture for Picasso, jazz for Stravinsky), they also shared—for better and for worse—a mutual romance with the primitive. T. S. Eliot's early avant-garde work was influenced by F. H. Bradley's philosophical views. I think this same intellectual curiosity holds true for many of our most inventive poets; these artists on the margins all reflect on experience as mobile, which is to say they make themselves available to how experience continually alters us. This kind of innovation provides a temporal syntax, which in music we experience note by note and in poetry word by word as the work of art develops by associative logic; in a larger sense, that syntax simply means building on personal and artistic history: extracting what's useful about the past and attentively revising those views as experience continues to unfold.

Many avant-garde poets also regard language as performative—that is, poems enact experience rather than reproduce or summarize it representationally. For these writers, a poem, like experience itself, is a process in motion, not movement toward closure and resolution through illumination. Many of the poets included here have benefited from that mobile perspective, leading to more open-ended poems, emphasizing a poetry less thematically and more dramatically centered. By tracking some key figures in modern and contemporary American poetry, I hope to argue that their flexible and often associative imaginations reflect and respond to our age: in both worldviews and artistic practices, they dramatize flux, contingency, and the volatility and instability of the self; they also reflect those stances in the plasticity of their syntax, in their use of collage or disjuncture, in their willingness to break down the artifice of the fourth wall in poetry and the fiction of the lyric as a coherent substitute voice for the poet. These poets are also influenced by aspects of the outside tradition, in either free verse or a bastardized or original transformation of received form that reflects the density, contingency, and sometimes the required irony of contemporary experience.

Certainly every age and art form has its conservators, accomplished poets whose obsessions and devotion to craft flourish within the bounds of the dominant conventions of the culture; the most accomplished of these poets manage to write moving poems because of the breadth and scope of their imaginations, the eccentricity of their diction, and their capacity to formally surprise. But these poets, most of whom are fifty years old or older, are not part of my current project and others have written well about their accomplishments. I have no wish to lay claim as to who writes the best or worst poetry today. Nor will I suggest anything like school of *margins* poetry as if the poets represented here had a single project. Rather, I believe that poems require acknowledgment and integration of their literary antecedents because poets compose in a medium that makes reference to their linguistic as well as personal experience: the range of the poets here shows remarkable diversity in their allegiances to that history. All the poets whose work I admire here also interrogate that history, and to varying degrees they advance it, both conceptually and in their praxis. I underline virtues of this adventurousness, and a consciousness of history, literary and cultural, and will frame some of those poems in those aesthetic and historical contexts.

I will also concentrate on some of the difficulties and consequences of resisting historical change in favor of stabilizing literary conventions. In the first chapter, I elaborate on how those conventions are primarily representational, emphasizing form as a fixture. Their dominant mode is the voice poem, which both depends upon identification with a lyric speaker and harmony among the poem's moving parts: so-called organic unity. Among representational poets, one finds significant discussion about the value of clarity, accessibility, and universality, but rarely will those poets investigate the ideological assumptions behind those terms. And for those representational writers in contemporary culture who still cling to the values of romanticism, depending on the fleeting illuminations of a heightened individual in a world where the individual "I" has been rendered relatively powerless, the resulting work is often melancholy, alienated, replete with stasis and resignation. Many poets and critics have already interrogated the limits of confessional or so-called postconfessional poetry; my critique of this kind of voice poem here is its lack of scope, its reliance on the "I" as a unitary self, and the consequential narcissism of aggrandizing sensitivity or victimization.

As for those who retain the formal conventions of the British enlightenment, end-rhyming iambic meter, the resultant poems often suffer from literariness in its worst configuration: a ghostly replication of a music and system of values that were once vital and integral to another culture (Walt Whitman first addressed this issue in his 1855 preface to *Leaves of Grass*). One wonders how poets now can reflect on current artistic and personal experience using either the modernist aesthetic of Robert Frost (the poem as a "momentary stay against confusion") or the transcendent harmonies of the New Critical paradox, when those literary values grew out of their own historical experience. To use another example regarding rhythm and meter as signposts of form, while we certainly enjoy the formal meters of Johann Sebastian Bach today, we would surely never compose like him.

In the case of modernism, the barbaric and inchoate experience of World War I served to underline the failure of the already nostalgic pastoral values of romanticism. For the New Critics, their ideas about harmony and transcendence and their standards for universal masterpieces—in short, their ideology (although contemporary formalists protest "theory" as if they were exempt from systems of value)—developed in a culture that was racially segregated and masculine: other voices and the rhythms that accompanied them were devalued or invisible. There were essentially only two sources for poetic speech and music: William Wordsworth's mythic "common man" or the ornate diction favored by the late Victorians and the Pre-Raphaelites.

As poetry in America has become more and more marginalized, virtually absent from major cultural forums, we encounter yet another cultural transformation that alters how we speak and who we address in our art. In Whitman's and Emerson's America, the poet was the privileged spokesperson for the self and the country: hence, the idea of the American poet as visionary, best exemplified in Emerson's 1844 essay "The Poet," where Emerson asserts that the poet

> stands among partial men for the complete man, and apprises us not of his wealth, but of the commonwealth. The young man reveres men of genius, because, to speak truly, they are more himself than he is. They receive of the soul as he also receives, but they more. Nature enhances her beauty to the eye of loving men, from their belief that the poet is beholding her shows at the same time. He is isolated among his contemporaries, by truth and by his art, but with this consolation

in his pursuits, that they will draw all men sooner or later. For all men live by truth, and stand in need of expression. In love, in art, in avarice, in politics, in labor, in games, we study to utter our painful secret. The man is only half himself, the other half is his expression.[1]

We have much less faith in the stability of correspondences between humanity and nature; we no longer reside in an agrarian culture, and most of us visit nature much the way tourists visit the tropics. We no longer share Emerson's faith in universality or the value of expression ("half a man"). How likely, then, is it that a contemporary poet will feel that kind of ultimate authority in his or her voice? When conservative and populist writers maintain that poetry can create a greater audience in the culture if the work is memorizable or more accessible, they betray a kind of naïve omnipotence: it is frankly not within the contemporary poet's power to influence our culture with that kind of authority now. So in sections of this book I try to address the question of audience implicitly acknowledging those cultural changes. Simply put, when we are listened to, we speak with more authority. When we are not, our discourse is privatized, often more resigned; or, in more repressive regimes (most obviously during social realism in the Soviet Union, but true of virtually all such regimes) artists find themselves in more polar ways resisting or acceding to the dominant culture. The relatively middle-class "I" in a particular American poem of our age is often forced to negotiate the seemingly unbridgeable distance between the personal and the social; the cultural forces that penetrate the "I" either seem like mere abstractions (like "globalization") or seem empty or unpleasant (increasingly materialistic, puritanical in its dualistic obsession with sexuality—shame and titillation). Experience, therefore, appears necessarily more privatized, or in the case of those moved by injustice, often formally and in terms of treatment of subject, willful and predetermined.

Words are the poets' medium, like paint; they are the vehicles of consciousness and always circumscribe our vision of the world. If we efface the differences between words and the world we miss the self-conscious pleasure of process, the being and becoming as well as the arrival. We also uncritically accept the conventions that pressurize our thinking. Energetic art reflects the complexity of its age and tests it. It teaches us to be voracious, to absorb and appropriate, to argue with ourselves and our past, but also to leap off of the known, to be open to possibility and not to merely enact unexamined law. Lyn Hejinian says that form is "dynamic" and language represents "a great curiosity,"[2] and more poets associated with the avant-garde and those associated with more mimetic poetry are crossing over, challenging their own previous assumptions about the art, transgressing the strictures of inside or outside writing.

Many of the poets whose work I discuss in *History Matters* remind us that we don't have to choose between mimetic writing and "a self transformed by language," any more than we have to choose between "word" and "world": those distinctions, echoed by avant-garde poets and conservative poets alike, lack rigor and discrimination. Historically speaking, while doctrinaire proponents of the avant-garde create works of art as illustrative, as exemplar, or as a systematic act of will (which is why André Breton's surrealist poetry is less moving than either Robert Desnos's or Paul Eluard's, or why Coltrane's a more sustaining artist than Ornette Coleman, or why Salvador Dali and Réné Magritte repeat the same strategies in painting after painting), those working on the margins, those borrowing and altering artists, manage to create models of imaginative freshness and transformation. Finally, the passionate integrity of their art requires them to reflect in their praxis a willingness to engage, probe, and play in a world that begs for us to inhabit and not resolve it, where the extremes of pleasure and pain will not be managed or tamed but rather dramatized and lived.

1.

....

ON THE MARGINS

Verse Poems

NO OTHER ART FORM clings to representation—what we think of in fiction as realism—like mainstream poetry. In visual art, figurative painting—representation's equivalent—has fallen in and out of favor regularly since Paul Cézanne, and painting has shifted from abstraction to cubism to expressionism and back. Classical music has abandoned and occasionally returned to tonality; modern dance has made ample use of abstraction since Isadora Duncan, from Merce Cunningham's chance collaborations with John Cage to Alvin Ailey, Paul Taylor and Twyla Tharp and beyond; and contemporary theater routinely blends realism with surrealism and the absurd.

Representational poetry is built on the metaphors of dream and narcosis: it provides the pleasure of suspension of disbelief and recreated characters and events. In a lyric poem, representation depends upon a reader's desire to identify the speaker with the poet, placing great faith in verisimilitude. It assumes, too, that conscious or self-conscious use of the medium (language) will distract from and diminish a reader's experience. Although one can posit any number of theories as to the persistence of representation in poetry, one factor might be connected to poetry's diminishing role in culture. Although it seems naïve to believe poets have the power to alter historical, economic, and social circumstances well beyond their control, many poets worry about difficulty further depriving them of an audience—so a new wave of well-meaning populizers like Garrison Keillor and Robert Richman promote clarity and directness, advocating the fiction of accessibility and authenticity. I say fiction for obvious reasons: experiences are filtered through consciousness, so no memory actually recreates experience or escapes subjectivity or distortion. And when narrating memories we select some details, omit others. Secondarily, it is difficult to imagine how the many competing truths of modern life and the increasing complexity of an individual's relationship to language and the world can be portrayed directly without seriously reducing experience.

Arguments about representation present a vexing question: by what means are we moved in art? How are we changed? Is it by our stories, themes, and the music behind them, or are those changes more unconsciously and irrationally rendered by the present-tense encounter with language and the unfolding arrangement of the words themselves? In music (despite the "programmatic"), we're clearly moved by the medium and not by subject or story. In poetry, though, two legitimate but contrary aesthetic stances shape the controversy: those who wish to advance the art form and those who wish to conserve it. Further, those poets who write representationally believe either in universal truths or in the romantic convention of illuminated and heightened moments. Avant-garde poets, for the most part, believe in the fluidity and relativity of truths about form and experience (Lyn Hejinian's essay "The Rejection of Closure" articulates this point of view). Most poets actually fall somewhere between these two extremes, but the central focus of most of these essays will explore the territory of poets who make use of avant-garde techniques without fully abandoning the above-mentioned pleasures of representation.

There is a truism about art that systematizers do not produce the most textured and suggestive art; perhaps it is an arguable truth, but the poets under discussion here have created moving poems of surprising depth and imagination by absorbing those aspects of literary history they can use and then extending them. These artists make use of image, metaphor, music, and narrative, but they also deploy modernist and postmodernist techniques: collage, fissure, multiple voices, and an unfolding syntax that explores and resists cohesion. I make no value judgment about those who work inside the tradition, but artists like Picasso and Stravinsky provide models of artists who went out of their way to see the world freshly, not to repeat themselves, changing artistic strategies when their view of experience changed. They continued to reinvent themselves, learning from— among others—contemporary movements in their arts: impressionists, dadaists, cubists, the surrealists, "the primitives," and neoclassisists. As a result there's no *one* Picasso or Stravinsky, which is one reason why we can be constantly surprised by the body of their work. In poetry, too, we can learn from responding to the historically altering medium as well as the wildness (imagination) and the kind of extension that comes from long-reaching and difficult connections and gaps at least as much as from the pleasures and comfort of shapeliness we find in a more-traditional lyric or narrative poetry.

Many contemporary avant-garde writers believe that writing is performative, that drama and feeling emanate more from the words themselves and their placement rather than from their signification, their rhetorical or symbolic content. After all, poems are made of words: the effect of a poem comes from the arrangement, sounds, dictions, and imaginative perceptions in and behind the words. The so-called L-A-N-G-U-A-G-E poets are often conflated with (and blamed for) all avant-garde writing, even though they belonged to a specific writing community for a brief time in the early 1970s and were named L-A-N-G-U-A-G-E poets by a hostile critic. That they theorized their aesthetic made more traditional poets even more hostile, even though the theorizing premise behind much representational writing is formalist or New Critical; that writers like Lyn Hejinian, Rae Armentrout, and Bob Perelman are as different from one another as Robert Duncan is from Allen Ginsberg also seemed lost on more defensive poets and critics. Arguments against L-A-N-G-U-A-G-E writing included its self-reflexivity, obscurity, and overdose of intellection. Their poems were elitist, self-conscious, self-referential, and, once you understood them, repetitive: language was their only subject. Furthermore, critics of L-A-N-G-U-A-G-E writing maintained that it is impossible to escape signification: our associations with words and things are often lightning fast: otherwise we wouldn't be able to communicate with one another at all.

I remember voicing many of those same concerns. It's been more than twenty-five years since I attended a talk titled "The Lyric Speaker," given by poet Bob Perelman. But one section of the talk critiqued William Stafford's well-known plain-style voice poem, "Traveling through the Dark," which had been formative in teaching me how to write. In retrospect, it is easy to see what drew me to the poem. Most of us begin writing poems as vehicles of self-expression: we tell stories and want to suggest their import. The poem's images were clear and pointedly observed; the structure, transparent; its sentiments, seemingly noble (read as my own) and respectful of the environment. The talk drew attention, though, to two problems with representational lyric poems like Stafford's: first, the narcissism of the lyric "representative" speaker: the romantic lyric always places him at the center of all knowledge, wisdom, and sensitivity ("I thought hard for us all . . . /

then pushed over the edge into the river"); second, like all representational poems, the truth of the poem is not so much enacted or lived but reported, mediated, and summarized. The resultant experience is more of a product than a process: it is packaged and compartmentalized. The drama (and therefore the emotional volatility) of the poem happens before and after we get to the illumination. The harmonies of the Stafford poem now seem to me too facile, the easy reversal of nature and machine (the "doe a heap," "the car purring") too clever and symmetrical, the ironies too neat. Oddly, one justification for this kind of writing is as poetry of "self-discovery." Whatever else the joys of "Traveling through the Dark," it is hard to imagine its making many discoveries. Stafford's poem could have used a second voice unraveling the man-versus-machine myth, questioning his moral authority when the speaker has just gotten out of a car. Then the poem might have put to the test its claims about where grief ends and resignation begins ("It is usually best to roll them into the canyon" and "my only swerving").

In the intervening years since I discovered that poem, I've become less interested in a poem of reportage, to quote Lowell, one that "say[s] what happened."[1] Partly out of faith in the medium of poetry, I find myself responding more to imaginative and linguistic surprise and transformation than to "wisdom" and illuminated truths. If I can articulate a poem's strategies, its design, its conceptual meaning, or its theme too quickly, I know only my intellect and ego have been engaged: it tells me what I already know and, in most cases, agree with. Some representational poems, like Stafford's, feel that way to me, and many others don't. If I want to be moved by a poem, the poem itself generally must be *moving*, which is to say mobile, emotionally, linguistically, and syntactically. I may have come to this view in part because reading so many representational poems over the years has made their strategies begin to seem predictable. As Stanley Elkin once quipped to me in a conversation about science-fiction stories, either we go there or they come here. Either this happened to me or them and then this—in image or statement—is the consequence of that drama or plot. The fiction of "sincerity" and "the real"—the vehicles of persuasion in the Stafford poem—is one important voice for our poems, but surely it is not the only one. More crucially, I have come to believe that we are changed by what we witness and experience directly, not so much by what we recollect, picture, resolve, or instruct. I find myself drawn to poems that seem to reflect more of the world where we actually reside: a world of great speed, a world suspicious of truth and ideology, a world where the medium can be acknowledged and explored as artifice as well as be seamlessly invisible. I often admire a poem unfolding and snagging before my eyes, including sometimes breaking through the fourth wall (the fiction of narrative event), or one that layers contrary voices and actively wrestles with cohesion and difference. And one reflects and interrogates fixity as a metaphysical and verbal experience.

Although Joanne Kyger's work is too various for a sweeping overview (she is one poet whose style has evolved and transformed from her early days, associated with the Beats and the Black Mountain poets), her poems are almost always simultaneously straightforward and prismatic, serious and playful, representational and self-conscious about process and changes of mind. She uses the geography of line often as a musical measure, a pause, or an aside. Her layering of contending voices, though, experientially brings the reader with her. The colloquial elements and her emphasis on the valences of diction reflect Jack Spicer's and the New York school's influence, but they also reflect an integrated absorption of Zen. The poem "September," written in 1973, contains elements of traditional narrative but also breaks with both sequence and the univocal voice.

> The grasses are light brown
> and ocean comes in
> long shimmering lines
> under the fleet from last night
> which dozes now in the early morning
>
> Here and there horses graze
> On somebody's acreage
>
> Strangely, it was not my desire
>
> that bade me speak in church to be released
> but memory of the way it used to be in
> careless and exotic play
>
> when characters were promises
> then recognitions. The world of transformation
> is real and not real but trusting.

Enough of the lessons? I mean
didactic phrases to take you in and out of
love's mysterious bonds?

Well I myself am not myself

and which power of survival I speak
for is not made of houses.

It is inner luxury, of golden figures
that breathe like mountains do
and whose skin is made dusky by stars.

The poem begins mimetically enough through the first two stanzas (except for the foreshadowing of "long shimmering lines," which introduces suggestions of both poetry and composition), and is enlivened by the syntax and breath rhythms until the line "On somebody's acreage." All of a sudden the poet's confidence in naming and placing falters—here the poem interrupts itself to question its "intentions": the diction shifts too, with the elevated word "desire." At this point the interruption forces the reader to suspend the narrative, though our curiosity is raised: perhaps she didn't want to describe—she's turning away from nature, from the exterior world to the interior. But she takes a narrative leap that moves us to the past, to the church voice of the repressive and archaic "bade." It turns out that the present-tense sequence in nature is Edenic, a place of "careless and exotic play," a call away from the institutional, the spiritual wrenched from the natural (as landscape and as in spontaneous). The reader at this point suspends judgment, doesn't quite know what to make of the flashback or change of voice. The abstract meditation that follows metaphysically registers the import of those changes. Memory is tricky, the lines suggest: the nostalgia for the past as possibility, as the unfamiliar becoming familiar, is both real and Maya. But the speaker is not satisfied with any New Critical wisdom about the scene: the postmodern moment in the poem interrupts the poem in midthought: "Enough of the lessons?" The judgments are temporal, a form of removal as well as engagement from "love's mysterious bonds." In other words, the easier connections the speaker has tried to register won't suffice to enliven, to keep her in the perpetual now.

The curious intensifying and shifting of the mystery of the poem comes from the colloquial "Well" followed by how she is implicated in this shifting landscape of the temporal and eternal: the iambic "I myself am not myself" is simultaneously Eastern and Western: it expresses both alienation and distance and at the same time it acknowledges the difference between identity temporal (in the body) and what "survives" (not for houses, the house of the body).

It is difficult not to think of Whitman's "Crossing Brooklyn Ferry" or other "Eastern" Whitman poems as predecessors here. This lyrical overflowing allows the speaker to see the material world differently—the poem has brought us somewhere new by its changes of stance and dictions, by its shifting music (from the iambic to the anapestic to the more prosaic abstract diction of stanza 5 which cues the reader to the speaker's rejection of those lines as a resting place). The speaker is surprised then by the expansion of her vision: in short, the speaker now sees more beginnings of "souls" in the present, not in some Edenic origin (read as Christian paradise). The tortoise on the shore of this poem becomes an apt metaphor for the body carrying the soul in its sleigh: September, mythically a time of moving away from origins and spring, carries with it its own song, leaving the speaker feeling blessed because she is inhabiting the world differently than she did at the beginning of the poem. And Kyger's choice to inhabit rather than to resolve, to interrogate the poem's premises, to break into multiple tonalities and voices, vastly expands her resources as a poet.

James Galvin's early work, allied with the neosurrealists, was influenced—as with many of his generation—by W. S. Merwin's work in *The Lice* and *The Carrier of Ladders*. Very soon thereafter, though, he found his own gifts, and as his writing became more individuated, it also became more adventurous: sometimes foregrounded language. His poem "Meteorology" offers as one of its subtexts language itself. The poem suggests assertion and indirection, evasion and the power of the irrational, the heart and its accompanying hurt. The emotion is powerful enough so it cannot be addressed directly, and since it cannot be authentically resolved in its closure, the poet refuses to do so. The deception that the speaker names is also self-reflexive. The poem is wildly associative and imagistic: feeling syntactically accrues and intensifies as the poem changes its mind, as it moves closer or further from the poem's softer and more idealized assertions. The poem sees as its failure and its authenticity as its inability to match up its figures, its metaphors with its heart. The motives: deception, the desire to romanticize, history itself. After all, the meteor falls to the earth and burns out: the poem is a study of that arc.

> The heart is such a big awkward girl,
> I think it's a paper cup of gasoline.
> The floor dozes off when I walk across it.
> And the windows turn opaque
> When they are sure no one is around.
>
> At night when no one sees them
> Lovers write each other's names
> With black volcanic stones
> On the white salt flats.
> There were slamming doors and flowers,
>
> A cup of milk left on the stove too long.
> There was all the wind in Wyoming.
> No one saw anything.
> We were not evil enough to make decisions,
> But able to let things happen
>
> Evil enough.
> We are learning that weather
> Is always merciless—
> Even if you don't mean weather—
> Even the best days.

The first two lines war with one another: the image of the awkward "girl" as shy and vulnerable transforms into volatility and danger. The speaker's indecision and the imaginative gap between the two perceptions create tension and surprise, alerting the reader to the poem's ongoing process. The surreal personifications (the claustrophobia of the moving floor, the closed-down windows) serve to suggest the speaker's paranoia and unreliability, as well as the lack of stability—or visual field—in the domestic sphere.

In the lines that follow, the poem seems to dismantle the figures' idealized writing each other's names in volcanic rock (permanent? archaic?) with domestic neglect. Crucially, "no one saw anything" as the great nothing of wind or fate swept over them. Small and helpless the figures, but the speaker finally cannot bring himself to face his own language, the language as metaphor that is a coefficient and distant substitute for engagement, for seeing, for owning up. So the poem ends up not with the illumination of the new critical paradox but with an acknowledgement that the correspondences in both the couple and the language do not match up and cannot be spoken of. The poem straddles the representational and the foreground of its medium, language, to make for a concentrated and passionate poem that anoints both expression and repression.

Barbara Guest often broke up representation with jagged and surprising syntax and often viewed her poems in terms of shapeliness and composition. In interviews she made clear her allegiance to modernism's exemption from experience, but some of her later poems resisted that willful authority. In *Fair Realism* she directly confronts the temptation and desire to gravitate to the known, to the light, to knowledge, and away from the fear of ecstasy, death, and the uncultivated, or as she calls the desire for legibility in "Wild Gardens Overlooked by Night Lights," "the grip of realism." She confronts the modernist temptation (her origins) to replace the wild gardens with color (the sensory form of art), as well as the comforting sequence of narrative.

Wild gardens overlooked by night lights. Parking
lot trucks overlooked by night lights. Buildings
with their escapes overlooked by lights

They urge me to seek here on the heights
amid the electrical lighting that self who exists,
who witnesses light and fears its expunging,

I take from my wall the landscape with its water
of blue color, its gentle expression of rose,
pink, the sunset reaches outward in strokes as the west wind
rises, the sun sinks and color flees into the delicate
skies it inherited,
I place there a scene from "The Tale of the Genji."

An episode where Genji recognizes his son.
Each turns his face away from so much emotion,
so that the picture is one of profiles floating
elsewhere from their permanence,
a line of green displaces these relatives,
black also intervenes at correct distances,
the shapes of the hair are black.

Black describes the feeling,
black is recognized as remorse, sadness,
black is a headdress while lines slant swiftly,
the space slanted vertically with its graduating
need for movement,

Thus the grip of realism had found
a picture chosen to cover the space
occupied by another picture
establishing a flexibility so we are not immobile
like a car that spends its night
outside a window, but mobile like a spirit.

I float over this dwelling, and when I choose
enter it. I have an ethnological interest
in this building, because I inhabit it
and upon me has been bestowed the decision of changing
an abstract picture of light into a ghost-like story
of a prince whose principality I now share,
into whose confidence I have wandered.

Screens were selected to prevent this intrusion
of exacting light and add a chiaroscuro,
so that Genji may turn his face from his son,
from recognition which here is painful,
and he allows himself to be positioned on a screen,
this prince as noble as ever,
songs from the haunted distance
presenting themselves in silks.

The light of fiction and light of surface
sink into vision whose illumination
exacts its shades,

The Genji when they arose
strolled outside reality
their screen dismantled,
upon that modern wondering space
flash lights from the wild gardens.

The poem begins with an almost objectivist description of limited visibility of a city at night. But two key pieces of diction—"overlook" and
"escape"—carry the density of the subjective lyric. To oversee is also to
overlook; the escapes are fire escapes but they syntactically foreshadow
one motif of the poem, the desire to escape the instability (darkness) of the
world and the text. "Amid the electrical lighting" the voice is tempted to
look for "that self who exists," joining that fictive self with one who fears
the "expunging" of light, which signifies here excising and erasure and also
resonates with exacting from the writing process its desire to define and fix.

Her first attempt to replace the puzzling natural/civilized landscape is
with a painting whose "expression" represents light and color, but art too
gravitates toward dissolution, reaches outward, flees into the delicate skies
it inherited (the fleeting temporal), and, just as in the preceding stanza, the
ineffable overtakes the poem. When surfaces and color fail her, she tries
another strategy, what she calls later in the poem "the light of fiction."

Here the poem opens up into a rhetorical flourish, reminded of a story
where each turns away from so much emotion (that *chora* Guest also resists).
The effect of this repression, though, is a picture in profiles, "floating / elsewhere from their permanence." Colors here displace and intervene, and as
she tries to move from the descriptive to signification, black will not hold
still. The hair, which she first associates with a feeling and then changes
to a clinical, distant objective diction (a stable vision of black "recognized
as remorse, sadness") brings us back to that "self who exists" and fears the
expunging of light. The word shortly becomes a headdress, a ritualized
word with so many significations, from covering to ritual to the ceremonial, the poem is forced to acknowledge the instability: "the space slanted
vertically with its graduating / need for movement."

She is frustrated both by the need to harmonize and the impossibility of doing so; what she calls the grip of realism is the desire to impose one landscape on another, to use art to transcend, "establishing a flexibility so we are not immobile / like a car that spends its night / outside a window, but mobile like a spirit." In a syntax that moves so quickly from flexibility to immobility to "transcendence," the poem dramatizes the impossibility and the temptation to impose, to make art instrumental in pinning down identity: the more she flees or displaces the wild gardens, the more she is subject to its darkness.

The poem as dramatic process, as repetition, qualification, transformation, has it both ways: it is a representational poem with some of the pleasures of plot and narrative—a person looks out the window at a scene that she believes evokes sadness and a sense of an ending, then attempts to displace it with art, to make order out of that which resists order—but Guest also takes what she has learned from Gertrude Stein's "Writing as Explanation" and uses the eternal present to move the words across the poem, to destabilize significations. Moving from clinical diction to intimate speech, moving from the scientific objectifier ("ethnologist") to the engaged participant ("puzzled inhabitant"), she recognizes that illumination exacts its shades, shades that form a barrier to vision. There's no unmediated vision here; even attempts to mediate vision through screens fail the poet. Time and space are conflated; inside and outside lose their definitions (interior life, the life of imagination, is out trying to give form to the world through art). The poem closes with the wonderful diction of that "modern wondering space," where lights flash this time from the wild gardens' space without the artist imposing light, order, art, or representation on them.

D. A. Powell must drive some people wild in terms of his aesthetic allegiances: he is simultaneously a poet with great formal control and wild, transgressive impulses that make his poems bristle with energy, horror, sadness, and surprise. They simultaneously honor and satirize received form. One would almost want to apply the classical cliché that the tight form holds the explosive material, but the generalization does not really hold up. The wide range of dictions and meters creates the poetic tensions. Scanning the lines of "dogs and boys can treat you like trash, and dogs do love trash" is tricky: the first line is essentially trochaic, the second iambic, the third anapestic. Everything in the poem keeps the reader off balance: the erratic repetitions and transformations, the first sing-song line, and the assonance of the first two lines crash with the phrase "that smell like their nuts." Here the animality, lucid and grotesque, creates a shift, a descent into vulgar slang. This poem transgresses most obviously the romantic notion of form as being in the service of truth and beauty: you don't get any less transcendent than this poem. "Dogs and boys" is poised between the almost-innocent sadness for the lost and betrayed lover's feelings of victimization and a more punctuated animal rage and ironic humor directed at the "nature" of "boys" (mutts, sluts, butts, putz, all one-syllable hard rhymes).

dogs and boys can treat you like trash, and dogs do love trash
to nuzzle their muzzles. they slather with tongues that smell like their
    nuts

but the boys are fickle when they lick you. they stick you with twigs
and roll you over like roaches. then off with another: those sluts

with their asses so tight you couldn't get them to budge for a turd
so unlike the dogs: who will turn in a circle showing & showing their
    butts

a dog on a leash: a friend in the world. he'll crawl into bed on all fours
and curl at your toes. he'll give you his nose. he'll slobber on cuts

a dog is not fragile: he's fixed. but a boy: cannot give you his love
he closes his eyes to your kisses. he hisses. a boy is a putz

with a sponge for a brain. and a mop for a heart: he'll soak up your
    love
if you let him and leave you dry as a cork. he'll punch out your guts

when a boy goes away: to another boy's arms. what else can you do
but lie down with the dogs. the hounds and the curs. with the mutts

Remarkable too is Powell's ironic linguistic use of the musical echo and shifts in voice: "a dog on a leash" is followed by "a friend in the world," repeating the meter exactly, arguing and complicating the first phrase's description of the lover with the second. The instability of the language helps the reader simultaneously feel the degradation and the fatal attraction of sex and pain. The signifier for the boy also shifts. When the poet talks about "boy," sometimes he refers to the other, at other times to the speaker. Because of the instability of the diction, it becomes impossible to discern who's the victim, who's responsible for the abjection. The very end of the poem offers a false ending, like Beethoven's Seventh Symphony: here the rhythm relaxes to three anapestic phrases, all repeated to offer equivalency; all the sadness and shame rises up in those repetitions: but the boys do love trash, and lying down with the mutts brings us to a circular ending: the boy gets to have his muzzle nuzzled while simultaneously feeling dirty and debased.

Sentence and syntax, rather than line and image, give thrust to Arthur Vogelsang's work. Vogelsang's poems are often seriously playful, the humor a dark veil over his anxiety about intimacy, contingency, and the temporal; his poems thrive on enigma and impersonality ("I'd like to know a secret and have wealth at the same time," he says in "Gods," and "secrets" is a repeated mantra through the body of his work). Influenced by the colloquialisms of Frank O'Hara and bearing some resemblance to the surrealism of James Tate, the postmodernism of John Ashbery, and the ironic humor of both, his poems' difficulties—their wide-ranging leaps—are offset by their playful and seductive surfaces.

He often uses the sentence tonally to achieve irony as well as the impersonal authority of the flat, deadpan voice. Reading tone (which shifts often in a single poem) helps cue the reader as to how closely one should identify with or assent to the speaker's assertions and observations, which are often in the third person. His sentences frequently serve as distancing devices, not so much to keep the reader emotionally distant from the poem but almost to hover above his characters, their authorial pronouncements and anxieties. Vogelsang makes use of the idiom and the transposed cliché (he opens "Sessions" with "Fully awake as if pregnant with an idea sharply,") and the repeated phrase or the play of pun or homonym to cue the reader that speech is always part of the subject and artifice of his poems. As with Stein, the author wants the reader to know the poem is like an action painting, a made thing, a thing in the making. "Brutal Lesson," from *Left Wing of a Bird* (a poem that echoes other work at the end of the book in its obsession with the finality of death), echoes Derrida's well-known comment, "In a sense, it is always too late to think about time." The speaker begins the poem wanting to be dismissive about choices and "the truth," to distance himself from their impact (It "was not his problem," "it didn't matter," "and that was fine"). The defensive humor is emphasized with the homonym of Hopper and Big Bopper—the serious and the pop cultural— as if the speaker were comfortable with the relativity of the postmodern. What seems not to matter—what he remembered—turns out to matter a lot. The subjectivity of memory—the distance, the fiction of it—is indeed his "problem," for in this poem he needs to decide how to live in time and space. Should he live in the present, without self-consciousness or history? The acting teacher advocates that "You don't select object correlatives, you just get your head right." But since memory can serve as a veil, a lens that either brings you closer to or further away from the "figures" (other people), the teacher's advice is simultaneously insufficient and indispensable. The acting teacher, one of many apparent "experts" who make quoted cameos in Vogelsang's poems, becomes both purveyor of a truth and an idealization.

> Whether what he remembered was bent to the chew and digest of his
>   line,
> Or was true like a photo, or an aerial photo or a TV show,
> About it, was not his problem. His mother painted from life
> Or from memory, it didn't matter. It came out like Hopper
> Or the Big Bopper and that was fine. This is an apple, he could say,
> Yeah, and after you eat it, it *was* an apple, dig? Dig
> Is what we said in the fifties in Philadelphia or California like alors
> In Paris or dig in Paris, like cocksucker at the bus station
> Where I actually worked, bless *me*. He advised, where you get into the
>   big scenes
> You don't select object correlatives, you just get your head right
> And put everything in that voice that blesses everything
> Which is why it's easy, really, and you don't have to remember
>   anything,
> Or memory is a veil, simple enough, but memory is never a gauze
>   stage curtain
> From behind which figures walk, embed themselves,
> Do a show on the thick threads,
> And then walk toward us, who said that?

The middle of the poem pursues the question of how we talk about experience, how it is both located in a particular time and space (the "fifties in Philadelphia"), or how it may provide a more indefinite sense of our location ("or California"). Do our signifiers have the same meanings over time and space, in which case we can understand one another, or are they transient, like the speaker's employment in a bus station? The reader is reminded of the diction of the first line and of the speaker's line (his dogma, his ritualized point of view, his subjectivity, a line delivered in a play, his line in a poem? – no single way of seeing be located with certainty). The poem argues both for and against those positions. If one lives in the present tense, one can deliver one's lines blessing everything, but to do so is to dwell in the general, the universal, where he or she lacks the capacity for distinctions ("bless *me*"). That these are "lines" puts the patina of artifice over all these positions: they become simultaneously posed and inauthentic, though they represent, metaphorically, the high-stakes drama of human experience. We understand that what keeps us from the present tense is the particular and the historical: the Edenic apple becomes the "was," the gone. And gone matters.

The lessons of the poem are brutal both because they are irresolvable (more than one of Vogelsang's poems end with questions) and costly: the recognition of how figures, people, and metaphors are kept by consciousness at a distance, as on stage, where they feel "real," but those selves on stage—the stage too of the world—cannot be distinguished by their speech. "Who said that?" casts the whole poem into doubt: the speaker, one person from another, who puts words into others' mouths to make them think and feel the way they do. As readers we move from ironic dismissal, the breezy and idiomatic, to the dangerous. As soon as we see the figures (others) through a veil, all this happens in the enacted and layered diction of the poem, which requires us in process to refer backward and forward, from where we've been to where we're going. The poem enacts its questions about the instability of time and space and what it costs us as human beings, because figures "embed themselves" in our consciousness and memories.

When the sentence displaces the metered line as a rhythmic and tonal vehicle—as it sometimes does in Vogelsang's work—poems approach the seemingly indeterminate boundaries of the prose poem (the last section of *Left Wing of a Bird* begins with a prose poem). We see this same blurring of boundaries in a number of plain-style poems, such as in Mark Strand's *Darker*, where Strand emphasizes his obsession with disembodiment in flat, almost deadpan verse—often relying almost exclusively on the caesura. Vogelsang's syntax is more jagged than Stand's, and he makes fewer concessions to narrative, but he may provide a flashpoint for traditionalists who view the sanctity of the verse line as grounded in rhythm and meter. Taken to the extreme, one outcome of such rigid doctrines of definition and classification would be metered prose (Robert Pinsky's early *An Explanation of America* evolves from that eighteenth-century, Alexander Pope–like sensibility). That is to say, there are many sources of poetic tension in a line: ranges of diction, the lilt in a caesura, the syntactical juxtapositions of one line set against the next. Just because a poem is written in prose, as Lyn Hejinian says, doesn't mean it's not poetry.

2.

....

ON THE MARGINS

Prose Poems

CHARLES BAUDELAIRE, MAURICE DE GUERIN, and Aloysius Bertran are usually given credit for giving birth to the prose poem form (Michael Hamburger, who translated Baudelaire's poems, calls it a "medium").[1] Borrowing freely from the metaphoric compression and the heightened diction of poetry and from the narrative elements and voicings of prose, the sentence, rather than the line, serves as lever of music in a prose poem; rhythm is established by sound, beat, and the pacing of the sentence (or from sentence to sentence). The twentieth-century prose poem has been advanced early on most obviously in America by Gertrude Stein and in Europe and Latin America by surrealists like Robert Desnos, Paul Eluard, and César Vallejo, as well as by parablists Julio Cortázar, Italo Calvino, and Zbigniew Herbert. The American prose poem has become part of the arsenal of those interested in expanding the range of poetic forms, those exploring the tonal possibilities of the sentence rather than the line, as well as those experimental poets who make use of theoretical frameworks that are skeptical about classification and genre.

Historically poised on the margins since its inception—formally walking the tightrope between poetry and prose—the modern prose poem may often imitate the archetypal with parables (Franz Kafka, Zbigniew Herbert, and Robert Bly) or it may parody contemporary prose. Spurred on by postmodern satires of the separation of high and low culture, poets like Russell Edson use either the arch diction of the comic book or the more clinical, mechanical, or journalistic prose. Beginning with Gertrude Stein's *Tender Buttons*, the prose poem becomes a medium for enacting the pleasures of language itself, creating drama by sculpting syntax, transformation, and repetition. Contemporary experimental prose poets make use of modernist collage techniques, interrupting narrative with rhetoric or recurring image (as in Lyn Hejinian's *My Life*) or disassociative syntax and diction to reassemble and refresh constituted meaning.[2]

It is difficult, then, to agree with David Mason, the latest formalist reviewer to claim that "the verse line is all poets have to distinguish what they do from prose."[3] Setting aside the tone of this comment, "all" conjuring up a poet's scant resources, what should one make of William Carlos Williams's *Paterson* or other modernist (no less postmodern) poems that use prose inside poems to create multiple voices? Such rigid classification is not only ahistorical (after all, "definitions" of poetry have been mobile well before Sir Philip Sidney), but such *ex machina* definitions exclude the extension of the medium and risk formula and stasis. I am reminded of a story told about Eric Dolphy, who, when lectured by a journalist who claimed that "free jazz" wasn't jazz (Dolphy was apparently listening to Stravinsky's Ebony Concerto at the time), he just shrugged and said, "Okay, it's not. It's all music, man."[4] The experimental poets under discussion in this chapter prove to be less interested in "what it is" than "what it does," and they will fall more easily into the category of "it's all music" than the strict meters of swing.

Anne Waldman grew up poetically among the East Coast Beats, but her recent work, wide in range, ambition, and tone (informed both by Buddhist practice and the relaxed colloquialisms of the New York school), includes a series of prose poems and counterlyric voices in a collection playfully and angrily called *Marriage: A Sentence*. The poems and their corresponding prose poems carry on a conversation, personal and mythic, about love, masculine economy, autonomy, language, and time.

The dramatic premise of "Stereo" traverses marriage as a dialectic, shifting from moment to moment from repetition to the boundless, from the replete to the emptying. Waldman has in interviews referred to "Two-ness," "the Buddhist belief in *yab yum*," or what Waldman calls "both both," which "provides a means for looking at binaries, even the gender binary, as a non-hierarchical entity."[5] In the prose poem "Stereo," Waldman writes, "When you are married married there will be handsome gifts for the kitchen kitchen sometimes two of every thing." Domesticity here, in the rhetoric of repetition, simultaneously dramatizes fullness while preparing the reader for replication: "Two two two two lines lines lines lines" alludes to the need for watchfulness (the need for privacy and autonomy in phones, e-mail accounts *and* poems) that's released in the closure of the poem.

Marriage marriage is like you say everything everything in stereo stereo fall fall on the bed bed at dawn dawn because you work work all night. Night is an apartment. Meant to be marriage. Marriage is an apartment & meant people people come in in because when when you marry marry chances are there will be edibles edibles to eat at tables tables in the house. House will be the apartment which is night night. There there will be a bed bed & an extra bed bed a clean sheet sheet sheet or two two for guests guests one extra towel. Extra towel. How will you be welcomed? There will be drinks drinks galore galore brought by armies of guests guests casks casks of liquors liquors & brandies brandies elixirs sweet & bitter bitter bottle of Merlot Merlot Bustelo coffee. Will you have some when I offer. When you are married married there will be handsome gifts for the kitchen kitchen sometimes two of every thing. Everything is brand brand new new. Espresso coffee cups, a Finnish plate, a clock, a doormat, pieces of Art. And books of astonishing Medical Science with pictures. Even richer lexicons. When you are married married there will be more sheets sheets & towels towels arriving arriving & often often a pet pet or two two. You definitely need a telephone & a cellphone when you are married married. Two two two two lines lines lines lines. You need need separate separate electronicmail electronicmail accounts accounts. When you are married married you will have sets sets of things things, of more sheets & towels matching, you will have duplicates of things, you will have just one tablecloth. When you are married married you will be responsible when neighbors neighbors greet you. You will smile smile in unison unison or you might say he is fine, she is fine, o she is just down with a cold, o he is consoling a weary traveler just now, arrived from across the Plains. She my husband is due home soon, he my wife is busy at the moment, my husband he is very very busy busy at the moment moment this very moment. Meant good-bye, good-bye. When you are married married sex sex will happen happen without delay delay. You will have a mailbox mailbox & a doorbell doorbell. Bell bell ring ring it rings rings again a double time. You do not have to answer. That's sure for when you are married married people people understand understand you do not not have to answer answer a doorbell doorbell because sex sex may happen happen without delay delay. You will hear everything twice, through your ears & the ears of the other. Her or him as a case case may be be. He &

he & she & she as a case case may be may be. When you are married married you can play play with names names & rename yourself if you like. You can add a name, have a double name with a hyphen if you like. You can open joint accounts when you are married. Marriage is no guarantee against depression. A shun is no guarantee against anything. Marriage is no guarantee against resolution. Revolution is a tricky word word. Here, you hear here? Marriage is sweeter sweeter than you think. Think.

Tonally, Waldman recalls Stein—repeated or transmuted phrases take on new meaning in the context of the new sentence. Like Stein, too, Waldman relies on the associative and the simultaneous pleasures of pun and homonym. Here, the repetitions echo and shadow one another, syntactically reinforcing, ironizing, and blurring with ambiguity the speaker's initial perceptions. The self finds pleasure in the other through the play of language and communication ("Even richer lexicons" and "When you are married married you can play play with names names & rename yourself if you like"). Naming, of course, is classification, and it resides at some distance from the palpable and particular. The speaker is enriched by the expansion of points of view ("You will hear everything twice, through your ears & the ears of the other"). But pleasure is shared at the same time individuality diminishes: "You will smile smile in unison unison." In marriage, an encounter with the other proves predictable and erotic and surprising all at once ("sex will happen happen").

The repetition of need ("You need need separate separate electronicmail electronicmail accounts accounts") dramatizes how marriage also blurs the boundaries: the individual is in danger of losing a sense of herself as an autonomous being. When "accounts" echoes in the above sentence, the diction resonates with clinical and social. First of all, there is accounting for; then the arrangement of marriage, after all, requires accounting in all sorts of ways, not the least of which is economic. One of the pleasures/burdens of marriage is material: "you will have sets sets of things things . . . you will have duplicates of things." It doesn't escape the speaker's consciousness that marriage is historically an economic institution, and the effects of that (masculine) economy enslave as well as insulate.

The beginning of the prose poem makes tentative and shifting equivalence among night, apartment, and marriage. Night, for the couple that works all day, becomes their apartment. The universe shrinks: they can't see out. The marriage bed provides a respite from work. Night, for the couple that works all day, becomes their apartment. Domesticity, the world of towels and sheets, provides a repository (the ideal and the real) of gifts and burdens: the self overflowing, the self disappearing.

The closure keeps the dialectics in motion: no resolution, no revolution (that "tricky word" that is irresolvable, altered by commerce); the ending implies both change and ownership. Thereby, the pleasure lies elsewhere than in thinking. "Here" (present tense) gets set against "hear": listen. Ending with "think. Think" again intensifies the pleasure and danger of thinking, necessary as consciousness is necessary to monitor experience, but it also provides distance, removal. To experience doubleness, the other in marriage is simultaneously predictable and surprising (the eros of sex anytime) as well as replete with sweetness. The poem acknowledges the desire and need for safety and insulation from pain, but it warns, "Marriage is no guarantee against depression." On the other hand, to refuse intimacy, to push away or displace, has a similar effect. "A shun is no guarantee against anything." In either case, experience comes with no guarantees.

Like much experimental writing, Anne Waldman's prose poem makes use of the self-conscious play of language at the same time the language enacts—rather than represents—meaning. Furthermore, the closure doesn't resolve or illuminate: it leaves the reader active, questioning, and engaged without reducing truth to an illumination or resolving paradox.

L-A-N-G-U-A-G-E poets share with other poets on the margins—in their own words—their "awareness of the materiality of language—in its sonic materials, in its syntactic materials, in the way sentences are built."[6] Like Stein, they view the sentence as a "landscape" and attend to the way a sentence or sentences transform(s) what has already been written—what Lyn Hejinian calls "linkages." Of those works identified with the school, Hejinian's poetry, veering in and out of the representational, appears among the most approachable, especially in the "autobiographical" *My Life*. Hejinian's early work (more recent work is more abstract and philosophical) is influenced by Stein, but no other poet I know has made such original or imaginative use of Stein's stylistic techniques. *My Life* began as a formal exercise: skeptical of the objectivity of memory and the truth of reporting (two issues consistently negotiated in the poems), Hejinian revised the conception of autobiography as a self-consciously fictive act. In *My Life*, narrative and plot are interrupted and altered, often with repeated phrases, such as "As for those of us who wished to be astonished" or "I found myself dependent on a pause, a rose, something on paper." As with jazz, before or after a solo, these phrases return the improvisations to the head, the recurring melody, the narrative. These recurring clauses provide the pleasures of ritual and grounding (although the statements themselves are always transformed by syntax, resulting in the reconsideration not only of the phrase but also of the passages that precede and follow them). The desired effect is not so different from the Songs of Lorca, such as "Romance Sonambulo," where each time the refrain is repeated ("Green, how I want you green"), it intensifies and alters the speaker's longing and the emotional ark of the sentence.

Hejinian's lyric gifts, her pacing and rhythmic variations in sentence structure, and her powers of observation all contribute to the freshness of her imagination, as in the following passage from "As we who love to be astonished," reconstructing a memory simultaneously public and private:

> The pilot of the little airplane had forgotten to notify the airport of his approach, so that when the lights of the plane in the night were first spotted, the air raid sirens went off, and the entire city on that coast went dark. He was taking a drink of water and the light was growing dim. My mother stood at the window watching the only lights that were visible, circling over the darkened city in search of the hidden airport.

Hejinian creates this voice primarily by using warring dictions and employing variations of anapestic rhythms, many of which are softened by the dactylic and are set against a number of spondees, reinforcing the clash of the tender and tough-minded, the nostalgic and the analytical. But the coordinate clauses simultaneously create causality (equivalence) and undermine reason with irrational surprise ("he was taking a drink of water *and* the light was growing dim").

Of course, these narrative moments are followed by more difficult and contrary interjecting voices. The rhetoric of "Unhappily, time seems more normative than place" both frames the sentence's antecedents and refutes the objectivity of those "memories." Using more abstract and elevated diction, the speaker steps out of narrative: tension in Hejinian's poems (as in Ashbery's) often arises from the gap between colloquial particulars and the conceptual generalizations about experience. Neither level of diction, neither way of speaking or being, takes dominion over the other.

"Like plump birds along the shore" tells a story about storytelling, subjectivity, and the irreconcilable gaps between memory and imagination.
The family mythologies are colored by "everyone in the family had a version of history and it was impossible to get close to the original, or to know
'what really happened.'" Mirages serve as a metaphor for the impalpable
as well as the illusory; because of the lively imagination of the speaker, her
"version" of reality, acquired from literature, where "camelback riders approach in the factual accounts of voyages," the so-called factual accounts
make her life both less stable (which reality can you trust?) and less vi-
carious, which is a tribute to the power of imagination. When she tries to
uncover the authentic by an act of memory, the images are vivid but don't
necessarily "add up." "The pair of ancient, stunted apricot trees yielded
ancient, stunted apricots," is glossed by the more abstract "What was the
meaning hung from that depend."

> Summers were spent in a fog that rains. They were mirages, no differ-
> ent from those that camelback riders approach in the factual accounts
> of voyages in which I persistently imagined myself, and those mirages
> on the highway were for me both impalpable souvenirs and unstable
> evidence of my own adventures, now slightly less vicarious than
> before. The person too has flared ears, like an infant's reddened with
> batting. I had claimed the radio nights for my own. There were more
> storytellers than there were stories, so that everyone in the family had
> a version of history and it was impossible to get close to the origi-
> nal, or to know "what really happened." The pair of ancient, stunted
> apricot trees yielded ancient, stunted apricots. What was the meaning
> hung from that depend. The sweet aftertaste of artichokes. The lobes
> of autobiography. Even a minor misadventure, a bumped fender or a
> newsstand without newspapers, can "ruin the entire day," but a child
> cries and laughs without rift. The sky droops straight down. I lapse,
> hypnotized by the flux and reflux of the waves. They had ruined the
> Danish pastry by frosting it with whipped butter. It was simply a
> tunnel, a very short one. Now I remember worrying about lockjaw.
> The cattle were beginning to move across the field pulled by the sun,
> which proved them to be milk cows. There is so little public beauty. I
> found myself dependent on a pause, a rose, something on paper. It was
> a way of saying, I want you, too, to have this experience, so that we
> are more alike, so that we are closer, bound together, sharing a point

of view—so that we are "coming from the same place." It is possible to be homesick in one's neighborhood. Afraid of the bears. A string of eucalyptus pods was hung by the window to discourage flies. So much of "the way things were" was the same from one day to the next, or from one occasion (Christmas, for example, or July 4th) to the next, that I can speak now of how we "always" had dinner, all of us sitting at our usual places in front of the placemats of woven straw, eating the salad first, with cottage cheese, which my father always referred to as "cottage fromage," that being one of many little jokes with which he expressed his happiness at home. Twice he broke his baby toe, stubbing it at night. As for we who "love to be astonished," my heartbeats shook the bed. In any case, I wanted to be both the farmer and his horse when I was a child, and I tossed my head and stamped with one foot as if I were pawing the ground before a long gallop. Across the school playground, an outing, a field trip, passes in ragged order over the lines which mark the hopscotch patch. It made for a sort of family mythology. The heroes kept clean, chasing dusty rustlers, tonguing the air. They spent the afternoon building a dam across the gutter. There was too much carpeting in the house, but the windows upstairs were left open except on the very coldest or wettest of days. It was there that she met the astonishing figure of herself when young. Are we likely to find ourselves later pondering such suchness amid all the bourgeois memorabilia. Wherever I might find them, however unsuitable, I made them useful by a simple shift. The obvious analogy is with music. Did you mean gutter or guitar. Like cabbage of collage. The book was a sort of protection because it had a better plot. If any can be spared from the garden. They hoped it would rain before somebody parked beside that section of the curb. The fuchsia is a plant much like a person, happy in the out-of-doors in the same sun and breeze that is most comfortable to a person sitting nearby. We had to wash the windows in order to see them. Supper was a different meal from dinner. Small fork-stemmed boats propelled by wooden spoons wound in rubber bands cruised the trough. Losing its balance on the low horizon lay the vanishing vernal day.

The power of this prose poem, like others in *My Life*, comes from this alternation of voices and transformation of the particulars by the abstract and vice versa. The particulars serve as examples; the aphorisms and repeated rituals serve as framing devices and inadequate generalizations—like the colloquial "can 'ruin an entire day'" to account for the vast range of sense experience. Where the poem dramatizes its instabilities and complexities, the writing gloriously unfolds and argues with what we already know by syntax. The remarkable sentence, "It was a way of saying, I want you, too, to have this experience, so that we are more alike, so that we are closer, bound together, sharing a point of view—so that we are 'coming from the same place,'" fills the reader with layers of meaning. The author, who directs the experience, wants to both share and control, wants to share a point of view. That point of view is hers, and the rest of the prose poem lets us know that there are competing versions of stories, and her desire to control must be mediated by an acceptance of flux and difference. Implicit in many of Hejinian's poems and prose poems is the reader's and writer's need to understand, control, or tame, which is tempered by the desire to embrace the gulf between articulation and experience and to immerse oneself in those complexities.

After the above lines, the arc of the piece becomes clear: the speaker loves the repetitions and rituals ("the flux and reflux of the waves," which prevent her from being "homesick"); contrarily, she loves adventures, the unfolding story, the unbound imagination, play that depends upon subjectivity and whimsy. So what they "always" had for dinner, in and of itself a distorted generalization, is set against her father's silly and deflating joke, "cottage fromage." Ultimately, the speaker requires the distortions of memory for balance and the fantasy of the imagination for both stimulation and insulation from the dangers of change and the boredom of repetition: "it had a better plot." This prose poem is full of accrual and turns: its shifts bring reader and writer together in midair while an emotional argument blossoms in the open spaces the poem provides.

One of the most adventurous, ambitious, and uncategorizable uses of the prose poem form has been Claudia Rankine's *Don't Let Me Be Lonely*, which her publisher mysteriously calls a poem/essay. The book freely mixes verse with prose narrative, pseudodocumentary, and commentary, supplemented by visual images, mostly from the media. A naïve reader might confuse it with a confessional narrative. It is clear, though, that Rankine's interests transcend the definitional: what concerns her are the materials she conjures to imaginatively shape her project. The story is told as a broken series of flat voices in the service of confronting the speaker's alienation and loneliness, as well as by braiding those apparently private feelings with public events from September 11 on. The range of dictions and perceptions move from the lyrical to the metaphysical to the postmodern integration of the daily (popular culture and the metaphors it provides). The speaker confronts an emotional deadness, enacted in the repetitive rhythms of the sentences, in the preponderance of weak or passive verbs, and of course in the perceptions, observations, and narratives themselves. The visual images serve to echo and intensify or argue with the speaker's accountings for her emotional state. Television is a virtual character, one source of the deadness, a background noise whose ambiance is everywhere. No single passage accurately represents the work, since echoes, foreshadowing, deferrals, and releases abound, but to demonstrate the range of the work, I've taken this following excerpt, which ends with an actual graphic image of the TV (*Don't Let Me Be Lonely* is in many ways a collaborative work: metaphorically, it uses overheard conversation; literally, John Lucas supplies the visual images).

Life is a form of hope?

If you are hopeful.

Maybe hope is the same as breath—part of
what it means to be human and alive.

Or maybe hoping is the same as waiting.

This relatively abstract meditative verse (reminiscent of some of Robert Creeley's middle period) frames the prose narrative that follows. The linguistic pleasures of the verse lie in its ironic reversals and halting single-clause sentences, abstract premises followed by their complication or dismantling.

The prose section dismantles its strategies and voices as it unwinds, as if to suggest the fiction of identity has been corrupted by contemporary culture's assaulting sense data.

When she comes toward me I stiffen. But it's all right. It's nothing. The pamphlet says in bold letters, **BE LIKE JESUS**. Because I was brought up this way, I wait two blocks before tossing it. Be your own Christ. I'll remember that or I remember that. As if it were a soul memory, I say aloud to Neo, be like Jesus. I am on my way home from seeing *The Matrix Reloaded*. The film's superhero, Neo, can't save anyone; Morpheus will have to have another dream: the one in which salvation narratives are passé; the one in which people live no matter what you dream; the one in which people die no matter what you dream; or no matter what, you dream—

When the speaker is approached on the street with a religious flyer (bringing her back to the/her past), in Steinian fashion the speaker says, "Be your own Christ. I'll remember that or I remember that." Thus, the past becomes present; and when the archaic motto becomes contemporary, it is filtered through the cheapened myth of the movies but also reflects a personal and cultural consciousness of helplessness: the speaker's loneliness, then, is relational—it is neither personal nor existential. What follows is a miraculous linguistic leap, again making use of Stein-like transformations. The disconnection between one's dream-life and the reality principle has been severed. The speaker's voice hovers about the narrative, above memory, to gloss a theoretical account of the experience: "salvation narratives are passé." What an odd juggling of voices that sentence reflects: "salvation narratives" is straightforward, elevated, and professorial, while the colloquial "passé" (the world where the individual is being her own Jesus) both reflects the fading truth of the advice and issues an ironic understanding of fashion. The paragraph ends by positing two different possibilities: dreams don't transform, or we keep dreaming—which becomes for the speaker elsewhere dangerously dissociative and emotionally numbing. The break in chronology of the lines that follow make connections between public and private life, the media (the passage ends with the TV graphic), money, and insulation.

When she experiences that mourning directly—her own father—dissociation coalesces into numbness and distance: the short sentences and weak verbs here reflect the coldness of the speaker. An embedded narrative about "purchasing" mourners turns into a narrative about replicants, reflecting the metaphor of the parallel science-fiction fantasy: *The Matrix Reloaded* (in this way, the media reflects cultural feeling at the same time it alters and distances us from experience). Mourning is blurred by use: the distancing device is money. One is reminded of how soldiers bought their way out of the draft in the Civil War, sending others—replacements, poor and black—to fight in their place, a practice that has been modified, but only in its indirection (the poor now often gravitate to the army to economically survive). Rankine's view—when it comes to distancing ourselves from the lives of the poor—mirrors that indirection exactly.

> At night I dream about my replacement mourner, a woman. She has lost her mother years before and because she is already grieving she just continues attending funerals for a price. Like a wet nurse, the prerequisite is a state of "already grief." Still, all the narrative control in the world does not offer me insight into her occupation. One creates her motivations and her tears, but cannot understand why she stays by the corpse—"with him" is the phrase no one utters, especially not with him "gone." Or one looks into the mourner's face and wants life to matter more. In the dream we talk about what a lonely occupation she has chosen. No, she says, you, you are the one with the lonely occupation. Death follows you into your dreams. The loneliness in death is second to the loneliness of life.

And here is where writing, where "narrative control," doesn't suffice, because there's too much distance and replication: dreaming outside the self, imagining the interior of the other, is available to neither mourner nor writer. Becoming compassionate, "inhabiting," becoming less lonely, then, is problematic in a culture where defensive distancing strategies dominate: individual salvation cannot transform. Imagination fails, reality distances. The project of the book becomes in part facing and avoiding this condition, trying to take flight from it, trying to fix it, trying to survive, trying to live.

Jean Day's prose poem sequence "Narratives from the Crib" works off the witty French tradition of the form (Desnos and Max Jacob come to mind). From the surreal point of view of a preverbal infant, Day explores the gap between the sayable and unsayable, wrestles with representing nature and time, and ironizes the economy of possession (loosely connecting death, money, and time). All these metaphysical issues are framed, mirrored in, and mediated by language. The speaker is beyond her years and the words are beyond her reach. What better vehicle and voice than the infant to tackle this material in a postmodern fashion? After all, the self-conscious wit of the sequence underlines how we always project onto the other; projection onto the infant is patently absurd; the poem's serious play emphasizes the impossibility of possessing the child's interior life (or, metaphorically, bridging the distance between words and experience). But even with this most theoretical construct, we have more than the skeletal remains of representation, a narrative whose syntax imitates temporal sequence: the babe is looking around the room, "meditating" about it (the poem seems based on some careful observation of an infant as well). So this poem's inside/outside moves negotiate the "field" of nature at the same time the poem decodes it. Here is the second prose poem in the sequence.

> 2. I was asked to be specific but could only wave my hands. A contemplative, I am like the artist who paints from a picture of nature because the real thing's too breezy and, besides, they're afraid I might destroy the original. The black dots represent birds; the names of those others I do not yet understand. Quiet and commotion, energy and rest; it looks simple, doesn't it? It's not. The clock has so far taken no notice of me (a sort of slug on the face of time), yet the struggle is already over the direction of my gaze. Before that, yesterday somebody tried to sell them a $65 spider, French, that spun like a lunatic while ringing a bell. Death might be thought of in such terms, or at the end, simply, of experience. This is what makes me a being that can speak of itself in the first person, though I have heard there is more to speech.

In the middle of the poem, the infant begins to learn the connection between signifier and sign, as if she has faith in them and in the figures of the birds. "Looks simple," representing, but it isn't, because what follows is "Quiet and commotion, energy and rest," figures of cycle and flux. Implicit in that sentence is the origin of the temporal. The poem next declares the clock has so far taken no notice of the speaker (for the moment the child remains uncoded, pretemporal). That perception snaps off because, in fact, "Before that, yesterday somebody tried to sell them a $65 spider" (now the reader's located *in* time). With the consciousness of time comes money (in my favorite episode of a 1950s TV show, *My Little Margie*, the bird in the cuckoo clock reveals the key to the treasure by saying, "time is money, look in the clock"). Of course, *in* time is where death lies: where the speaker can think of herself as having an identity formed by time, the first person. Before language, before time, there is no first person. At the end, there's experience.

But thinking of oneself as an "I," a unitary self, and being one are quite different. The whole prose poem breaks down with the qualification, "though I have heard there is more to speech." The poem's closure lives with its incompletions, its half-knowledges, contained in the Gregor Samsa–like fiction of the infant's voice (except Day dispenses with the modernist internal consistencies).

It is challenging to try to inhabit all of Diane Williams's jarringly difficult postmodern prose poem or poetic prose. A reader may move in and out of making connections while at the same time certain passages read as if overhearing someone's private conversation. Using the prose poem to resist deciphering and analysis is part of her project, just as her character's sexuality resists definition and comprehensibility. She does have the verbal authority to know where she takes the reader. That trust in structure originates in choral dissonance: hearing a voice come back later, intensified or contrary, hearing some of the armor drop, despising the character, feeling pity, absorbing the self-knowledge. "Dear Ears, Mouth, Eyes, and Hindquarters" is like a photographic negative. Gone is the traditional dramatic monologue, and the reader can't avoid the knowledge that the author is a woman investigating maleness. The speaker is all need, and the mixed tones reflect the mixed feelings: the animal rage (the bitch is a dog, the dog is a bitch), the pleasure, his powerful powerlessness, and most of all a lack of self, a neediness alternately disguised and laid bare.

She crossed the main street, which is enlarged by sexual stimulation. Then that's settled and I want to use the word sexy. I go for the rather thick bitch with my beloved arms and hands.

I have a job and I have a large flat sea beside us with its operation of forces.

When I was young I was more interested in this mother. I went straight for Cornelia across the fantastic steps stretching out on the sea. Hidden among the views, she is now climbing, now running, I say, trotting, penetrating different experiences, typically swelling so that she can be seen. It is called profane. It's not such a time-consuming process. Imagine spending part of every day after her. She is completely different with Mr. Reinisch. The two of them were laughing at something dirty. With her short nose she looked rested. He was conducting her through the isolation and the cool. What is there that is good about her? I wanted to kiss her but thought she would recoil. Something important—this is in the land of your bitch.

I hate her too. My cock is too tough and too long. It must be nice to be the one who's rushing, is always rushing. I had hoped to get those boners. All that puckling, it doesn't matter. You don't forget the sea water, the chase. I want Mr. Reinisch to tell this—he has the true interest to tell this.

Mr. Reinisch, as I tell it, has lived with the woman for many years. She has been perfection. That is unbelievably still true. She is great shakes. She did not die before he does. He always has access to her friendly hubbub and he is undisturbed by his being cared for.

I have never been a man desiring more, either, of the red fur around the mouth. My cock—slightly rounded at the tip and set high—I hold it high, so contentedly.

What happens when you get the bitch—if I meet her, if I really meet her rising just out ahead from the glorious past? She says, "That's a very gaudy thing. Tell me the ways it can hurt me." This is the patriotic center. If I am in love I cannot be sad. I am very happy our lives are unruined. I don't get money out of it. I have my hat and my coat on and my cock in a hand. This is a case of ensorcellment if there ever was one. This is my sky and my favorable opinion of a leaf over there. This is my mother, not your mother. You would like to stop this. I would, too, but not just temporarily. But stop it as in please stop! You have your own work, your own mother, the terraced land with vined bowers—your own certainty by the water, the scanty water. The street runs along by many hotels. Don't bother to remember that.

I've walked toward the object and the big fat skkkkky—past the sucker. The shapeless flora becomes a curse or something. It is all so multi-colored. I like the stick part and what's underneath it. I just don't like the decoration on top.

The surprises—free and vigorous and normal—are as plentiful as good fruits. The steep, famous slopes, the colored rocks, the sides of hills, the flax, the wheat—the gaudy things—I don't want to recast those so that I am ashamed and concerned about them. However— you—I miss you!—and I want to see you! That is not such a good feeling to have. It shocks me at the end of the valley, at the last spur of the ridge.[7]

From the beginning of the piece, we reside in the world of metaphor, negotiating the will—power over self, over other—while examining the value of and limit to assertion. From the opening sentence, we not only talk about the will, represent it, but also experience it. "She crossed the main street, which is enlarged by sexual stimulation." Here the metaphor has parity with the literal (thanks to the coordinate clause), and the multiple strategies, a woman being watched and sexualized language, are underlined by disassociation. We are talking about the street, but we are talking too about the man's vision of the woman as street. The woman as he wants her, the woman he wants to clinically watch and later—in his powerlessness—needs to demean. It is a magical opening—even if it overbrims with intelligence—because it sets in motion the multiple openings and orifices and gaps alluded to in the title. As with the mother, the origin of "openings" and his separateness. And the diction? "I go for the rather thick bitch with my beloved arms and hands" is certainly mixed if not mixed up, satiric but menacing. This sentence is followed by the fissure of having a job and a flat but boundless sea "with its operation of forces," so more voices and poetic arguments are unleashed, making it impossible and undesirable for the reader to extract a single moral construct. The piece offers up simultaneous points of view, and after all, simultaneity, the great pleasure of metaphor itself, provides one of the central pleasures of poetic writing.

In one way, this piece is also about writing, writing as a process: what to admit, when to release it, when to take action, when to acknowledge that the overpowering leaves one alone and powerless and not "unruined." "To be in love," the speaker says: this job is not within the speaker's power, because he only understands conquest and assertion (verbal as well as phallic). "As I tell it," "I want to use the word sexy," and similar assertive phrases self-consciously reveal the simultaneous desire for and lack of power to locate and control. Language can be invented or stumbled over but can't be pinned down: in that sense, the piece wants to reach beyond the explanations that words provide.

Mr. Reinisch, the male speaker's alter ego, is capable of care and being loved and remains "unruined." He seems to possess (the speaker misunderstands) the mythical she, the enlarged street, the sea: "and he is undisturbed by his being cared for." As for the speaker, he would like to meet her, he wants his "boners"; he wants to hear her say about his cock, "That's a very gaudy thing" (later the natural world is the gaudy other). " 'Tell me the ways it can hurt me.' This is the patriotic center." Williams yokes sexual, social, and linguistic imperialism. Reinisch was hoping to get those boners from that bitch, the street and the sea. To be stimulated and satisfied.

But the he remains the watcher, the he who has no self and so needs to be completed. He pushes with his tirades about the "you" (the reader, too) including, "You have your own work, your own mother, the terraced land with vined bowers—your own certainty by the water, the scanty water." We too try to possess our certainties: we too are separate and solipsistic. He asserts, "My cock—slightly rounded at the tip and set high—I hold it high, so contentedly." The cock is flag, phallus, prideful self-assertion. But he confides in the closure, "However—you—I miss you!—and I want to see you! That is not such a good feeling to have. It shocks me at the end of the valley, at the last spur of the ridge."

Williams's strategies do not account for—and do not create—a monochromatic or "realistic" landscape. They create linguistic conflict on the word stage. They take us to the brink where language and experience are enacted and refuse each other. Where language stays language, where the other stays the other. We are moved sentence by sentence, but always remembering and bringing the past into the present. Always dragging the associations of signification behind it. Williams reveals, I believe, a complex understanding of structure that includes fluidity, echoes, intensifications, variations on a theme, moving from distance to closeness within the confines of a single sentence. We don't come out of the piece, if we are careful readers, with one feeling, with a coming to, but we end up *having been somewhere.* The surprises, as she says, are plentiful, and as with Hejinian's prose poem, the reader receives narrative fragments, but the ethos behind these prose poems challenges both chronology (narrative) and the work of art as a reproduction of experience.

Resistance to prose poems and prose poem experiments emanates from its rewards: difficulty and the complexity of fluid boundaries. There's no arguing the difficulty of these works, and they're certainly not poems every reader will like or be able to approach; but in our current climate, accessibility has taken on great currency, though the subtext for accessibility is usually a white, middle-class audience. How complexity can be used as a criticism of poetry and how that standard is applied with such inequality is mystifying: that criticism is rarely leveled at Eliot and Pound, for example, and it should be noted that most avant-garde work has been met with such opposition (the audience fled in panic from Igor Stravinsky's *The Rite of Spring*, early abstract expressionists dismissed Jackson Pollock's "squiggles," and contemporary jazz critics considered Charlie Parker's solos "noise"). Often enough, one person's "difficulty"—as Stein suggested in "Composition as Explanation"—becomes the next generation's literature.

It's no secret that we live in an age where resistance to increasing difficulty and complexity extends everywhere, from government to the classroom, to the media, to medicine (where GPs routinely prescribe antidepressants often without understanding the source of those depressions). Many of my colleagues worry about including Joyce, Melville, or Stein in their syllabi for fear of losing student enrollments. One might argue that these prose pieces are so difficult that their pleasures, intellectual and otherwise, can only be discerned by a few. But even if one were to take, say, one of Stein's well-known prose poems like "Picasso" and read it to a child, the pleasures of language play would surface, and the feeling that erotic play refers to (what Norman O. Brown called, borrowing from and altering Freud, "polymorphous perversity") would be partially absorbed. Relaxing the super-ego in reading poems—that desire to conceptualize or thematize or otherwise reduce by comprehension—serves as counterbalance to the need to immerse oneself directly in experience without transcending it. Yes, these poems are difficult: in the days of the old *Norton Anthology*, that would have meant "worthy of study." I make no such claims for these works. Rather, they remind us of the rewards we miss if we narrow our interest in art to what's easily accessible. A bad life lesson, to always reside in the familiar, indeed the familial—it's the lesson of the insulating and multiply replicated suburban landscapes as well as most American movies, where we sit back and receive (consume) what's readily available, rendering us passive creatures of ritual and cliché. Our lives, feelings, and relationships, when most vibrant, are virtually always tangled, enmeshed, complex, fleetingly comprehensible, and, as I've alluded to heretofore, virtually always revised: we require a highly attuned and attentive consciousness in our lives and art to attend to and expand our lives.

All the poems and prose poems in these first two chapters dramatize the sculptural pleasures of a work of art being made in the present tense: we travel with the poet as he or she constructs, advances, or retards and disbands what precedes or follows. We concentrate less on the poem's product, conclusion, or illumination than on its investigations: its range of feeling (a graph that's *in perpetuum*), its syntactical transformations and repetitions. In many ways, Dickinson and Whitman foreshadowed these poems: Whitman most obviously in the way he—like prose poets—alters the poetic line, but also in the way inside his coordinate clauses he modifies, blurs, or intensifies an originating phrase or claim. But Dickinson's imagination too, at its liveliest, alters formal expectations and freely acknowledges instability and flux, not only in her many crossings out and tentative appending but also in the work itself (fortunately so difficult to thematize and, yes, even understand).

'Tis this—invites—appalls—endows—
Flits—glimmers—proves—dissolves—
Returns—suggests—convicts—enchants—
Then—flings in Paradise—

Here, as elsewhere, imagination—the foundation of poetry—allies itself with the made-up, the made, and the being made. It's one way of many to consider the flight of art.

3.

....

MIXED MESSAGES

Hearing Voices

NOW I'M HERE TO WATCH my tone of voice. But what *is* my tone (ironic, self-conscious, chastised, vigilant?), and why can't it contain multitudes? Why, on the other hand, do young writers so often search for their "voice," as if a voice emanated from a private self, as if constancy reflected that self, a self that, taken to extremes, becomes rigid, fixed, monotonic? Tone is the most elusive of poetic terms, though muddled attempts to fix a definition seem to originate with I. A. Richards's *Practical Criticism* (1929). The *New Princeton Encyclopedia of Poetry and Poetics* suggests that "Tone's multiple nuances" are "often felt to pervade and 'color' the whole, like a mood in a human being, so that the tone becomes its pervading 'spirit.' . . . More specifically tone means tone of voice . . . the tone of the speaker's voice. . . . [Tone] thus reveals information about her attitudes, beliefs, feelings, or intent."[1]

The most recent, sophisticated, and qualified New Critical revision of Richards comes from Ellen Voigt. In *The Flexible Lyric*, she rejects Richards's rigidity—in part because she recognizes that tone shifts in process. Ultimately, in apparent anxiety to move toward "clarity" (echoing Frost's "momentary stay"), she maintains, "Tone in a poem expresses the form of the emotion in that poem and is lodged primarily in the poem's non-discursive elements, especially in its music. Music is meant here to include both the broad units of repetition, sentence structure, and lineation and the small units of syllable, vowel, and consonant." Anchored in the conviction that "voice" in a poem progresses toward clarification, and using as one example Dickinson's "My Life had Stood—a Loaded Gun," Voigt makes music the primary stabilizer of tone. She maintains that the poem's "progression becomes more and more clear, more and more precise . . . and we plummet . . . into a reversal."[2]

Voigt's attempt to locate tone in a particular craft vehicle wards off the entropic and dissonant, assuming closure as an arrival point offering the clarity of resolution. Such New Critical ideas about tonal control don't examine assumptions about stability of identity and hierarchy; Voigt substitutes "progress" and "movement" for Richards's "fixity." This chapter proposes a more fluid reconsideration of tone, one that includes multiplicity in diction and embraces tonal dissonance, one that considers, as Mikhail Bakhtin does in *The Dialogic Imagination*, the contingent and social context of language.

Indeterminacy and linguistic instability both serve to dispel the illusion of a single voice. For an artist to create voice, he or she utilizes several timbres, several tonalities, all in the service of sequence and drama. Voice becomes language unfolding and unraveling. Bakhtin uses the term "heteroglossia" to refer to the role of indeterminacy in style and voice. He writes,

> At any given moment, at any given place, there will be a set of conditions—social, historical, meteorological, physiological—that will insure that a word uttered in that place and at that time will have a meaning different than it would have under any other conditions; all utterances are . . . functions of a matrix of forces practically impossible to recoup, and therefore impossible to resolve. Heteroglossia is as close a conceptualization as is possible of a locus where centripetal and centrifugal forces collide; it is that which a systematic linguistics (the origin of the idea of a unitary voice) must always suppress.[3]

Bakhtin suggests, then, that language is social and reflective: there's no individual voice separate from our social contexts or communities. Therefore all speech is "polyphonic," made of multiple voices. "Every word tastes of the contexts in which it has lived its socially-charged life. All words and forms are populated by intentions."[4] As Linda Park-Fuller points out, "Polyphony refers not literally to a number of voices, but to the collective quality of an individual utterance; that is, the capacity of my utterance to embody someone else's utterance even while it is mine, which thereby creates a dialogic relationship between two voices. For example, I quote or report someone's speech and thereby 'dialogue' with his/her opinion; I appropriate the speech pattern of an admired person and associate myself with that person's linguistic-ideologic community; or I mock someone and dissociate myself from him or her."⁵ In our daily life our speech comes from various sources, historical and social. Listen to the coded speech of adolescents and you will hear in their diction their anxiety to belong to a particular ideological community. As we inhabit more and more social communities, then, those boundaries continue to break down: we listen to the way our parents talk, we pick up speech from work and bring it home. We read newspapers; we listen to our children, friends; we integrate the diction of public figures. It's impossible to repress the range of those voices and to maintain an allegiance to one community of voices without the interjection of others.

These factors complicate, blur, and disrupt the fiction of tone and the unified voice or utterance. Moreover, each poet, consciously or unconsciously, psychologically seeks out the bounds (and in the process searches out of bounds) of his or her tonal range. Temperaments play a crucial role in deciding the range of "authentic" levels of diction and rhythms, but this range also depends upon history, cultural as well as linguistic. Each of us has many originating voices. To use myself as an example, part of my labor as a poet is to attend to, to hear and express, a range of voices that reflect the incongruities of a single identity. Since I was born in Brooklyn, *Fuck you, Senorita* was adjacent to Picasso's late drawings in the Brooklyn Museum, where in sketches *the human animal resisted and indulged in the retrospective, regressive impulse of infantile desire.* I was the first person in my family to finish college, an Ivy League one at that, so I learned to listen to the charming and restrained seduction of the articulate and well-educated voices of long-term wealth. In college I tried to segregate my voices because I had no place to put them. No one on Stillwell Avenue seemed to want to hear about Picasso; and my English professor, as he told me snow was a symbol of death, hardly wanted to know I thought that his literary criticism was not merely faulty, but *fucked.* And "fucked" said it better than, say, "cerebral," because it contained more. My case may be obvious, but we've all been somewhere twisted, diction-like, syntactical and historical, where a range of voices is required to reflect the fullness and particularity of our experience.

Moreover, since a voice has dimension and range (in diction we talk about range as wide or narrow, high or low, formal or informal, as colloquial, mechanical, or slang), the repression of this range in favor of consistency and universality (the canon, the King's English) diminishes a poem's capacity to create linguistic and emotional mobility—a variety of stances—

making it more difficult for a poem to reflect more than one emotion at a time or to inhabit a conflict. It also renders a poem monochromatic. Frostian "clarity" often reflects this reduction with summarizing "wisdom," inadequately closing off the emotional flux and simultaneity raised by the diction and syntax of a poem. Multiplicity is by no means anarchic—but to extend Ellen Voigt's musical metaphors, many of the poets discussed in this book make conscious use of polyphony in the musical sense: symphony. Poets who consciously use these polyphonic strategies complicate the emotional life of a poem and make the reader work to experience the imaginative gaps and fissures as well as more linear connections.

Imitating the associative process of the mind at work in time, these poems dramatize *shifting* and *colliding* points of view, tracing developing attitudes, exploding the myth of the single point of view we usually associate with voice. I mean point of view, quite literally, as a way of *viewing* one's material. The writer's shifting emotional stances, his or her poetic argument, create the fictive voice. We hear those voices most often in relation to some of the following categories: distance—how close or how far away is the speaker; focus—who does the writer and speaker look at and how do we as readers view the speaker; power and hierarchy, addressing issues of size and scope; intimacy—how formally or informally does the speaker present his or her experience, and to what degree does he or she ironically deflect feeling, distort fact, and display pleasure and pain. If the painter Robert Motherwell is right, and writing, like art, is "organizing states of feeling," point of view, the writer's stance, becomes a central vehicle of the fictive voice.[6]

Our willingness to include and address obstacles to the harmonious, the closed, the resolved, then, is instructive. More conservative critics may often be disarmed by tonal dissonance, may find it difficult to contain the tension and nuances of wide-ranging diction, jagged music, and syntax without attributing it to tonal violation or decadent formlessness. "Most poets since the Modernists," Christian Wiman has recently said in *The Sewanee Review*, "claim not to aim at particular forms. Ecstasy affords the occasion, expediency determines the form, and all that."[7] Ecstasy here suggests the inchoate rather than the sublime. Wiman's archaic assertion about "occasion" derides the poem as process and ties poems to a nameable event of feeling; it also misunderstands a primary source of drama in poetry, which is neither *a priori* narrative nor lyric urgency, but rather the word stage.

I suggest the metaphor of the word stage because as readers we know nothing until we read the first word of the poem; feeling accrues syntactically, from one word action to the next; feeling is altered by syntactical movement and accumulated (inside the history of the poem) narrative or lyric. The stage metaphor *does* imply distance, because words are not things—elementary structuralism—but it also implies an intimate fiction because the order, range, and associations of words create a feeling that helps us forget words are words and not experiences. We have an experience, obviously, *of* words. I see "mixed tones" in a poem as choral dissonance; multiple voices—sopranos, altos, tenors, baritones; happiness, unhappiness, melancholy and even ecstasy reside in the same poem, even the same lines—address one another in the body of a poem while acknowledging, advancing, accepting, and/or defending against their differences. The words create intensification and tension but do not *require* the old behemoths, clarity or resolution.

I have listened, intermittently, and with varying degrees of comprehension, to John Coltrane's 1964 recording of *Ascension*: I have heard it as noise, as musicians tuning up, as anger and aggression, as a collage of musical phrases, some repeating, others accelerating; sometimes the piece seems symphonic, tones drawn from the horns trying to outrace the rhythm section. The more attentively I listen, the more I hear motifs dropping in, being inverted, being played in a minor key, and purposively breaking off (fragmenting) into chaos. The piece inhabits the insoluble: it takes us there.

My point is that music, like poetry, can be an adventurous process for writer and reader, a simultaneous moving toward and away from origins and occasions. In bebop, a fixed rhythm, often established by a comping piano, a recurring rhythm from the bass, and meters from the drums, may be set against the "free" improvisation of the horns. But in more contemporary "free" music, the chaotic warring resides simultaneously with the attempt to clarify. The drama is fluid, and as with all the arts, it has been historically transformed, reflecting its time. So Frost's clarity ("a momentary stay against confusion"), a romantic concept already nostalgic in the mid-twentieth century, spoke to a particular historical moment. As others have pointed out, the promulgation of New Critical values, with its emphasis on paradox and resolution, is an attempt to compose ahistorically while ignoring or at least effacing temporality. Robert Schumann once wrote, "We may be sure that if a genius like Mozart were alive today he would write concertos like Chopin's and not (like) Mozart's!" Louis

Armstrong would never have thought of it Coltrane's way. He would have more likely demanded a "clear, contained expression."[8] And although we may listen to Armstrong with pleasure today, we cannot compose with his harmonies, or improvise like him without ignoring what we know has come since.

Shaping any work of art is a sculptural process, responding to what has preceded and then advancing the given (or retarding it with complication or contradiction): that process forms the basis for the structure of poetic argument. Attending to the syntactical movement from word to word as the poem continues to change, readers may not receive a single voice, but will find an architecture that holds the abrading voices in tension. The lyric can no longer be seen solely as a single impulse relentlessly pursued. It works better for Dickinson's "I Heard a Fly Buzz" than Whitman's "Crossing Brooklyn Ferry." On the other hand, what about her parenthetical phrase in the line "With blue—uncertain stumbling buzz"? Here, for at least one moment in the poem, the tone is interrupted with this odd telegram-like talk of Dickinson's; then it retrieves its elegance and passive melancholy in "The windows failed—and then / I could not see to see." The poem's effect is puzzled and hence intensified by its stuttering, its interruption, its grammatical dissociation.

To use a more dramatic Dickinson example for the presence and pleasures of multiple voices, I want to expand upon and diverge from Ellen Voigt's interpretation of "My life had stood—a Loaded Gun." The poem changes its mind and stance almost from line to line, but it never lands in the clarifying reversal Voigt suggests. It simultaneously explores rage, a humble connection with god, and an ambivalent power relationship with language and with a lover. The speaker negotiates feelings about sexuality and power but also tries on a phallic fantasy to see if it brings her what she wants, which is (not only alternately but simultaneously) equality, power, submissiveness, autonomy, and merging with an other. The poem does not end in tragedy or reversal but rather without the possibility of closure ("the power to die"), precisely because any one of those choices excludes the rewards of the other. The poem could not dramatize this intensity of simultaneous desires without open-ended multiple stances and attitudes—which is why the speaker moves not merely from anger to ecstasy but also to feeling conflicted and incomplete but not resigned. Resignation assumes the closure as an arrival point; but rather than resolve the conflicts of the poem, Dickinson leaves the reader with the dilemma intensified but unfixed. The poem takes us where her speaker has been—on an irreconcilable quest for the sublime with her lover, with a fantasy self, and with god.

> My Life had stood—a Loaded Gun—
> In Corners—till a Day
> The Owner passed—identified—
> And carried Me away—
>
> And now We roam in Sovereign Woods—
> And now We hunt the Doe—
> And every time I speak for Him—
> The Mountains straight reply—
>
> And do I smile, such cordial light
> Upon the Valley glow—
> It is as a Vesuvian face
> Had let its pleasure through—
>
> And when at Night—Our good Day done—
> I guard My Master's Head—
> 'Tis better than the Eider-Duck's
> Deep Pillow—to have shared—
>
> To foe of His—I'm deadly foe—
> None stir the second time—
> On whom I lay a Yellow Eye—
> Or an emphatic Thumb—
>
> Though I than He—may longer live
> He longer must—than I—
> For I have but the power to kill,
> Without—the power to die—

In the first two lines the speaker shifts from stasis and shyness to anger, then from being owned to being released and swept away. She feels the pleasures and pains of the sublime, which is why "My Life had stood" is ultimately a love poem. At this syntactical moment in the drama, in the world of love or paradise or eternity, the speaker feels powerful, grandiose, male, connected to the natural; she can speak for the lover (if this is a poem that brushes against the immortality of poetry, she changes her mind and her tone in the closure when she loses the power to die). She smiles; she is even happy. But the tone changes quickly with its "Vesuvian glow," which suggests the violence of gunfire, the explosion of the violent eruption of orgasm; in stanza 4, as often happens in an experience of the sublime, the speaker is restored to a sense of power, then softens her stance to "have shared," which is to say be an equal partner to her partner. And how is her loyalty rewarded? With an understanding that her desire for equality is blurred by her desire for power and control (which, in its explosions of passion and little deaths, the sublime never offers). She ends up without symmetry, understanding (in love) her dependency; and although she has acquired power, it cannot bring together all the dissonant wishes of the poem. We have been through a journey here without the "illumination" of unification or of paradox (paradox implies resolving feelings, making them congruent, erasing differences).

Since words are not things (sensory data, referents) and are always charged with multiple resonances, language creates discrepancy by nature. As Voigt points out, irony cannot account for shifts or transformations in attitude; the speaker is not only contradicting but also modifying what has already been said, as Whitman, for instance, does all the time. Irony, understood as a binary, blurs ambivalence, conflicted and unresolved feelings (which imply the opposite of removal: they require what Keats famously called Negative Capability).

Irony also fails to account for simultaneous feelings, which is required to consider Judith Taylor's poem "Natural Woman." Despite the fact that this is in some ways a conventional narrative poem, traditional definitions of verbal irony—representing discrepancy as the distance between what is said and what is felt—are insufficient to account for the way it deploys pleasure, power, self-satire, and terror simultaneously.

Snails spit glistening threads on my poor pansies, chewed to lace.
Let me not hear one more rattler when I walk up the canyon!
Darwinian nineteenth century crepuscular dread overcomes me when
    the sun goes down and some *thing* scuttles in the attic.
That's a bit of a lie, but I've succeeded in saying crepuscular.
You could say I've a yes/no relationship with nature.

Sunning themselves on the patio, geckos, of whom I'm fond, do
    insouciant push-ups.
I swoosh my broom around, a warning to centipedes oozing their way
    across the carpet.
This is the deal: we all stay where we belong, and no one gets hurt.

"Insouciant push-ups" is certainly clever, but beyond that it emotionally serves as a purposeful, insufficient, and temporary distancing device
from the speaker's fears. The yes/no relationship with nature suggests, on
the one hand, playfully funny, and on the other, the defensiveness of play
(the function here of language). I mean defense as guarded against the literal: nature destroys beauty, threatens with deadly and mostly unknown,
unseen force unless you project with language onto it. Look at the consonant music of the first line and you can hear the damage nature does—
intensifying in the second line with the rattler. The shifting levels of diction provide cues for how the speaker feels toward her subject: her elevated
diction is playful and distant, sometimes satiric, sometimes self-effacing,
but also formal in the way a handshake is formal.

The question this poem asks of its readers is *Can we simultaneously or alternately reside in play and terror?* The closure of the poem, spoken with the
immediacy of slang, offers a questionable assertion of power with the recognition that the phrase comes from the movies (the art and culture part).
"This is the deal: we all stay where we belong, and no one gets hurt." Of
course, you can't make deals with nature, and the bravado of the threat/
plea for boundaries resides delicately on the brink of terror and laughter.
Art provides a defense against danger, a removal through words. But the
sound of words (pure Eros in opposition to the literal) doesn't console the
speaker; rather, it yanks her into the domain of art and play. The erotic
world of language gives her sensual connection and some of the control
over nature that she lacks. It also allows her to play, to fantasize by making
connections with what is entirely other in the poem: the notion that the
geckos are doing push-ups tames them.

For Taylor, the function of metaphor is to temporarily domesticate and
thereby do battle with nature in her imagination. Our traditional view of
irony as removal and discrepancy doesn't account for this closure, which
refuses to choose between irony and the straightforward lyrical impulse.
It accomplishes this complex stance mostly by manipulating diction and
attitude as well as—as Voigt might suggest—by its music (flatness set

against consonance); but here music is utilized in the service of creating a tension between tones. This speaker's fears cost her terror and armor. She means what she says with conviction at the same time that she tries to fend off her feelings of helplessness and terror.

In "No More Marriages," also clearly representational, Linda Gregg subtly shifts tone to move from being confident and well defended to critical of convention to a straightforward plea and then to out-and-out doubt, which is where her vision splinters: she is both resolute and resigned. At first, Gregg's speaker appears to be assertive, all tough and all country.

> Well, there ain't going to be no more marriages.
> And no goddam honeymoons. Not if I can help it.
> Not that I don't like men,
> being in bed with them and all that. It's the rest.
> And that's what happens, isn't it? All those people
> that get littler together. I want things
> to happen to me the proper size.
> The moon and the salmon and me and the fir trees
> they're all the same size and they live together.
> I'm the worse part, but mean no harm.
> I might scare a deer, but I walk and breathe
> as quiet as a person can learn.
> If I'm not like my grandmother's garden
> that smelled sweet all over and was warm
> as a river, I do go up the mountain
> to see birds close and look
> at the moon just come visible and lie down
> to look at it with my face open.
> Guilty or not, though, there won't be no post
> cards made up of my life with Delphi on them.
> Not even if I have to eat alone all those years.
> They're never going to do that to me.

If the speaker seems ironic but absolutely resolute in the opening one and a half lines, her resolve weakens at the end of line two, "Not if I can help it." Then she begins to waver, and when men in bed appear, things get messy. Tones of voice modulate and shift. Get messy to the point of a question mark on line 5. Lines like "The moon and the salmon and me and the fir trees / they're all the same size and they live together" make it appear that the poem's speaker is very confused. She appears to confuse size and scope, becomes soft, part of nature, quiet, receptive, and open. So we have now two apparently contrary voices. But all along the speaker has intended for her life to loom large (meaning open), wanting to experience life directly, without postcards "made up" of her life, without the protection and diminishment of marriage. And she has always known, ever since "people / that get littler together" in lines 5–6, that she needs to do it alone. But how do readers feel about the speaker's coming to that decision? Pleased, saddened, proud, fearful. Here again, Gregg achieves voicings primarily through arguments in diction but also through arguments of sound, in assonance ("that smelled sweet all over and was warm") against the consonance ("being in bed with them and all that"). Gregg establishes her fictive voices, her points of view, the writer's contextual stance toward intimacy and vulnerability, by enacting the flux of poetic argument and by closing with the unspecified "*they're* never going to do that to me," which is both resolute, helpless, and paranoid concerning the culture's capacity to coerce.

"Phantom Pains," from *Design with X*, is one of Dean Young's most emotionally direct poems, and while it may lack some of the improvisational invention of his later poems, it also precedes those moments when the joke sometimes overwhelms the poem. This father-son poem retrospectively circles around disembodiment and distance, as well as distance over time. The speaker's ambivalence about wholeness, about the value or possibility of knowing one's father after he's gone (and he appears as "an ache," a feeling rather than an image), makes the speaker alternately playful and theatrical or fragmented and lost. After the opening couplet's "ache" and the difficulty of deciphering the tone there, the speaker playfully deflates the memory with distraction and demarcates his youth with school activities: in the world of play (and the play), the speaker offers a miracle narrative of good over evil and the sing-song rote and meaningless memorization of Columbus discovering America.

But what follows is spoken in a different voice; the playfulness is troubled as he developmentally "killed things for study." Literally, we associate this "killing" with dissection (here a trope for examining or inspecting), but this moment foreshadows the fragments of photographs the speaker studies as an adult, this time trying to "piece" his father together. In those lines of the second stanza, the tone is completely straightforward. These stops and starts, frequent Dean Young strategies, sometimes accomplished by Frank O'Hara–like and James Tate–like enjambments, are here composed for the purpose of changing one's mind. How seriously does the speaker take the loss of his father, how does he revise his view of time? How much ironic distance and playfulness is required to even look at these "phantom limbs," whether they're portrayed in the father's photographs or the father's shadow as the speaker's own phantom limb?

> Sometimes I remember my father
> as an ache low in the throat
> from a long time holding up my arms—
> the part I played in the kids' play
> as a small flowering shrub
> around which Fox was outwitted,
> the lame walked and Brother Chicken
> restored. In 1492 Columbus sailed
> the ocean blue and year by year
> I grew into my growing-into coat
> and killed things for study.
> Found the digestive system of the worm,
> the eardrum of the grasshopper.
> Found reproductive organs in the squid.
> Passed the test on the four prongs of the heart.

At the end of the first stanza, the speaker's training in biology becomes his mode of discovery and measure of self. He finds and passes things; the tone modulates here: it is lighthearted but distant, descriptive, and, as the diction of the four-pronged heart indicates, clinically disinterested, of minimum scale and value; it is nothing more than "the eardrum of the grasshopper."

The adult melancholy that begins the second stanza represents another shift in voice: the "sad man's photos," associated with a "father" (is the speaker also a father or are we considering a generic father, since the speaker uncovers no image or relationship between father and son?).

> In this rainy winter light
> I've been looking at
> a sad man's photos of himself,

each entitled Father: close-ups blown up
and never a face: back desolate
as moonscape, foot a monumental
prop, cock garishly haired
as monster under big-tops.

These fragments are "blown up," "desolate," "alien"; with the metaphor of his father's cock as "monster," the poem turns theatrical and playful again. The speaker is moving to imagining the circus in the same tone of voice as the play (his retreat to childhood) with "imagine . . . the floods," but it quickly turns seriously again when the father is transformed into the speaker: the image as absence movingly "persists." The entire drama of the poem revolves around exploration and repression, play as defense, as "happy ending" to tragic human events.

Imagine
the naked setups under tiers of floods,
the hours watching a part of yourself
lost from yourself as it appears
in the chemical baths. Imagine
cradling it out of the darkroom
like an amputated limb, the itch
that persist.

In the last stanza, play is no longer possible: resorting to rhetorical repetition, acknowledging his helplessness, only using the subjunctive can the speaker create the fantasy of a just world; in actuality, the poem implies, the world isn't made to be just; pain isn't compensated or transformed. The speaker ends with those animals as a child he used to kill.

If God stood on the corner of Pearl and Commercial.
If God rang a brass bell like the sea
and gathered us in to decree:
for the plumage of the nightjar
you are given eyes,
for the abundant rush of pine forests
you are given ears,
for the brilliances of nosebleed and sudden snow

you are given heart
and those dashing shapes you fear
each time you turn out the light
are only zebra
who are always gentle with their young.

The nosebleeds and the explosions, the aches and the fragments finally lead the reader to a violent and unpredictable father: the speaker's wistful childlike wish to be treated with kindness ends the poem with melancholy. The potential sentimentality of the poem is mitigated by the speaker's own inability to decipher the scale of his ache or his playful attempts to transform it into play, made all the more tragic by the unattainable longing and the recurring fearful darkness of the last stanza. This longing, this indecipherability, gives this poem vitality: it refuses to fix the unfixable.

Cole Swensen takes us to a more difficult place with many gaps. Her "April 3," seemingly an idea-driven poem, at first leaves one far away and full of obvious fissures, grammatical, rhetorical, and narrative:

Curve
now my
love these trees, three
careful arcs
arching away

from

create the space of

the way that turning your back on

The small
trees that border worlds on

Two men alone in boats.

This poem accomplishes its density, its multiple tones and voices by the strategic breaking down of syntax and diction, shifting and stirring the known. The poem seems to eschew regularity or pattern, or does it? It has created a pattern of change, from the lyric opening five lines to the change in perception that involves lots of space in couplets and single lines. The poem begins located in time and ends up watching in the distance men alone in a boat, or the speaker sees the trees as men in a boat.

Tonally, the lines "Curve / now my / love" are almost Shakespearian: intimate but formal. The syntax requires us to ask, is it trees the speaker loves, or is it love that is curved? Both? Yes, because there's an arc as there's an arc to the poem, to "careful arcs" further out from "create the space of," which breaks with the grammar of the sentence and interrupts the emotional inquiry. The speaker desires both closeness and distance, wants to accept, embrace, and resist the motion of the love and the world, which exist outside of her. And the fractured syntax serves as a stutter and a slowing down, a tentativeness, one that we experience but that is not formally accounted for by traditional meters, narrative, or a pursued lyric obsession.

We move from the intimate opening lines to the distant spatial, but the speaker and reader also become observers: two men alone in boats. The love and the trees, the person and the natural, all which began with closeness and love, end up in solitude, partly at the calling of the speaker who is asking for change, who observes change in the trees, and then finally resists it, seeing the "space" as other than it is: the trees, the love, are two men alone in a boat, a contained space, yoked together but separate. As for the richness of the poem's journey, the gravity, the austerity, the shyness, and the withholding, I find it both melancholy and emotional, the way Elizabeth Bishop's poetry is emotional. Once a reader understands her restraint as only apparently formal and descriptive, once a reader hears the parenthetical slips in the voices almost as stutters, one can grasp the way in which emotional suggestion appears in this poem as shyness, an interruption, an aside.

As with Swensen's poem, poems often take shape in their seemingly casual or half-conscious digressions and interruptions. This is the way—not coincidentally—readers track a poem or story: not only by its associations but also by its dissociations, its occlusive and abrasive syntax. A poem's density is amplified by its collected counterharmonies and dissonances.

When I asked Stanley Elkin how he shaped a story, he told me, "I write sentence by sentence: is there another way to do it?" Would that I had understood then the syntactic journey, nurturer of Eros and invention of writing: a reader is stirred by the principle of adjacency. We are moved moment by moment; we are not made whole by the end of an experience.

I'm not suggesting employing dissociative language, segregating the writing experience by taking the body/poem and removing it from the mind; I'm not advocating accident or even necessarily the distant, self-conscious postmodern break; but surely we can reflect experience more fully than by the reification of tonal definition. We can live inside, beside, being intimate with and attending to a poem's fluid and unfolding language—its improvisations, its associations, its multiple resonances. On the word stage, feelings reside transposed: not *represented* the way we are by congressmen and the concomitant corruption of commerce (that gladiola's a stand-in for spring!), not *symbolic* with an equal sign, but inhabited.

Every poem has a change of mind or it's static and "store-bought." But many poems contain many minds that both reflect and embody the instability of language and experience. Certainly multiple tones of voice can be formulaic, subject to the postmodern conventions, and should not escape scrutiny. But we do hear voices. We are not composed artistically or experientially of a single voice: we create tension in poems by memory and suspension, by allowing gaps, by frustrating as well as rewarding expectation. This is an essential element of what we used to call "imagination." If we listen for the dissonant, if we camp out where it's slippery, where the other lives, where discovery and contradiction wrestle with one another before our eyes and ears, where the metaphors are mixed but not random, then the ecstatic and catastrophic can coexist in the same sentence, just as they may live in the same literal moment. And if we listen more attentively to these clashes and nuances, as poets and readers we will experience the world differently, because we're enriched by a consciousness of complication and qualification, by the multiple and the difficult. In this way, perhaps we won't confuse harmony (definition) with neatness, with a desire to dress up the twins in pink so they look alike or to obsessively clean the surface of the counter with a dishrag, to bleach out the stains that might show someone actually lives here.

4.
....

FORM

Neoformalism Revisited

DURING THE HARLEM RENAISSANCE, a passionate aesthetic debate among African American writers centered on two ground-breaking
poets, Claude Mckay and Langston Hughes.[1] In plain terms, McKay,
trained in canonical English by Walter Jekyll, wrote an integrationist poetry that he believed would not only give expression to black experience
but also be accessible to whites. Some associated with the New Negro
movement claimed that Mckay's work demonstrated what W. E. B. Du-
Bois called "double-consciousness," which is to say, aesthetically he saw
himself "through the eyes of the white person"; he wrote about black subjects but employed the diction and received forms (sonnets, etc.) of canonical English. McKay's work, which was thought to be more "universal"
and is ultimately more essentialist in its premises than Hughes's, shared
James Weldon Johnson's controversial criticism of black dialect; Johnson
also maintained that eventually Aframerican poets would be absorbed
into mainstream American poetry: "I do not wish to be understood to
hold any theory that they (Aframerican poets) should limit themselves to
Negro poetry, to racial themes; the sooner they are able to write *American*
poetry spontaneously, the better. Nevertheless, I believe that the richest
contribution the Negro poet can make to the American literature of the
future will be the fusion into it of his own individual artistic gifts."[2]

What differentiated Langston Hughes's views from McKay's was a belief
that African Americans' history differs from that of whites, and so-called
universal expressions of art produced, for black artists, selfless replications
of a culture that didn't speak to their music, art, or experience. When he
published *The Weary Blues* in 1927, Hughes was berated as the "poet low-
rate" by white and black critics alike, because they thought Hughes's por-
trayal of the ghetto would reinforce racial stereotypes. He wrote poems in

the black vernacular based on blues meters or free verse rather than iambic pentameter or traditional end rhyme; moreover, his poems were antitranscendental, celebrating bodily sensuality, leisure, and play.

In his influential essay "The Negro Artist and the Racial Mountain," Hughes made clear the nature of his disagreement with Johnson and his followers: aesthetically his work emphasized racial difference and challenged conventional ideas about audience. Rather than disassociate linguistic practice from his subject, Hughes wanted his poetic discourse to correspond to the rhythms, structures, and experiences of his racialized subjects and culture. If white people labored to embrace the different rhythms, speech patterns, and levels of diction of African American poets, they might absorb some but not necessarily all of what the poet intended, because much of his discourse and experience was alien to them. In the essay, Hughes rhetorically maintains indifference about white acceptance. In reality, all through his career Hughes was deeply divided about audience. He appears to have considered it virtually every time he published: some poems addressed whites—those pleading for equality—while others consciously excluded them. His essay maintains that poets who refuse racial identity are necessarily filled with self-hatred.

In any case, Hughes's aesthetic implicitly critiques liberal humanism's assumption that rich and poor, black and white, share the same language and experience—and are therefore accessible to all—as patently ideological. Historically, canonical culture's claims for universality are sophistic, because they set the standards for value, and thereby their voices are authorized and given currency. In "Criteria for Negro Art," W. E. B. DuBois maintains that "All art is propaganda," reflecting on both the ideological nature of experience and the artist's desire to change consciousness. "I do not care a damn for any art that is not used for propaganda. But I do care when propaganda is confined to one side while the other is stripped and silenced."[3]

The terms of this Harlem Renaissance argument illuminate a discussion that still permeates American poetry today. The implication behind these two positions informs questions of form and accessibility as well as the more obvious and crucial question of how to portray art racially. What does this have to do with neoformalism? For one thing, the current advocates of received forms replicate seventeenth- and eighteenth-century British Enlightenment values disguised as constant and universal truths (Walt Whitman and William Carlos Williams had many of the same objections to these poetic values). These poets are nostalgic advocates for an aesthetic that serves to stabilize and conserve form as well as ideas about culture, at the cost of effacing history, complication, and change (change more radical poets have been resisting since Blake and the advent of romanticism).

Neoformalist David Mason, in *The Hudson Review*'s poetry round-up, says, "I have been reading Arthur Schopenhauer to cheer myself up." Later he explains why: "Schopenhauer believed in masterpieces and the viability of poetry that could reach readers everywhere in the stands. To many contemporary minds, this is a contradiction, but as the philosopher said, 'nothing is easier to write so that no one can understand; just as contrarily, nothing is harder than to express deep things in such a way that everyone must necessarily grasp them.'"[4]

In these few sentences, Mason lays bare some of the ideological underpinnings of neoformalism. Schopenhauer's view of art, that "contemplation of the object of aesthetic appreciation temporarily allowed the subject a respite from the strife of desire," turns art into transcendent flight. Truth is beauty here. "The aesthetic experience temporarily emancipates the subject from the Will's domination and raises them to a level of pure perception."[5] Additionally, "we forget about our individuality, and we become the clear mirror of the object."[6] Art, then, in its purity and segregation from desire, becomes a way to access "the thing itself." Schopenhauer's idea of artistic genius was someone who accessed the universal truth of the thing.

Mason links this view of art with Schopenhauer's valuing accessibility to "everyone in the stands." Using Schopenhauer's aphoristic assumption that writing of the highest ("deepest") order is accessible to all is linguistically naïve, filled with a disregard for history and cultural differences, unexamined ideas about race, class, dialect, and the difference between the referent and the signifier. Using his own metaphor, "everyone in the stands" is so culturally specific that those unfamiliar with Western athletic stadiums might not even understand what he's talking about. And that's a small part of what's wrong with his ideas about "Masterpieces," because he also neglects the power, premise, and authority of those who authorize those masterpieces. One look at the last half dozen *Norton Anthologies of Modern Poetry* indicates the place of commerce, editorial bias, and dictates of cultural fashions (most recently, fewer African Americans, more Native Americans and Hispanics) as much as it signifies "masterpiece." When Dana Gioia edits those anthologies, a reader will notice the virtually complete absence of postmodern poems among his "masterpieces," though he himself appears in the anthology.

More recently David Mason has expressed with greater clarity and less subtlety his advocacy of accessibility and his disdain for difficulty. He proclaims, "In our time there are precisely two kinds of poets: populists and snots. The populists believe that something generally referred to as 'the world' is more important than their poetry. The snots believe their poetry is more important that 'the world.'"[7] Now he means this comment to be humorous, but he also believes it: he uses the review of X. J. Kennedy's light verse to support this contention. For neoformalists who consider themselves populists, poets who compose difficult poems "in our age" (i.e., modernity) use language as an assertion of ego. This absurd judgment implicitly associates difficulty with that anti-intellectual conservative buzz word "elitism" (an accusation often used by radical right-wing commentators like Anne Coulter, but one that had also spread to populist poetry commentary).[8] One could argue contrarily that Mason's moral superiority forgoes the possibility that one project of contemporary poetry might be to negotiate the relationship between word and world, to render the labyrinthine connection between the two rather than to choose one over the other.

Timothy Steele, one of the more articulate and intellectually rigorous of the current wave of neoformalists (many of whom emulate or replicate Ivor Winters's conservative aesthetic and cultural values at Stanford—Robert Pinsky, Ken Fields, and Christian Wiman are among some of the others), claims:

> Versification benefits from both rhythm and meter. Without rhythm, verse is lifeless. Without meter, verse risks sacrificing memorability, subtlety, force, and focus. If the experiment of the 20th century was to separate rhythm and meter, the challenge of the 21st century may be to re-connect them in a vital and fruitful way, so that poets again may, as Thom Gunn writes in "To Yvor Winters, 1955,"

> . . . keep both Rule and Energy in view,
> Much power in each, most in the balanced two.[9]

These absolutes are surely open to question: first, the classical advocacy of balance reflects nothing more than an Enlightenment view of the value of harmony; Steele's notion of rhythm is iambic. He views twentieth-century poetic practices as an aberrant "experiment" and elsewhere views the history of British standards of meter from Sydney to the end of the nineteenth century as eternal, making clear his wish to restore those values to poetry. His assumption that subtlety, force, and focus are the purview of metered poetry also suffers from high-level generalizations: setting aside the troubling charged masculinity of "force," even if he is thinking of the intensifying effect of poetry or of subtlety as complexity, how would he account for multivalent writers like John Ashbery, Lyn Hejinian, or Susan Howe, or how could he embrace the diversity of musical notations in other cultures (e.g., Asian poetries or reggae music in the Caribbean) equally persuasive as our own iambics?

"Memorability" as a product of cadence certainly served the oral tradition beginning with the troubadours, but surely there's as large a difference between memorizable and memorable as there is between artisanship and artistry. Memory is also partly subjective and associative: it isn't limited to the capacity to reproduce a repeated cadence. Personally, I remember Mozart Kochel listings and the taste of exceptional wines. I remember Federio Garcia Lorca's poem "A Moon Rising," but I could not begin to recite Tennyson's "Locksley Hall," so pertinent to Steele's literary memory and equally pertinent as inspiration for the title poems of his latest collection (to be discussed below), although I studied the poem in three different courses and twice had to teach it. Of course, it's easier to remember simplicity, and there's nothing wrong with simplicity per se, though it's hard to imagine its appearing on a checklist of *a priori* aesthetic values. But experience is complex, multivarious, rich, and difficult, and often so are its textures and rhythms: sometimes we require a language and music that reflect the density of that experience to capture it more fully and authentically.

Then there's that "balance" quotation from Thom Gunn: a classical notion, the tension we hear in Mozart piano concerti: the left hand steady, the right hand seemingly free to move up and down the keyboard. There may be nothing wrong with writing "classically"—it's the very premise of New Criticism—but one wonders why in other art forms classicism was transformed into romanticism and then modernism, what contemporary artists may view as neoclassical (say, the neoclassical works of Stravinsky, whose Pulcinella Suite improvises off a theme attributed to Pergolesi and which employs many of the same rhythmic strategies—some parodied—

Stravinsky had used in *The Rite of Spring*). Actually, in the case of neoformalists, they replicate the mode of British poetry from Sydney to Hardy. To view that history as universal and eternal ultimately represses evolving formal concerns and practices in our and other literary cultures. Unlike the accomplished "neos" in other art forms, most of the self-identified neoformalists are working with a poetic vocabulary that ignores the history of the art since the origins of romanticism.

Steele's title poem of his newest collection, "Toward the Winter Solstice," dramatizes the problem with making claims for accessibility, memorability, and universality.

> I make adjustments. Though a potpourri
> Of Muslims, Christians, Buddhists, Jews, and Sikhs,
> We all are conscious of the time of year;
> We all enjoy its colorful displays
> And keep some festival that mitigates
> The dwindling warmth and compass of the days.

In the above lines, Steele clearly doesn't mind being a spokesperson for all nationalities and religions; he doesn't mind asserting not only that everyone is conscious of the colorful lights (read metaphorically in part as the "Christmas spirit") but also that the lights are enjoyed by everyone. This "festival" symbolically "mitigates" cold (emotional as well as the thermometer) and transcends time!

First, there's the greeting-card quality in the music of the poem:

> Some say that L.A. doesn't suit the Yule,
> But UPS vans now like magi make
> Their present-laden rounds, while fallen leaves
> Are gaily resurrected in their wake;

Steele employs the pathetic fallacy (a "weeping birch's crown") and reinforces the magi and the "resurrected" Christian symbolism; lines are overloaded with clichés ("And as the neighborhoods sink into dusk"), telling adjectives and adverbs that act either as emotional directive or filler for the meter of lines ("Will accent the tree's elegant design"). The poem's closure, though, is probably most instructive and a product of its claims for universality:

Some wonder if the star of Bethlehem
Occurred when Jupiter and Saturn crossed;
It's comforting to look up from this roof
And feel that, while all changes, nothing's lost,
To recollect that in antiquity
The winter solstice fell in Capricorn
And that, in the Orion Nebula,
From swirling gas, new stars are being born.

Here the poem rhetorically makes its essentialist claim for the eternal ("It's comforting to look up from this roof / And feel that, while all changes, nothing's lost"); of course it might be comforting to some to feel nothing's lost and that the Star of Bethlehem still instructs, and, thanks to the correspondence with "antiquity," we have recurrence; how different the sky may have looked, that the relationship between signifier and referent might suggest that it is possible that "back then" people didn't have the same feelings about the connection between the sign of "summer solstice" and the constellations, never intrudes on this act of faith suggested as eternal truth.

What is most intrusive about this poem is the implication behind its assumptions about universality: it authorizes the poet to represent, to speak for, everyone—at the same time it assumes that the speaker's values are indisputably shared. On a daily basis, I can say I associate colored lights (appearing earlier and earlier every year) with American consumerism, but that association is as subjective as Steele's: I wouldn't claim that perspective in any way as universal. Nor would I put my faith in Christian metaphors as if we all shared and participated in those religious values or those conventional and familiar archetypes.

What makes this poem so flat and predictable, aside from its myopic vision, is both its insistent ahistoricity (this poem could have surely appeared in one of those tepid academic anthologies of the 1950s, another epoch whose cultural aspiration was essentially to "comfort") and Steele's faith that twentieth-century poetry represents an aberration in the history of all of poetry. One might consider it an aberration if high modernism didn't grow directly out of a response to the failure of romanticism, or if Langston Hughes and others from the Harlem Renaissance didn't bring the language of the urban Negro into the world of poetry (those poems also developed out of a response to Paul Lawrence Dunbar and other writers at the turn of the century). Poetic practice doesn't evolve from merely some inner, insular set of constant principles: it responds to experiential changes in the word and world. In fact, Steele's inspiration for this poem draws on Tennyson's imagery and ideas in his bitterly nostalgic "Locksley Hall." Orion in Tennyson's poem suggests a similar dilemma concerning constancy and the temporal and also solves its dilemma with assertion and rhetoric. Tennyson's nostalgic and mythic poem uses the constellations to enlarge the bitter speaker's feeling about loss of a childhood love and his accommodation to accept the virtues of civilization (so Steele's speaker won't have to worry about "unsuitability").

O, I see the crescent promise of my spirit hath not set.
Ancient founts of inspiration well thro' all my fancy yet.

Some of Tennyson's speaker's opinions are so repugnant (degrading images of a romantic fantasy with a primitive) that advocates of the poem have perhaps appropriately made distinctions between the speaker's and Tennyson's views (although paired with the later poem "Locksley Hall Revisited," the parallel is at least worrisome). But one doesn't have to tag Steele with Tennyson's conservatism to suggest that using Tennyson the way he does, the poem seems archaic or at best ahistorical—because he's repressed all the complications of linguistic and personal experience that has followed that poem.

Why ahistorical? Let's take a thumbnail history of another art form: jazz. At the turn of the century, ragtime became the first popular cross-race rhythm for jazz. "The resultant music created a 'ragging' effect or embellishment to the music by combining spontaneous melodic variations with syncopated rhythms."[10] The syncopation is regular, but the defining characteristic of ragtime music is a specific type of syncopation in which melodic accents occur between metrical beats. Elements of the blues and ragtime in particular combined to form harmonic and rhythmic structures upon which to improvise. Social functions of music also play a role in this convergence: whether for dancing or marching, celebration or ceremony, music was tailored to suit the occasion. Ragtime was followed historically by what is retrospectively called classic jazz, a kind of collective improvisation made famous by—among others—Louis Armstrong's Hot Five. One historical explanation for the shift from classic jazz to swing or big band jazz, in the late 1920s and early 1930s, was the impossibility of microphone placement for larger bands. Collective improvisation sounded merely chaotic. So most famously Duke Ellington transformed the music into more of a concerto form, with continuing dialogue between soloist and orchestra. The rhythms, while less syncopated than ragtime rhythms, were relatively regular. To compare them to poetic rhythms, they might sound something like this: stress-slack-stress-slack-stress-slack-stress-slack, with a heightened emphasis on the third beat. Swing was dominated by eighth notes and regular beats from the rhythm section to support the improvisation of the soloists. One can see the correspondence between these musical principles of classic jazz and the classicism of classical music. In the work of Haydn, Mozart, and others, the left hand remained steady while the right hand improvised. This shift one might find also mirrored in eighteenth-century painting, when the baroque gave way to the rococo. But returning to the mutability of jazz as a medium, in the mid-1940s Charlie Parker and Dizzy Gillespie introduced complication to that meter, playing off chord changes with much greater variation, really changing jazz forever. The next movement was called hard-bop, followed by free jazz, and so on. This chronology doesn't indicate "progress" in the liberal sense of improving the art, but it does represent the kind of continuing complication of artistic movements through time. The point is, as I've suggested earlier in relation to Bach, no serious contemporary jazz artist would consider writing in the meters of Duke Ellington or even Charlie Parker. The musical language of Thelonious Monk, the inventions provided by Miles Davis and John Coltrane and later by Cecil Taylor, David Murray and the Art Ensemble of Chicago, all became part of the vocabulary of the art of jazz. In classical music, a contemporary composer might return to tonal music, but he would have in his repertoire Schoenberg, Dodge, Elliott Carter, and others who compounded the art. The history of an art form—just like history itself—brings with it the burden of listening and paying attention to its transformations as well as its constancies.

When neoformalists write in a style and with a vision unmediated by the increasing vocabulary of the art and complexity of the age, though the artisanship may be accomplished, the art is, for the most part, composed in a dead idiom with a network of symbols, images, and archetypes that are academic in every sense of the word. In this context, the final death knell for the legislation of received forms in contemporary American poetry probably came in the late 1950s, when poems that had currency in the dominant culture were virtually indistinguishable from the poems written now by the neoformalists. Donald Hall, Robert Pack, and Louis Simpson's *The New Poets of England and America*, published in 1957, was really the last anthology to refuse the diversity of writing practices in its age. Dominated by white males (forty-five white males to seven women and perhaps one African American), its assumptions included the transcendence of culture and the universality of its judgments. In later anthologies, like the Pack and Leary's 1965 *A Controversy of Poets*, what we might now call the "culture wars" surfaced (more accurately, early challenges to the premises behind the canon were in some small degree recognized, making room for some diversification and more inclusiveness—including the contemporary avant-garde, which primarily consisted of Black Mountain poets and the Beats). It is not an accident that this anthology appeared at the same time of the civil rights movement and the beginning of the resistance to the Vietnam War: cracks in the armor of New Criticism were visible in the culture and were increasingly criticized by artists in all art forms as well.

When I characterize the neoformalist movement as conservative, I mean that they're aesthetically conservative and historically reactionary; I would also maintain that their vision of experience is conservative as well. Neoformalists balk at the notion that their poems are "conservative," pointing to a handful of formalist poets (like Marilyn Hacker) who claim progressive or left-leaning politics. If poems were essays, one might find this argument more persuasive; but in any art the mode of address matters: assumptions about constancy, about representation and the right to speak for everyone, these are also conservative values. In Cézanne's paintings, his view of how we perceive the world is implicit and central to his artistic vision, his way of seeing the world as mobile, flux-filled, and subjective. In this regard, I take more seriously—and am more transformed by—the means of expression (praxis) than the rhetorical opinions and observations of poets.

Perhaps no neoformalist makes fewer distinctions nor is more disingenuous than Dana Gioia, in his attempt to flex his diversity muscles by appropriating black art and rap. "Is rap an extension of formal academic poetry of the 1950s because it uses rhyme and meter? It's a silly argument."[11] First of all, rap is an oral art, a performance art, often accompanied by music, and like drama its effect must be immediate as well as long term: there's no question rhyme and beat make an important contribution to rap songs. Second, while rap artists predominantly depend upon end rhyme, their rhythmic practice is rarely iambic, and inside the verse line a reader will find incredible diversity, often including the rushed laxity of prose. Finally, ask a rap artist what he or she considers the resemblance between the dictions, rhythms, and syntactical movements of rap and those much more metronomic verses of neoformalism. It doesn't take a highly discriminating intelligence to recognize the essential difference between Gioia's "The Next Poem,"

> How much better it seems now
> Than when it is finally done —
> the unforgettable first line,
> the cunning way the stanzas run.

and say, this brief excerpt from the far from universal 504 Boyz's "Holla."

> These little niggaz can't take it anymore
> I push thru the club iced out low key wit my P. Miller velour
> Hoes breakin' down the doors uhn
> Because the 504 Boyz here, they can't wait til' we get on
> It's Curren$y the muthafuckin' rookie of the year
> This ain't the WNBA ain't no pussy's over here
> Yeah I'm makin' figgas fuckin' wit the Ghetto Bill
> In a truck wit some rims that's bigger than ferris wheels holla[12]

If anything, like most rap artistry, "Holla" more resembles Hughes's view of cultural specificity: its ideas about form, culture, and the function of rhetoric have more in common with the postmodern than they do with neoformalism. But the idea of groups like 504 Boyz appreciating poets like Steele and Gioia would, I think, provide the kind of absurdist entertainment as those professors in the Marx Brothers' *Horse Feathers* romping through the classroom singing "Whatever it is, I'm against it."

Poets are a strange breed, often conflating responsibility for the implications of their vision with some kind of political test. So while in my original essay on this subject I talked about neoformalists as being nostalgic essentialists, some critics thought my labeling them as conservative made a direct link to their political stances, when in actuality I was questioning their aesthetic assumptions in a cultural context. My premise for that essay was as follows: in a conservative age (the end of the Reagan era) art will to varying degrees reflect the cultural milieu. The desire to write in fixed forms in the twentieth- and twenty-first centuries is often a nostalgic attempt to make poetry more accessible and (according to their writings on the subject) recapture universality, concepts that—as I suggest here and elsewhere—require unpacking. The neoformalists confuse the idea of form with writing in rhyme and meter, when form ultimately reflects the architectural (again, it is not a fixture) and is much more fluid than neoformalists acknowledge. Form contains discovery, intensification, structural diversification, and reinforcement (a dialectical tension between the subject that is revealed and transformed and a willingness to entertain the multiple textures of experience using *all* vehicles of the craft). Rhythm in our historical moment is much more diverse than the predominant conservative association with the iamb. A poem that is written in received forms but that has progressive or radical sentiments still accomplishes its task conservatively, often with rhetorical strategies held up—like Alexander Pope's "Essay on Man"—by a scaffolding of meter. So the more sensual and sensory aspects of writing experience—those strategies that are more densely textured, less immediately decipherable as a single thing—may be effaced. A rhetorical closure is an opinion, no matter what the substance of the opinion. And if the closure is accomplished emblematically, with metaphor or image, as I suggest in my discussion of Stafford's "Traveling in the Dark," it can more immediately be translated into a message or an idea, so that those who already agree with those sentiments will register comfort and pleasure in recognition; those readers who wish to be moved, however, might prefer to accompany the poet on his or her journey, by what happens *performatively* in a poem.

As I pointed out in the chapter on prose poems, there are always some artists who temperamentally belong more to the past than their present moment and write well because those allegiances are products of personality and a conviction that the purpose of art is to preserve, but it is difficult to find those artists among these contemporaries. Ultimately, the proof of the value of a movement is in the work itself: those American poets who wrote formally with success mostly come from the generation of poets born in the 1920s (Elizabeth Bishop, though her late free verse work probably offers the pinnacle of her work, Richard Wilbur, Donald Justice, James Merrill, Derek Walcott, and Ronald Jarrell).[13] With very few exceptions, those who have followed, including Steele, Gioia, Mary Jo Salter, and lesser lights, often seem like imitative artisans or dilutions of earlier formalists. Not that writing in received form is to be *a priori* dismissed, but those who write formally now, like the aforementioned D. A. Powell, Ted Berrigan, Olena Kalytiak Davis, Ben Lerner, or Gerald Stern in his *American Sonnets*, extend their imaginations not only to subject but also to the medium itself and make use of knowledge gleaned from the changes brought forth by literary history. For the rest of those poets, it is difficult to find a neoformalist poem that contains a freshness of mind or imaginative technique in the service of vision that would make me change my mind about my 1990 essay on the subject. In the ensuing ninteen years, the movement has been given a breath of extended life by formalist Christian Wiman, who took over the editorship of *Poetry* magazine around the same time the magazine was given a multimillion dollar donation (with an advertising budget that made possible an increase in their readership several fold). In fact, if anything seems to unite neoformalists, it is their considerable entrepreneurial skills: in their many anthologies—mostly by Gioia and R. S. Gwynne—they have promoted one another with the kind of exclusive cadre-based social network that defines many of our different poetry clubs. In fairness to Wiman, *he* is not responsible for the financing (the Lilly foundation is). But Gioia's switching the funding of the National Endowment for the Arts from contemporary artists to programs centered on reading Shakespeare in schools—for whatever the merits of the programs he established—diminishes opportunities for support, attention, and audience for more adventurous contemporary writers. John Rockwell is one of many who laments this cultural shift: "one hopes that Mr. Gioia at some point can find a way to push his consensus toward helping artists create the masterpieces of tomorrow, masterpieces that challenge or even scare the assumptions of today. That would be a win-win policy not just for the present, but for the future."[14]

Even so, the neoformalist movement is passing into obscurity without creating a significant body of work: it reminds me why I objected so much to Robert Richman's *The Direction of Poetry* in the first place. In a conversation, experimental trumpet player Dennis Gonzales told me he stopped touring and playing in clubs for a while because Wynton Marsalis (the neoconservative jazz trumpeter, who uses his funding to perform the work of Duke Ellington instead of original or contemporary work) "took up a lot of air space." And those who get a lot of air space tend to frame the terms of an argument.

5.

HISTORY MATTERS

A Minority Report

IN THE BRILLIANT RUSSELL Banks short story, "Sarah Cole: A
Type of Love Story," the protagonist Ron, a self-described extraordinarily
handsome upper-middle-class white man, has an affair with a very ugly
(as described by Ron) lower-class woman who packs *TV Guides* in boxes
for a living. This is the kind of narrative—where love supersedes time and
station—fairy tales are made of; in the middle of this short story, for a
brief transcendent moment, again according to Ron, the "magic" works:

> We stood across from one another and watched while we each simul-
> taneously removed our own clothing . . . until we were both standing
> naked in the harsh gray light, two naked members of the same species,
> a male and a female, the male somewhat younger and less scarred than
> the female, the female somewhat less delicately constructed than the
> male, both individuals pale-skinned, with dark thatches of hair in the
> area of their genitals, both individuals standing slackly, as if a great
> protracted tension had at last been released.[1]

Had this been the end of the story, we might be tempted to believe
that the naked human animal, having effaced the "scars" and refused class
difference, had indeed transcended culture, attaining the blessed state of
universal love. But one paragraph later, Ron tells us "During the next few
weeks, we met and made love often, and always at my apartment." From
that moment, the moment they reenter the world on his "closeted" turf,
they live in history.

What eventually complicates their romance is their different pasts and
divergent class differences. Sarah had a bad experience with an abusive
husband; Ron became uncomfortable about "showing" the unattractive

"trophy" of Sarah in public; they had sex but nothing to talk about. Their interest in one another partook of colonizing: they came together because of their curiosity about each other's strangeness. Sarah had approached him on a dare from her fellow women workers. Ron initially found himself curiously drawn to this "unattractive," stationless woman in cowboy boots. When it came to eventually making a commitment (love over time) and Sarah told Ron he "owes her," narcissistic Ron threw Sarah out of his apartment, calling her an "ugly bitch." Sarah disappeared from view, rumored to be dead; Ron's bourgeois guilt and feelings of omnipotence make him feel responsible for her death, although he really doesn't know if she's dead or not.

I know of no more succinct critique of romanticism's transcendent moment of illumination than the above-quoted passage of Banks's story. In the twenty-first century, when the forces and velocity of culture make the whole notion of identity more unstable than ever, it is not only naïve but often self-serving to efface cultural differences and the influence of living in our particular historical moment. The signs and signposts continue to change; it is at least problematic to grant an individual sufficient consciousness or agency to decipher, direct, or control those changes. In other words, as this unreliably narrated story underscores, it has become more and more difficult to untangle the sources of our feelings and values: do they come from some inner place or are they infused into us by our surroundings? In Ron and Sarah's case, the terms for what they value—how they commodify one another—differ from, say, the qualities each would find appealing in a nineteenth-century partner. Banks's story dramatizes, in shifting from first to third person, that Ron's notion of a core self is relational, tentative, and entangled with an indecipherable social world.

Moreover, in mass culture, terms like "self" have been revised by magazines, television, the Internet, and so forth. While post–World War II existentialists might have meant one thing by "self," in our culture the term is often translated into taking care of *one's* self; in some humanistic therapies, we hear the aphorism, "Only by loving yourself can you truly love others." These solipsistic discourses enter "Sarah Cole" and, indeed, our contemporary consciousness: particular to our American culture (though cultures too are now more permeable), they mediate our very sense of who we are.

To take another kind of example, in Haydn's Symphony no. 22, "The Philosopher," the first movement calls to mind the sacred music of Bach, but more obviously you can hear Handel in the elegant stasis of the ceremonial horns. In the second movement, though, still some fifteen to twenty symphonies from the so-called Sturm und Drang symphonies, you can hear, with the bristling energy in the attack of the first violins, the characteristic wider melodic leaps and sudden contrasts in dynamics, a glimpse of the musical future. Like experience itself, the symphony doesn't fit into a rigid category or an immutable present. But the artistic present always absorbs the artistic past, processes it, and, in much of the most energetic work (more so in a restless age, like ours), manages to transform it. Art does live in history, dependent upon its antecedents and limited by its field of vision (which does not, temporally speaking, expand infinitely into the future). Every work of art participates in the conventions of its age: like Haydn's symphony, it may resist those conventions, but it will always reflect and revise what's already known. You would not hear Webern's twelve-tone scale in "The Philosopher" because Haydn does not receive his ideas about harmony from Arnold Schoenberg or his experience from twentieth-century Germany's growing empire and industrialization.

The subtext for these examples is twofold: just as we honor the importance of syntax as it unfolds in a poem and creates the poem's living and mutating history, in a larger sense *every* poem resides in its moment of history. So while we might wish for transcendence or the momentary illumination sought by the romantics to slow down history, or while we might essentialize our experiences as eternal and universal—as I pointed out in my discussion of the neoformalists—as readers and writers we always depend on looking backward *and* forward, revising what we already know by the next word, the next moment.

History Matters proceeds from the conviction that since we live and write in history, our artistry is circumscribed by and measured against the ways we traverse, resist, nostalgically reconsider, or unconsciously accede to the conventions of our age. The vision that artists conjure can never be completely stabilized, nor can any art fully transcend its cultural surroundings without the ensuing repression or displacement being reflected in the work. One may find a spectrum in terms of the role of culture (how central or peripheral it might be) in any particular poem's project, but even in a poem like James Wright's "A Blessing" (written during the Vietnam War, and foregrounding the speaker's longing and loneliness), the illuminating moment is only possible "Just off the highway" and past the "barbed-wire fence." The speaker steps away from the alleged boundaries of "civilization," for the much more civilized though isolated world of these horses that "ripple with kindness." Having given up on cultural models for love and openness, he seeks it out in "Whatever it was I lost, whatever I wept for / it was a wild, gentle thing" ("Milkweed"). The shadow of the Vietnam war is present in these poems. While a poet like Robert Lowell foregrounds his place in history, Elizabeth Bishop is enlivened and lost in large part because of her desire to escape America by "visiting" other cultures. She explores the consequences of spectatorship and exile in many of her poems, most obviously in poems like "Questions of Travel" and "Santarem." Even an aesthete painter like Morandi, whose obsession with bottles and muted interiors appeared during the most intense fighting of World War II (and led to his taking his family to Grizzana), reveals in his resistance to and repression of the chaotic world outside these great paintings his intense desire for harmony in his compositional structure. But as with many modernists, much of the world had to be left out for him to accomplish it and thereby might circumscribe the limits of his accomplishment. In the broadest sense, every artistic creation contains both the history of its art and of experience; in poetry it contains the cumulative history of its sentences in its syntax.

I am by no means suggesting that art's function is sociological but rather that artistic creation always receives nourishment and resistance from the world. Our cultural environment always contributes, consciously or unconsciously, to shaping our art. We take for granted these permeable boundaries in other art forms: in music, we can recognize Bach's music as originating in the baroque, bearing resemblances to the musical discourse of his age. His music differs from that of Brahms in part because they lived in different ages. Brahms heard and was influenced by different artists (including Bach), but Brahms also aspired to conserving his art while making concessions to *his* culture: he also made a secular living rather than one from the church (which explains why Bach cranked out more than two hundred cantatas while Brahms wrote popular waltzes).

Consciousness of these regulating cultural conventions and discourses can help untangle the expressive from the conventional while broadening and contextualizing our experience of a work of art. Minorities and women, in both their art and lives, have almost always consciously reflected on their relationship to history, because of their social position and because of the way history so palpably acts upon them on a daily basis. Equally important, they respond to how majority discourse shapes, authorizes, and regulates their own. Pamela J. Annas's study of Sylvia Plath underscores the way in which Plath, the married, ambitious woman poet in 1960, is circumscribed not only by psychological diagnosis but also by what the culture supplies or fails to supply.

> The dialectical tension between self and world is the location of meaning in Sylvia Plath's late poems. Characterized by a conflict between stasis and movement, isolation and engagement, these poems are largely about what stands in the way of the possibility of rebirth for the self. . . . in the post-*Colossus* poems the self is more often seen as trapped within a closed cycle. One moves—but only in a circle and continuously back to the same starting point. Rather than the self *and* the world, the *Ariel* poems record the self *in* the world. The self can change and develop, transform and be reborn, *only if the world in which it exists does; the possibilities of the self are intimately and inextricably bound up with those of the world.*[2]

In *Black Skin, White Masks,* Frantz Fanon provides an example of this dynamic between self and world applicable to race: "For it is implicit that to speak is to exist absolutely for the other. . . . The black man has two dimensions. One with his fellows, the other with the white man. A Negro behaves differently with another Negro. That this self-division is a direct result of colonialist subjugation is beyond question." Earlier, he claims that for "a Negro who is driven to discover the meaning of black identity . . . White civilization and European culture have forced an existential deviation. . . . What is often called the black soul is white man's artifact."[3]

Fanon's vision, which applies to other minorities as well, is reflected on and articulated most directly by Homi Bhabha, who also rejects the reductive binary of "oppressor" and "oppressed" in favor of a more complex dynamic, one he calls "hybridity," a concept that honors the continuing push and pull of those relationships. In its simplest terms, minorities cannot "escape" the dominant culture by resistance: they are always in dialogue with that majority culture, so their quest for autonomy—when the regulatory economic and social laws remain in place—is continually altered by those power relationships. In a similar fashion, a female artist also remains in dialogue with male artists (even if she addresses her work exclusively to women) because she inhabits a system of knowledge and discourse that still regulates and authorizes her. To talk about "freedom," therefore, one must confront and inhabit the shape of what the minority knows as law. Even our most ambitious and eccentric minority artists, directly or indirectly, address that set of power relations.

Langston Hughes wrote his famous poem "Theme for English B" in 1949. But the retrospective poem is informed by consciousness of two different eras. Narrative time is a composite taken from his time at Columbia in 1921–22 when Hughes (as I alluded to in the last chapter) was very much involved in a debate inside the African American community. Hughes's poems from this time, eventually published in 1926 as *The Weary Blues*, drew criticism from more "integrationist" writers like Claude McKay, who felt that Hughes's black slang and sensual characterizations played upon racial stereotypes. By 1949, the United States was in the middle of the cold war (and under the pressure of McCarthyism); Hughes had become more conservative and ambivalent about his allegiances to race and class (in the 1930s, Hughes had been sympathetic to the Communists and wrote about his visits to the Soviet Union). In a conservative culture, having lived through ruptured relationships with established white and black patrons (most importantly Carl Van Vechten and Charlotte Mason), he addressed his poem—in very mixed tones—to a white audience, a professor who had authority over him. Sometimes deferential, sometimes wrathful about his subjection and exile, sometimes imploring the professor for respect and equality (this being five years before *Brown v. Board of Education*), the diachronic poem is pressurized both by memory and the present tense, by two different historical moments: the resolution of the poem, couched simultaneously in negation and qualification ("somewhat"), acts out Fanon's dialectic of the minority's split-consciousness.

> I guess being colored doesn't make me *not* like
> the same things other folks like who are other races.
> So will my page be colored that I write?
> Being me, it will not be white.
> But it will be
> a part of you, instructor.
> You are white—
> yet a part of me, as I am a part of you.
> That's American.
> Sometimes perhaps you don't want to be a part of me.

Nor do I often want to be a part of you.
But we are, that's true!
As I learn from you,
I guess you learn from me—
although you're older—and white—
and somewhat more free.

This is my page for English B.

The poem is commonly read as a humanistic integrationist tract, but that reading is undermined by the stuttering couplet's guessing and double negative, "I guess being colored doesn't make me *not* like / the same things other folks like who are other races." The "melting pot" lines that follow ring hollow, since the dependent speaker "learn[s] from you" but again is forced to "guess" if the white man learns from him. And "although" defers to age and color, but not without resentment. Earlier in the poem the speaker says, "here / to this college on the hill above Harlem. / I am the only colored student in my class. / The steps from the hill lead down into Harlem." These lines simultaneously "educate" the professor, articulating differences in class and race privilege, but in "the hill lead down" the lines acknowledge hierarchy, and they emanate from a desire to be known by that authority. The speaker's assumption is that the professor knows nothing about the speaker's history or the import of where he lives. Ultimately, the "truth" of the poem/composition as suggested by the professor's assignment (*And let that page come out of you— / Then, it will be true.*) makes naïve humanistic assumptions about identity and "wholeness"; the speaker's response, moving back and forth between the two historical moments, past and present, affirms as much when he says, "I wonder if it's that simple?"

Almost half a century later, Yusef Komunyakaa is involved in the same struggle, narratively negotiating multiple historical moments, his racial loyalties, and the overwhelming force of history. In *Dien Cai Dau*, the poem "Tu Do Street," a pun on two-door street, recollects a black GI's experience of segregation and the confusing and shifting drama of being an African American in Vietnam while a race war rages on the American urban landscape. Although the poem's setting recollects the early 1970s, the story is told in the late 1980s, during the apex of the Reagan years. Komunyakaa holds these multiple historical moments in his "split consciousness": his childhood in the segregated South, the aggression of Vietnam, and the coming to racial consciousness and feelings of "black power," set against a disconcerting pessimism at the time of composition, living in a culture where the racial divide seems at least as virulent as it was in the past and leads to a more despairing rhetoric and vision. Komunyakaa's closure in this poem is informed not only by the tragic aggression in Vietnam but also by the stasis of race relations at the time the poem is written. After all, many of the African American poems published in the 1960s and early 1970s, some quite rhetorical (Michael Harper, Amiri Baraka, and Audre Lorde come to mind), were not only understandably angry but also optimistic about the possibility of revolutionary changes in race relations, which meant that respect for the African American was an assumption of the poems, not an aspiration.

The opening of the poem fuses multiple historic moments: in all these moments, America, the trope of which is its music, as Komunyakaa experiences it, is racist. The syntax of the opening lines not only brings the speaker back to his past but also diminishes him to a "small boy," as soon as he enters a bar for white soldiers.

> Music divides the evening.
> I close my eyes & can see
> men drawing lines in the dust.
> America pushes through the membrane
> of mist & smoke, & I'm a small boy
> again in Bogalusa. *White Only*
> signs & Hank Snow.

The poem is complicated by the triangulation of the Vietnamese mama-san, who, dependent on white business, refuses to recognize or serve the young black man. Interestingly, at the moment of the greatest racial divide, the speaker, empathizing with the Vietnamese woman (the syntax draws the parallel between those who "serve" when others have power over them), he takes responsibility for the violence and betrayals that make black GIs complicit allies with the white soldiers.

> We have played Judas where
> only machine-gun fire brings us
> together. Down the street
> black GIs hold to their turf also.

And although the speaker seeks out in the Vietnamese "a softness behind these voices / wounded by their beauty & war," ironically,

> Back in the bush at Dak To
> & Khe Sanh, we fought
> the brothers of these women
> we now run to hold in our arms.

The poem movingly concludes that "There's more than a nation / inside us," which for a moment seems to humanize the soldiers. But the following lines show that the humanity these soldiers share is nothing more than a kind of hell (the literal Viet Cong tunnels, the id, and of course Lethe).

> as black & white
> soldiers touch the same lovers
> minutes apart, tasting
> each other's breath,
> without knowing these rooms
> run into each other like tunnels
> leading to the underworld.

The helplessness and shame, the stasis and racism, are all concurrent with this poem: social programs had been mercilessly cut; the policies of the Reagan administration dramatically increased the gap between rich and poor; the promises of Martin Luther King and the Black Panthers had become more ghostly; these historical changes provide a backdrop and contextually frame the tone of "Tu Do Street."

In "Report from the Skulls' Diorama," these historical moments are consciously fused and noted: it is only by retrospective knowledge that we know that Hoover spied on King's private life, but Komunyakaa reports in the present tense of the Vietnam War.

> Dr. King's photograph
> comes at me from *White Nights*
>
> like Hoover's imagination at work,

dissolving into a scenario
at Firebase San Juan Hill

At the end of the poem, those moments are consciously gathered as scar-
ring memories: so history lives both inside and outside the speaker's
consciousness.

> When our gunship
flies out backwards, rising
above the men left below

> to blend in with the charred
landscape, an AK-47
speaks, with the leaflets
clinging to the men & stumps,
waving to me across the years.

Harryette Mullen's literary historical ancestors are Gertrude Stein and
the oral tradition in African-American poetry. Her work has always exemplified what Frederic Jameson calls, in *The Political Unconscious*, the
"schizophrenic text," one that speaks from several positions at once (if we
reject the ideology of New Criticism and its fictional notion of "organic
unity," all poems partake of such fissures and multiple sources). "Black
Nikes," a prose poem from *Sleeping with the Dictionary*, explicitly resides
in history as it revises it. Using jazzy diction that spars with the clinical
objectifying diction of the dictionary, this particular entry moves back
and forth between the signs for the goddess and the shoe company, moves
from the expansive Whitman to the "big-ticket item" diction of current
consumerist slang. It resides in our historical moment and comments on it
implicitly, racially, and otherwise; but more centrally, it uses these combat-
ing dictions to parody how romanticism's longing for transcendence com-
mingles with (and is corrupted by) the attachment to and fixation with
our crassly materialistic culture. Punning on the sneaker company and
the winged goddess of victory who fought for the Olympian gods against
the Titans, Mullen satirizes the hypocrisy of those who deride the material
world ("knowing money isn't what matters") while exploiting it for its own
use ("Please page our home and visit our sigh on the wide world's ebb. Just

point and cluck at our new persuasion shoes"). Nike, with its "revolution" advertising, is a perfect trope for this kind of entrepreneurial manipulation and disguise.

> We need quarters like King Tut needed a boat. A slave could row him to heaven from his crypt in Egypt full of loot. We've lived quietly among the stars, knowing money isn't what matters. We only bring enough to tip the shuttle driver when we hitch a ride aboard a trailblazer of light. This comet could scour the planet. Make it sparkle like a fresh toilet swirling with blue. Or only come close enough to brush a few lost souls. Time is rotting as our bodies wait for now I lay me down to earth. Noiseless patient spiders paid with dirt when what we want is stardust. If nature abhors an expensive appliance, why does the planet suck ozone? This is a big-ticket item, a thickety ride. Please page our home and visit our sigh on the wide world's ebb. Just point and cluck at our new persuasion shoes. We're opening the gate that opens our containers for recycling. Time to throw down and take off on our launch. This flight will nail our proof of pudding. The thrill of victory is, we're exiting earth. We're leaving all this dirt.

Here, this "comet" becomes a toilet bowl cleaner. The earth is, in Luther's terms, "filthy lucre," but the poem also ingeniously shows how focusing on "things" and "commodities" displaces our anxiety about death. The home becomes a home page, the gates of heaven become the "containers for recycling." And darkly, the prose poem's closure focuses on the fear of the "dirt," or the material body: the desire to transcend becomes the desire to die. The poem is a brilliant tour de force, using word play, the pun, dictions that ironize and undermine the "we" of the piece; the poem parodies fetishizing, corrupting literary myths. It is simultaneously playful and incisive, and, written in 2002, both speaks to and emanates from our historical moment.

In the nineteenth century, Emily Dickinson's "I cannot dance upon my Toes" confronts her historical moment, often negotiating masculine privilege with rich and shifting tonal gestures. Ambiguously, Dickinson opens the poem with "I cannot dance upon my Toes— / No Man instructed me," lines that bristle with rage, ironizing deferral and at the same time acknowledging her own powerlessness.

I cannot dance upon my Toes—
No Man instructed me—
But oftentimes, among my mind,
A Glee possesseth me,

That had I Ballet knowledge—
Would put itself abroad
In Pirouette to blanch a Troupe—
Or lay a Prima, mad,

And though I had no Gown of Gauze—
No Ringlet, to my Hair,
Nor hopped to Audiences—like Birds,
One Claw upon the Air,

Nor tossed my shape in Eider Balls,
Nor rolled on wheels of snow
Till I was out of sight, in sound,
The House encore me so—

Nor any know I know the Art
I mention—easy—Here—
Nor any Placard boast me—
It's full as Opera—

Eventually, after parodying the archetypally feminine—the kind of woman who pleases male instructors—she ends the poem with an astonishingly ambiguous off-rhyme ("Here" and "Opera") that indicates, in its fading dactylic meter, the speaker's own doubts; on the one hand, the closure echoes and releases the splintered self of "among my mind," transforming the phrase into polyphonic, seemingly self-sufficient private "voices." On the other, no one else knows she knows the art she "mention[s]" —and she mentions all of them, then turning on "easy—Here" to the solitary art of poetry. The speaker both boasts of her mastery of the art and attains moral superiority by satirizing the desire for worldly attention ("Nor any Placard boast me—"); at the same time she acknowledges that she "knows" the art (whether in dancing she can perform it or not is a different matter), she also understands that art without cultural response is "easy" and here, closed-off and insular.

There's no place in the world for her to enact her creative talents. By refusing the demeaning display of the feminine, which is both grotesque ("One Claw upon the Air") and infantile (as a pillow fight or cartwheels in the snow), the speaker ends up in exile, weakly proclaiming the untested power of her art. The poem rhythmically fades with its two final unstressed syllables and sounds a minor key among the more perfect early rhymes.

In "I would not paint—a picture—," Dickinson's speaker becomes the subject, subjecting herself to art rather than creating it. Again, though, the shifting diction and ambiguous tone blur the boundaries between maker and receiver of art. The first few lines draw parallels with the feminine, to be "dwell[ed up]on" and "delicious": the effect of the art introduces the ambiguity of a "sweet Torment" and a "sumptuous" "despair." While the oxymoronic pairings suggest the sublime, we find no Blake-like imaginative energy here: the poem more resembles Tennyson's "The Lotus Eaters," with its "weary" and decadent passive sensuality; here, the speaker's being "dwell[ed up]on" also becomes costly.

> I would not paint—a picture—
> I'd rather be the One
> Its bright impossibility
> To dwell—delicious—on—
> And wonder how the fingers feel
> Whose rare—celestial—stir—
> Evokes so sweet a Torment—
> Such sumptuous—Despair—
>
> I would not talk, like Cornets—
> I'd rather be the One
> Raised softly to the Ceilings—
> And out, and easy on—
> Through Villages of Ether—
> Myself endued Balloon
> By but a lip of Metal—
> The pier to my Pontoon—
>
> Nor would I be a Poet—
> It's finer—own the Ear—
> Enamored—impotent—content—

The License to revere,
A privilege so awful
What would the Dower be,
Had I the Art to stun myself
With Bolts of Melody!

The silenced speaker is in awe of the art: she transcends, balloonlike, impalpable, in that weightless painterly heaven, but again (as with many of her depressed poems where she aches to be raised out of the world) there is nothing material for her. Our first real clue comes in the diction of "endued," which means either a gift or faculty or assuming a role. So we're left questioning the ambiguous power of the speaker's imagination as possibly artifice. In the same way, the pontoon is either a temporary bridge or a small boat, just a "lip of Metal" (again the sensuality's artifice, inhuman, the mode of transport is slight). It is only when she uses the series of adjectives that resembles Whitman's catalogues in its blurring, intensifying, and contradicting motion that the reader understands how the speaker's willful attempt to assert her "awful privilege" diminishes her. She moves from "enamored" to "impotent" and "content": the dashes serve simultaneously as equivalence and change of mind. These domesticated adjectives oppose the earlier sublime moments in the poem: here the ego is used to tame desire and results in powerlessness and passive settling, an acceptance of the bourgeois (to be content instead of ecstatic). So the speaker comes to realize herself in the position of the widow, complete with dower, property permitted to her only after her husband dies. This "awful privilege," this "Dower," this cultural law that requires her not only to be the receiver of the art but also to be content instead of immersed (as she willed in the beginning of the poem) leads her to a masturbatory fantasy. Once again, the closure expresses a willful assertion of autonomy side by side with the pathos; it offers no corresponding love or audience for her active pleasure. Her wish to be Zeus is her fantasy to authorize and control, rather than being subjected to the "Dower."

In other poems, like "The Soul selects her own Society," the speaker rhetorically asserts her power and preferences, but she always pays a cost (there, turning to stone), in choosing self-denial and mutilation of the female body, as in "Rearrange a 'Wife's' affection."

Rearrange a "Wife's" affection!
When they dislocate my Brain!

Amputate my freckled Bosom!
Make me bearded like a man!

The problem for Dickinson and other women writers in the mid-nineteenth century was that since the culture provided no respect for the female artist—no hope or solution to the conflicts of dependence and autonomy, assertion and recessiveness—her imagination, even in her wide-ranging greatness, could only give shape to fulfilling the self in the earthly known. The terms of her subjugation resemble but differ from Sylvia Plath's because the cults of domesticity and femininity differed in their respective ages. Dickinson—because women were still considered property; because of the pressures of revivalism, the church, and her class circumstances; because of her depressive temperament and her isolation from family—faced some different conflicts than mid-twentieth-century women. Her strategies for survival, though, resembled other minority writers over time, including her penchant for irony, self-effacement, and flight through transcendence; her attraction to metaphors of the afterlife, and her adoption of the male voice of mastery (the same braggadocio that causes her—as it did with Langston Hughes—self-division, erasure, and ultimately self-hatred).

The narrative circumstances of Sylvia Plath's well-known "Tulips" brings the speaker to a hospital, where she finds herself desiring the anesthetizing benefits of illness: the erasure of identity and freedom from the burdens of domesticity.

I am nobody; I have nothing to do with explosions.
I have given my name and my day-clothes up to the nurses
And my history to the anaesthetist and my body to surgeons.

. . . .
The nurses pass and pass, they are no trouble

She prefers the numbing and the inanimate, the metallic glittery brightness that frees her from recognition, from her own interior terrors as well as from her own body:

My body is a pebble to them, they tend it as water
Tends to the pebbles it must run over, smoothing them gently.
They bring me numbness in their bright needles, they bring me sleep.

She desires purity even if it costs her those "loving associations." Until this point in the poem, one might read those associations without irony, but these domestic images provide their own nightmares:

> They have swabbed me clear of my loving associations.
> Scared and bare on the green plastic-pillowed trolley
> I watched my teaset, my bureaus of linen, my books
> Sink out of sight, and the water went over my head.

Having "lost" herself, these domestic images become the very source of her "wounds."

> Now I have lost myself I am sick of baggage—
> My patent leather overnight case like a black pillbox,
> My husband and child smiling out of the family photo;
> Their smiles catch onto my skin, little smiling hooks.

They provide their own burdens and nightmares, and suddenly the domestic images and metaphors become oppressive, like "an awful baby." And although at first the speaker associates the hospital with water and death, the tulips themselves, as well as being associated with the heart and the sensual, also correspond to her "wounding" and "drowning":

> Lightly, through their white swaddlings, like an awful baby.
> Their redness talks to my wound, it corresponds.
> They are subtle: they seem to float, though they weigh me down,
> Upsetting me with their sudden tongues and their color,
> A dozen red lead sinkers round my neck.

In this context, the sensuality inside this domesticated marriage offers the speaker images of "clutter" and "noise."

> The peacefulness is so big it dazes you,
> And it asks nothing, a name tag, a few trinkets.
> It is what the dead close on, finally; I imagine them
> Shutting their mouths on it, like a Communion tablet.

Certainly that peacefulness is caught up in the thanototic: she gives spiritualizing value to the silent "church" of the dead. It is also true that the roses offer flux and the vitalizing forces of life: part of the speaker's dilemma is related to her already having drowned and "rusted." She's exhausted and defeated. But in the past, the speaker claims she "had no face," wanted "to efface herself"; freed of her married life, she "was happy / Playing and resting without committing itself."

> Now the air snags and eddies round them [the tulips] the way a river
> Snags and eddies round a sunken rust-red engine.
> They concentrate my attention, that was happy
> Playing and resting without committing itself.

Critic Barbara Hardy believes that, in the closure of "Tulips," "there's a slow, reluctant acceptance of the tulips, which means a slow, reluctant acceptance of a return to life."[4] And certainly in one of the figures of the poem, the tulips become a trope for her heart. But accompanying that image is an animal of prey (They are "opening like the mouth of some great African cat"), devouring her (just as early in the poem she was snagged and hooked). These images and those that follow are densely ambiguous: after the tulips remind her of the animal, she comes aware of her heart: the syntax raises the question of whether she is aware of her heart because of the emotional associations with the tulips or because of her own frailty and vulnerability. Ultimately, she is a victim, surely of her own "unhealthy" past, but she is also a victim of domesticity, without a key to figure out how to live without being trapped and suffocated. While Plath's powerful persona helps us read the poem in the most psychological of fashions, the poem provides ample evidence that the artist/mother in 1959 cannot find satisfying figures for both being an artist and being a conventional mother. The same struggles go on in many of the *Ariel* poems, including "Lesbos," where the domestic landscape is both phony and threatening:

> Viciousness in the kitchen!
> The potatoes hiss.
> It is all Hollywood, windowless,
> The fluorescent light wincing on and off like a terrible migraine

This dilemma is echoed in much women's confessional writing from this time: Anne Sexton, Maxine Kumin, and others: women of enormous talent and matching unhappiness, trapped in a diminished life with no place for their worldly ambitions. So when the speaker closes "Tulips" with "A country as far away as health," she alludes to an alien condition virtually beyond her imagination. Without a "self," Plath's speaker cannot really entertain whether the desire for "health" is authentic or she is trying to adapt to the culture's definition of fulfillment for women. And no matter what other dramas went into the complex and individual personality of Plath, "Tulips" contextualizes some of the reasons why she cannot make her social world (the world that has devoured her) and the self mesh.

In the late twentieth century, for many women poets the struggle shifts to finding a language of their own, one not contaminated by the regulation of the patriarchal. Alice Notley, whose collected poems were recently published, advocates—sometimes directly in her poems—experimentalism. In later work in particular, she resides on the margins of representation; she often admits the reader into the self-conscious process of the poem, inhabits several time frames simultaneously, snaps off perceptions as they approach the "truth," and relies on sound and syntax to create multiple voices (tones that argue with one another, diction that moves swiftly from the highly romantic to the comic to full-blown rage). Retrospective events are never fully authorized, and predictive grammar and syntax are constantly violated. While each collection seems to take on a different formal project, including creating myths to revise the masculine, in a number of poems she directly navigates the problem of style and patriarchal authorities, from those who write in "the Iowa style" to her own poet husband, Ted Berrigan. These poems are filled with willful assertions of power and rage at those whose voices regulate recognition and the canon, but interestingly the poems alternately attempt to create a "style" that resists male authority before falling away under its gaze. At every attempt she makes to overpower that authority, she self-consciously must acknowledge its power over her. In the retrospective poem "Choosing Styles–1972," she writes:

I still get a thrill when I say, emeralds and topazes.
Who wants to say "freightage," what is the charge for that word
who wants to say "distress" and wear the black chiffon
scarf inside it
who wants to write in old long lines clearly and not be
slightly more inscrutable
askance in freaker
lines, in brilliance

In these lines she aspires to recover the sublime innocence of sound and sign (what Norman O. Brown calls "polymorphous perversity"). The power of her imagination is thrilled by those connections and by the strangeness and sensual richness of language without their representational codifications. As the poem's syntax unwinds, she willfully asserts:

> Choose sometimes more for beauty or for clarity
> or for some arbitrary reason—no reason I know go
> against word order: firstling you
> by dint of me, clean, sings up in the clerestory
> on the donned doom show. Worthless filmy daughterous

But the signs of meaning reassert themselves: she hears the paternal voices judging those playful choices and is restored, involuntarily, to history and the social world. A few lines later she says:

> There are these sides (I'm tired of it)
> Float in air liaison with illicit spirit
> Who cares how I write?

In wildly fluctuating diction, the poem continues to rearrange sense to attempt to create an identity not subject to social regulation, to dispel origin by going "underground," and at the same time to call up origins and the archetypally feminine:

> My style is to
> forget whence we came; the origins of
> my style. I'm gnarling at you.
> Moon and underworld, queen and cunt where the molten
> metal flows. My style comes from death.

Inevitably, in the poem's closure, Notley returns to a dialogue with the "you," the male principle, the poetry legislator, but again with the willful and repetitive assertion:

> I don't have to care
> how I write, in what manner—up-to-date *are you*

kidding? You're dead!
Menstruation covered with sand, garnets and amber.

But "dead" as he is, he reappears in the dialogue and consciousness. She buries him in the female (and the "emeralds" above become less "precious" stones), but she still needs to bury him in the present tense. There is no solution to the patriarchal; there is only a rising up, an internalizing, a resisting, and then, with some mourning, returning and resisting to the legislating "you," which even in 1998, when this poem about 1972 was published, still hovers above the female self.

Nowhere does Notley challenge the perspectival, patriarchal, and authorial authority (the power of words to represent her experience) more clearly than in "Experience." Though the culture maintains "experience" (with its faith in knowledge and progress through time) can authorize her as a poet and person, Notley's poem discovers there is no currency for her in either self-knowledge or the progressive syntax of sequence. Subjectivity, discontinuity, and false power regimes all intercede, superceding her own romantic vision with the corruption of the world's.

> though one's divided between
> if he tells you or you tell yourself—
> you know what I mean?—
> what's true.

The poem, in its desire to pin down experience, constantly changes its mind:

> the rest is a secret no it isn't . . .
> Why no secrets? Oh,
> who reads poetry anyway!

It moves from a parody of high patriarchal culture to the play of sound association (Phoenician to Phoenix) to her experience with its own share of paternal advice.

> I think this kind of tale is
> as important as a pompously cited

Phoenician myth, to poetry
in Phoenix I drink with my father
"You don't bruise the bourbon," he says.

Ultimately, "Experience" interrogates the act of composing: attempting
and failing to compose a stable interior self through language or otherwise.
The poem chronicles the frustrating impossibility of representing or recollecting experience. At every moment, the poet struggles to create a poem
that authorizes ownership of experience; at the same time, the experience
of the poem brings her to understand experience as a hoax, which ends up,
like the self, discarded. Here experience is male truth (as French feminists
point out, the value of agency figures differently for men and women); the
connections Notley wants to make between poetry and experience fail her:
her vehicles are words, assertions that are always syntactically undermined
by what comes next.

A sex isn't very deep but its
surface is armor ironmasked
like certain poetries I can't use
how be what you are what's experience but
a becoming acceptable to the keepers
of surfaces say this University

This poem climbs the mountain to self and rolls down again, subject to
social forces larger than the poem's orchestrating voice. Notley's subversive
authority, which she often doubts, is most powerful when it resists and
negates.

In "Colors 1973," Notley's speaker is explicit about her identification
with the female, which is in part her loyalty to the senses:

These petals are all my fingertips
if I don't think, don't remember myself I'm not a
woman by identity though I'm pregnant and obsessed with
the Feminine. Don't believe in it it's words, I
believe in the textures I like: cream of unyellow daffs,
apricot-pink roses, grain-of-wood voices my friends have
rock garden voices like efficaceous herbs and grasses

Her identification with the feminine is tied to not thinking, because the signs, the words, lack the immediate and palpable pleasures of the sensory; as the poem moves away from natural images to the metaphoric, to the wood-grain voices (the natural), the feminine acts as a figure, even though in the beginning of the poem she tries to treat "thought" as a male principle, as property; "Thought, as possession, my depression / does this to me." All further attempts to fall away from thinking, though, return to it, as a simultaneous liberation from the natural and being bound up in a desire for male mastery. This dialogue occurs in most of Notley's poems from this period, in the poems that constitute a poetic "autobiography," an autobiography that's no more autobiographical than Lyn Hejinian's *My Life*. Both books attempt to honor the fluxlike feminine of Julia Kristeva's concept of the *chora*, but they remained absorbed by, obsessed with, even in their resistance, male mastery.

As discussed in the last chapter, it is possible for an artist to try to take flight from the age in which he or she lives. But what often occurs is a diminished and narrowing vision, one in which love, family happiness, and, say, the valorization of nature in poetry might take on so grand a scale that given the world in which we live, poets may exclude too much difficulty. The poems then risk breaking faith with a contemporary audience by acts of either sentimentality or bourgeois insularity. When one considers the cruelties, violence, devastation, and disrespect for the planet caused by our own contemporary culture, a poem praising design and the harmonious in our age is at the very least problematic and accountable in some ways for its erasures. On the other hand, poems that address those conditions directly "as subjects," such as poets writing about the wars in Vietnam or Iraq, often suffer from liberal self-congratulation and rhetorical and moral superiority. It is not surprising that when artistic difficulty is circumscribed by a culture of selfishness and privatization, many of us find it difficult to negotiate a space that is simultaneously more or less experiential and yet reflects sufficiently intimate and tactile contact with a larger world. It would be naïve to think that this problem would remain invisible in the poems of our age.

When I think of our artistic age, I sometimes think of the recently remastered 1958 Prestige sessions, *John Coltrane: Fearless Leader*. In these CDs, you can hear Coltrane straining against the formal conventions of hard-bop standards. Particularly in midtempo and upbeat songs like

"Spring is Here" and "Come Rain or Come Shine," tempos are not only sped up (as Miles Davis subsequently did with his own compositions from *Kind of Blue*) but sound rushed, as if Coltrane were not only impatient but even frustrated with the constraints of convention. His solos seem jumpy and jittery, the trills ultimately don't lead him anywhere—that is, anywhere new. But you can hear the first signs of his odd fingerings and the beginnings of those rippling "sheets of sound" he became renowned for later in his own groups with "the quartet." Usually we think of 1961, specifically the Village Vanguard Sessions, as Coltrane's breakthrough into free jazz, but the earlier sessions are interesting not only musically but also because they reveal Coltrane up against the limits of his age: there were few models for what would come next. In the following two years he would work with Miles Davis and avant-garde players like Ornette Coleman and Don Cherry, so he seems in the late-1950s recordings, retrospectively at least, trapped in a musical culture that had exhausted its capacity for invention. The musical instrument and the word, in spite of our longing to make language an expression of individuality, do not exist in a vacuum, do not remain static, as in Blake's parody of the "crystal palace" of heaven. I am reminded of Mao Tse-Tung's famous aphorism: "Where do correct ideas come from? Do they drop from the skies? No. Are they innate in the mind? No. They come from social practice."[5] In our age we may dispense with "correct ideas" (excepting the evangelical), but it is important to investigate where and how *in the world* self and the word are generated.

6.
....

LOUISE GLÜCK

The Death of Romanticism

FOR MORE THAN THREE DECADES, poets and literary critics have been recycling an argument about the self and the historicity of poetry; narrative poets and avant-garde poets have both, for entirely different reasons, questioned the limits of the lyric "I" and the tenets of romanticism. Narrative and formalist poets have complained about self-absorption and excessive subjectivity. Experimental poets, as noted in the first two chapters of this book, find the concept of self problematic: the lyric "I" assumes a stable and coherent self and authorizes a kind of wisdom and authority that makes for a virtual hegemonic possession of experience. Both points of view express valid concerns, but I would also posit the problem historically: romanticism's reliance on epiphany and fleeting transcendence is inadequate to account for or decipher the pressures of cultural and historical change. Our relationships to nature and landscape have changed; our stake in government and community has diminished as we have migrated to cities and the suburbs; the many changes emanating from industrial and technological revolutions challenge and alter our understandings of self. Many poets who rely on romantic ideologies merely recycle the themes, values, approaches, and archetypes that belong to the early nineteenth century; this approach to experience serves to attenuate alienation and helplessness and to idealize the poet's privileged position as spokesperson for the individual.

Romanticism evolved "out of and against Enlightenment rationalism, which had deepened the skepticism, growing in the West since the Renaissance, about theological or philosophical absolutes capable of sustaining a reliable relation between subject and object, mind and matter, physics and metaphysics. The Romantic's response to this epistemological and religious crisis was to ground certitude not in reason or institutional systems of belief but in the felt experience of the individual." But "Romanticism put such stress on the individual's momentary experience that the Romantic synthesis of subject and object through the agency of the Imagination began to deconstruct almost as soon as it was ventured."[1]

The romantic sublime promises redemption based upon an individual's capacity to permeate experience and transform him- or herself through imagination and fleeting "higher consciousness." For contemporary American poets, though, trapped in a culture whose rhetoric elevates the individual at the same time it systematically devalues and regulates the individual's capacity to shape and participate in that culture, romanticism is a dead end, succeeding only to frustratingly paralyze and isolate him or her. The contemporary romantic poet, losing all sense of relation, becomes trapped in the two alternating poles of narcissism: grandiosity (my pain or joy is unrivaled) and self-hatred (I'm uncentered and have no sense of self).

Among contemporary poets, few pursue more obsessively the tenets of romanticism than one of our most skillful and accomplished artists, Louise Glück. Even though the aesthetic consistently fails her speakers, the urgency of her longing combined with her unflinching, skeptical self-consciousness makes her obsessions compelling even when they are paralyzing to her characters and on occasion seem sentimentally fatalistic. Glück brings into focus a whole generation of poets who valorize their own position as sensitive artists and attribute their loneliness and lovelessness to tragic fate and human nature. Their ongoing faith in self-reliance effaces social forces that contribute to their exile, including an ambivalent romance with patriarchal authority and deprivation caused by the economy of love and loss of community.

Glück's romantic sublime pursues both the Keatsian ecstasy of the heightened moment and Dickinson's darker, more annihilating flight from the material world. From the beginning of her career, in the Plath-like elements in *Firstborn* (1969), Glück has often presented a persona fluctuating from the fragile victim to the mythical goddess whose love bears tragic consequences. Throughout her work, but emerging clearly as a pattern in *Descending Figure* (1980), Glück has deployed mythology as an attempt not only to stabilize and universalize the temporal but also to deflect and reinforce the resulting "fated" stasis. The use of myth thus serves both to diminish choice and responsibility and to provide justification for grandiosity. When culture and the temporal get in the way of the poet's desires (as most often happens in *Ararat* [1990] and *Vita Nova* [1999]), Glück's speakers use self-dramatization or irony, blame or self-hatred, as alternating strategies to defend against a dependent and fragmentary self.

These stances toward the Keatsian sublime manifest themselves most explicitly and willfully in *Wild Iris*, which is an instructional volume in mapping out Glück's romanticism. In "Field Flowers," the flowers chide the human ego.

> What are you saying? That you want
> eternal life? Are your thoughts really
> as compelling as all that? Certainly
> you don't look at us, don't listen to us

Here the projection of the speaker as field flower is taunting; Glück capably critiques her speaker's human flaws (vanity, inwardness, and a contempt for the world), but the poem's insistent rhetoric, its dissonant dictions—the twangy idiom of the contemporary set against the lyrical moment of "the wild buttercup"—never fuse mind and body into a unified, stable, or credible self.

> Contempt
> for humanity is one thing, but why
> disdain the expansive
> field, your gaze rising over the clear heads
> of the wild buttercups into what?

The talking flowers (critical of the you's ego-bound desire for the sublime) offer nineteenth-century advice: the cycles of nature mirror the human, thereby offering lessons in scope, perspective, and acceptance of change: "Your poor / idea of heaven: absence / of change." It's no wonder that she—since the "you" is a gardener who has already attempted to order and harness nature in a civilized world—can't make use of nature's rhetorical wisdom. Glück acknowledges belonging to neither nature nor culture (you "who are neither / here nor there"), but she attributes the failing to the personal, to being an outsider or—as she says elsewhere—"a watcher." In *Wild Iris*, when Glück feels paralyzed by ambivalence, or when she proposes two seemingly irreconcilable simultaneous desires, to be safe and to feel ("Aubade"), she essentializes them. Though she poses the dilemma as tragic, it is her destiny, it seems, to kvetch.

Glück's personae of talking flowers create an almost Disney *Fantasia*-like caricature (while Keats and Whitman translate birdsong, Glück acknowledges no such medium). How could her speaker, two hundred years after the Industrial Revolution, accept such an archaic metaphysical lesson from an imagined agent of nature? In this and many other poems in *Wild Iris*, the obsessions that propel the collection seem rhetorical and almost external, as if Glück served as amanuensis for romantic poets. Dickinson speaks through Glück, as do Wordsworth and Keats. Nature counsels as if its cycles still correspond to the human—parallel to Emerson's essay "The Poet," where nature's regeneration not only is instructive but gives the poet dominion in his or her capacity to decipher it. Even in Glück's late work, as in *Vita Nova*, the speaker draws this archetypal causality between her emotional life and the natural: "Laughter, because the air is full of apple blossoms." Often when Glück recognizes this response as nostalgic, she frames the dilemma as archetypal or "fallen": in "The Red Poppy," the poppy speaks like a human because "I am shattered." Even when her skeptical intelligence acknowledges that nature cannot hold the correspondence, that it is an alien force, as in "Marina," her romantic longings remain, in her own words, rigid and unyielding.

> around the walled garden:
>
> there's nothing there now
> except the wildness people call nature,
> the chaos that takes over.

The Dickinsonian sublime emerges in poems like "The Jacob's Ladder" ("Trapped in the earth, / Wouldn't you too want to go / To heaven?") and in "Wild Iris" ("At the end of my suffering / There was a door"). Thanatotic desires, often conflated with the erotic, serve to release the romantic from earthly suffering. As Glück writes in "The White Lilies," "I felt your two hands / bury me to release its splendor."

At her most self-conscious, as in "Matins," she acknowledges her need to project and appropriate.

> Noah says this is
> an error of depressives, identifying
> with a tree, whereas the happy heart

wanders the garden like a falling leaf, a figure for
the part, not the whole.

There's no renunciation of romanticism in the above lines. Here the speaker ascribes her error to choosing the wrong metaphor to project: the falling leaf accepts flux and death, prerequisites for the sublime. Ironically, in her anxiety to embrace romanticism in *Wild Iris*, Glück depends much more on willful rhetorical assertion than on imagery or metaphor (the sensory world). In other—especially earlier—collections she retains much more inhabited, nuanced, and evocative stances toward these issues: she is well aware of the conflicting burdens and consequences of choosing this ethos or turning from it.

The utopian romantic vision fails her, though, for more reasons than willful intellection. The romantic ideal and the intimate sphere are corrupted by three cultural phenomena: the economy of love (Glück's conflation of Eros and currency), fixed sex roles, and a repressive, stabilizing mythological vision. Glück's approach often combines the mythic with the psychological. In "The Reproach" her speaker claims:

You have betrayed me, Eros.
You have sent me
my true love.

. . . .
All my life
I have worshiped the wrong gods.

But it is not Eros she worships. In poem after poem, desire is an object of exchange. In the marvelous, pivotal poem "Mock Orange," the speaker (who formerly hoped for transcendence through sexuality and the body) becomes angry, divided, and disappointed. The romantic self, seeking merging, the dissolution of self, ecstasy, and freedom, finds that sex does not provide her with the necessary exchange value—a promissory note—the promise of eternity or immortality.

It is not the moon, I tell you.
It is these flowers
lighting the yard.

I hate them.
I hate them as I hate sex,
the man's mouth
sealing my body, the man's
paralyzing body —

and the cry that always escapes,
the low, humiliating
premise of union —

Bound by the domestic world (the civilized yard), she finds her selflessness leads to irreparable ego damage: she feels silenced and paralyzed by
men. Though she must sacrifice herself to aspire to transcendence, the
premise of union humiliates this fragile self. The central metaphor provides the promise of transcendence and lasting sensual pleasure. In the
closure, the odor of the orange and of "sex in the air" reminds the speaker
that she has returned to the temporal world where the purity of sexuality
is contaminated by the earthbound (not the moonlight but *flowers*) and
by power-ridden gender relations with the other. Her anger externalizes
her bifurcated feelings about sex and love. On the surface, the speaker is
frustrated by sex not bringing her love, but she expresses her disappointment in terms of a need for rest and contentment, a displacement of feeling
turned into a desire for death or stasis. The promise of union is realized as
oppression. Phallic mounting only returns her to her divided self.

I hear the question and pursuing answer
fused in one sound
that mounts and mounts and then
is split into the old selves,
the tired antagonisms.

. . . .
How can I be content
when there is still
that odor in the world?

Here we find the slippage: these "tired antagonisms" demonstrate how
romanticism's temporary fusions fail to alter the speaker's alienation and

division from lover, self, and world. The speaker expresses the oppression as external ("I hate sex" and the man who oppresses her), but the closure of the poem indicates that the inescapable presence of materiality, the associations of the senses, keeps her from contentment.

The speaker here wants a debt paid: sex was supposed to provide for her "fusion," but it does not pay off. Often fueled by rage or disappointment, Glück's female speakers, in their need, often incur a debt. In an earlier poem, "Gretel in Darkness," Gretel says "I killed for you" to make Hansel feel guilty about abandoning her and leaving her powerless. In "Vespers," though referring to the relationship between the self and nature, Glück consciously uses the economic metaphor. "In your extended absence, you permit me / use of earth, anticipating / some return on investment." Most directly, in "Nest," she draws capital connection between the bird and the speaker/artist:

> my eyes fixing on each thing
> from the shelter of the hidden self;
>
> First, *I love it.*
> Then, *I can use it.*

Gender roles almost always play a part in Glück's conflicted attitudes about sexuality and power. In the poems where the female speaker is not a goddess (whose power enables her only to withhold or displace), females are passive and immobile, without volition. While Odysseus travels, Penelope feels abandoned. Or in another wonderful but melancholy poem, "Brenënde Liebe" (from *The House on Marshland*), the early-twentieth-century female speaker is passive and bedridden, held by the boundaries of the garden. She is shaded from passion by the umbrella and tree; the absent male lover is given the simultaneous erotic and thanatopic power to "*take*" her "*breath away.*" Women without men are empty, selfless. Glück writes in "The Untrustworthy Speaker," "People like me, who seem selfless, / We're the cripples, the liars: / We're the ones who should be factored out / In the interest in truth." Similarly, "A Novel" from *Ararat* contains these lines: "From this point on, nothing changes: / there's no plot without a hero. / In this house, when you say *plot* what you mean is love story."

Glück's selflessness is usually triggered by male authority figures: she externalizes her feeling of immobility with blame. In "Gretel in Darkness"

(*The House on Marshland*), she says, "My father bars the door, bars harm"; with typical Glückian doubleness, the patriarch protects by stifling, by holding the female prisoner in the domestic world. In "The New World" (*Ararat*), she reiterates,

> As I saw it,
> all of my mother's life, my father
> held her down, like
> lead strapped to her ankles.

Glück's escape from these imprisoning social hierarchies, her "authorization," comes through the entitlement of the artist. She echoes the romantic poet's faith in the special perception of the artist, who is often metaphorically if not literally Orpheus. "No one wants to be the muse; / in the end, everyone wants to be Orpheus," she says in "Lute Song": thereby Orpheus appears as Glück's masculinist hero. Invoking this Rilkean romanticism, in the capacity to see more deeply into both the ecstatic and abysmal aspects of experience, the speaker then suffers more intensely. Charles Feidelson distills Rilke's inner-turning vision of the artist (seen most prominently in *Sonnets to Orpheus*) in the introduction to *The Modern Tradition*:

> Outward events and circumstances are so engrossing that most people gladly dwell among them; but the artist turns away into the "abyss" of his own being to learn what is there and to become reconciled with his own latent powers. In this way he is able to surpass his ordinary self, to achieve a preternatural level of being and perception. . . . He does so by granting forms a life of their own, independent of their function or appearance in external nature. Judged in terms of nature, these forms are lies; but they are valid imaginative expressions, manifesting the distinctive world of the artist.[2]

But artistic form fails to bring meaning, fulfillment, or erotic pleasure to Glück. In "Celestial Music," Glück directly connects the love of form with the love of death, considering classic symmetries of form as closure and resolution. In "First Goodbye" (from *The Triumph of Achilles*), she says, "This / is mastery, whose active / mode is dissection." This skill to analyze is masculine and destructive: it picks apart experience rather than making it cohere. This vision of the artist dovetails with Glück's perception that being an artist *per se* removes one from engagement, from feeling directly, echoing her tragic ambivalence about wanting to be safe and at the same time to feel. In *Ararat*, she makes this romantic assertion, embracing being and doing as being essentially at odds.

Sometimes Glück believes the job of the artist is not only to divide but also to devour, as the mother does her children in "Appearances" from *Ararat*. "You could say / she's like an artist with a dream, a vision. / Without that, she'd have been torn apart." Here too art provides substitute gratification for love. Elsewhere in this volume, although Glück would not make the social claim, her mother's whole sense of self is enmeshed in what Glück sees as a pitiable relationship with her husband. She issues a bracing critique of the traditional nuclear family, but it is one the daughter is fated to duplicate later in her own love relationships.

This figure of the artist, who must escape such a family and the role assigned to her, leads Glück to an essentialist romantic isolation. In "Summer," she says,

> The bed was like a raft; I felt us drifting
> far from our natures, toward a place where we'd discover nothing.
> . . . .
> And in each of us began
> a deep isolation, though we never spoke of this,
> of the absence of regret.
> We were artists again, my husband.
> We could resume the journey.

Once again, Glück echoes Rilke's privileged view of the artist, perhaps still plausible at the turn of the twentieth-century but difficult to reconcile as domestic drama late in the twentieth century. To quote Feidelson again, "Rilke attests that an artist surrenders love and friendship to carry on his embattled search for the understanding of things. Artistic heroism is epitomized by Paul Valéry in his figure of Leonardo da Vinci, a type of the artist as universal man. Exploring the night of consciousness, the artist discovers that the reality to which we are accustomed is but one solution out of many possible ones. He is able to divest objects of their peculiarities and, at the same time, to sense what consciousness is apart from its objects, to reach 'the deep note of existence itself.'"[3]

In valorizing lines like "the artist lies / because he is obsessed with attainment," Glück implies that the artist's quest makes him or her a privileged being, a secular God, with a mission beyond the capacity to choose. In "The Mystery," her speaker says,

> I have acquired in some measure
> the genius of the master,
>
> . . . .
>
> My life took me many places,
> many of them very dark.
> It took me without my volition,
> pushing me from behind

Or in "Lute Song," the speaker proclaims: "Yet my anguish, such as it is, / remains the struggle for form."

Throughout Glück's work, her speakers maintain their longing for the ascendancy of the masculinist: the powerful individual, mythic or otherwise. Glück envies the power and mobility of men, and, when she doesn't mock them (with castration), she envies their capacity for departure. Glück's speakers, faithful to many of the paradoxical strategies of New Criticism, are caught in a binary: either the self is too fragile to enter the world or it must become so defended that only irony, deflection, and emotional deadness provide comfort. Only through the act of prohibition does a Glückian speaker become an agent of her own fate.

Here and elsewhere, the romantic artist fails for two reasons: first because in spite of her wishes, the selfless person/artist must live in the world. Second, because the "special" individual, artist or otherwise, is both powerless to inhabit her body or to reach beyond the self to an other. In the Pegasus poem "The Winged Horse," the speaker pleads, "Come, Abstraction, / By Will out of Demonic Ambition: / carry me lightly into the regions of the immortal." Ambition grows out of the resentful recognition that the discrete "self" in Glück's poems needs to prove herself in and to the world; she desperately needs acknowledgment because she cannot verify or justify herself. She takes a self-castigating stance, but rather than desiring to find a place "in the world," she requires taking her part above it. "Is this what having means," Glück says, smartly casting doubt on transcendence in "Condo," "to look down on? Or is this dreaming still? / I was right, wasn't I, choosing / against the ground?"

Lacking any resources beyond the self, Glück's speakers achieve neither ecstasy nor heightened consciousness: for the most part, they seem resigned to their fates. Fixed on a desire for completion by love and an idealized attachment to nature as an extension or projection of self, Glück's speakers turn to power to compensate for their powerlessness. Glück's double consciousness (a nostalgic longing for what is no longer possible simultaneous with her understanding that those desires cannot be met) brings Glück paralyzing ambivalence. In Glück's romanticism, time, the family, and the other all serve limited dualistic roles: either as a projection to identify with or as an obstacle to fulfillment. In "Paradise" (*Ararat*), Glück expresses the fated negative:

But I know. Like Adam,
I was the firstborn.
Believe me, you never heal,
you never forget the ache in your side,
the place where something was taken away
to make another person.

On the one hand, these lines powerfully reflect the lasting effects of psychic deprivation. But this poem echoes other poems where the other interferes with desires for attention and individuation. The desire to escape history through myth often traps Glück's speakers either in narcissistic display via the powerful heroine/goddess or as the powerless victim. Representation also fails her in these mythic stories: unlike in the *Odyssey*, telling these stories provides no illumination for the teller or listener but rather reenacts the same obsessions through different scenes. The ironic and often embittered refiguring of myth leads Glück to attribute fixity ("naturally") to social experiences.

In "Aphrodite," using strategies of recurrence, transformation, and resolution, Glück explicitly plays out an obsessive theme: the passive, immobile, and powerless woman must wait for the adventurous romantic hero to return. She retains power only by stoniness and withholding sex: "A woman exposed as rock / has this advantage: / she controls the harbor." Myth and dramatic monologue replace the earlier lyric speaker of

"The Apple Trees" and "The Letters" (from *The House on Marshland*), but the material remains unchanged. In this almost-transparent Freudian allegory, the speaker's already been disappointed by love over time: boredom has set in, followed by abandonment.

> Ultimately, men appear,
> weary of the open.

> So terminates, they feel,
> a story. In the beginning,
> longing. At the end, joy.
> In the middle, tedium.

Simultaneous with the appearance of men the story is terminus. They drift toward her, in imagination, which romanticism exalts; this narrative, however, follows romanticism's defeat: irony and cynicism replace imagination. The speaker does not believe in her capacity to change or affect the male other, and she is ambivalent about his seeing her as a goddess.

> In time, the young wife
> naturally hardens. Drifting
> from her side, in imagination,
> the man returns not to a drudge
> but to the goddess he projects.

As the syntax of the sentence reveals, it is not that the "drudge" is *not* a goddess; rather, she is clearly not the goddess he projects. The goddess's power is a substitute for any authority of self: control over the harbor or female sexuality. Therefore, her power is entwined with her powerlessness and prohibition. She is armless, she cannot welcome him home or hold him: all she can do is prohibit his penetration. The rock, an archetypal metaphor that Glück uses over and over again, represents solidity, stoniness, and cold-heartedness. The female sex is the flaw in the rock: her victory is, ironically, sealing up. This invulnerability results in damage and self-hatred (internalizing the flaw).

When she is disappointed in the failed strategies of romanticism, as she is in "Mock Orange" and "Aphrodite," Glück either chooses repression—externalizing rage, withholding and withdrawing from love—or, frightened of her own vulnerability, she emulates masculine powers of conquest and hard-heartedness. The female self is thus fragile and isolated, victimized by a desire to be completed, but actually selfless in—or contemptuous of—the social world controlled by men. As a result, Glück turns to the displaced desire for thanatotic permanence—sometimes expressed in the mythological sphere, where she can universalize her personal drama. Thus isolated, she subjects herself to adversarial power regimes and a repetition of flight, ironic defense, denial, and withdrawal, leading her simultaneously to circularity and stasis, as in this passage from "Unwritten Law."

> Interesting, how we fall in love:
> in my case, absolutely. Absolutely, and alas, often—
> so it was in my youth.
>
> . . . .
> Nor did I see them as versions of the same thing.
> . . . .
> And yet, the mistakes of my youth
> made me hopeless, because they repeated themselves

The female speaker, divorced from the social, relies exclusively on romantic love as salvation: she is without other mediating sources of fulfillment. Glück's poems persuasively argue against dependency and domesticity, social forces many of the women poets discussed in earlier chapters consciously resist. What the poems dramatize, despite rhetorical and mythological reframing of experience, is the impossibility of retaining a semblance of autonomy in the face of the social world's power relationships. One is reminded of Nagisa Oshima's film, *The Realm of the Senses*, where an obsessive couple pursues their passion in opposition to a culture consumed by militarism, only to eventually mutilate one another in the very intensity of their isolated love.

> I can imagine how my face looks,
> burning like that, afflicted with desire—lowered
> face of your invention—how the mouth betrays
> the isolated greed of the lover
> as it magnifies and then destroys.

Glück evokes the Platonic view of desire as illusory ("love is blind"), but here, focus on the two figures yields "isolated greed" and distortion. These dramas, depending on her power to seduce and refuse, recur throughout her entire body of work. From the beginning of her career, with the Plath-like elements of the aggrieved in *Firstborn*, Glück has fluctuated from the fragile victim to the grandiose goddess whose love bears tragic consequences. Deprived of scope and a sense of relation, finding no alternative models in the culture, her speakers are doomed to serially repeat failed attempts at intimacy.

Since Glück also believes she is destined to live by what she calls fate, she deprives herself of agency while the patina of myth elevates her helplessness into the realm of the tragic. Mythology helps fuel this nostalgic fatalism, while also emphasizing temporal decay—the present as a falling from the ideal. Theodor Adorno historicizes artistic obsession with myth as follows: "Whoever glorifies order and form as such, must see in the petrified divorce, an archetype of the eternal. . . . Fetishism gravitates toward mythology. In general, cultural critics become intoxicated with idols drawn from antiquity to the dubious, long-evaporated warmth of the liberalist era, which recalled the origins of culture in its decline."[4] Mythology thus reinforces a dead end for Glück, leaving her speakers hopelessly mired in a past that looms larger than the present; her revised heroines are abandoned to solitary, self-defeating desire for illuminating truth.

Ultimately romanticism itself intensifies these frustrations, resulting in an increasingly self-mocking inwardness. As in the late drawings of Picasso, Glück's vision metaphorizes the speaker's "animal" nature and derides her own feelings because she cannot give them expression or scope without melodrama or heroic dimension. The outcome of this degradation is expressed in the tonally complex and beautifully written "Vita Nova," the title poem of a recent collection:

> In the splitting up dream
> we were fighting over who would keep
> the dog,
> Blizzard. You tell me
> what that means. He was
> a cross between
> something big and fluffy

and a dachshund. Does this have to be
the male and female
genitalia?

"Vita Nova" is another variant of the parable expressed earlier in the collection (while once she found her parents' lives heartbreaking, she now
also finds them funny). One might argue that, in the Old Testament tradition, the ironic becomes a way of coping with pain, but here the closure
of the poem makes clear that human feeling has been diminished: in her
late work Glück turns to satire. She dismisses "daddy's" spontaneous ado-
lescent romantic yearnings:

the kind of love he wants Mommy
doesn't have. Mommy's
too ironic—mommy wouldn't do
the rhumba in the driveway

In the final couplet, she turns the cynical eye on herself:

Never
will I forget your face, your frantic human eyes
swollen with tears.
I thought my life was over and my heart was broken.
Then I moved to Cambridge.

Suffering here is transient, undermined by cynicism, and made to be forgotten. The poem, interestingly, alludes to the culturally current "inner
child," at first acknowledging her suffering and then "moving on."

Supposing
I'm the dog, as in
my child-self, inconsolable because
completely pre-verbal? With
anorexia! Oh Blizzard,
be a brave dog—this is
all material; you'll wake up
in a different world,
you will eat again, you will grow into a poet!

But lest the reader think the speaker has reached some mature integration of child and adult, one only has to look at the tonal fracture between "Never . . . Swollen with tears" and "*moved to Cambridge*": the speaker draws to our attention her unreliability. In this drama, daddy's heart is empty and mommy's heart is brittle and defended. Moving to Cambridge won't transform the hurt or deprivation dramatized by the poem. The speaker gains strength by an act of escape, repression, and ironic diminishment; she doesn't "heal" the child self but leaves it behind with derisive laughter. The effect, as in many of Glück's strongest poems, is chilling. But the narrative of this poem essentially rarifies a suburban midlife crisis: the shifting tone, momentarily acknowledging suffering and then parodying it, becomes the ultimate consequence of the failure of romanticism.

Glück's simultaneous contempt for, fear of, and desire to control such a world thus becomes comprehensible. Her retreat from the world is filled with strategies she learned from its corruption: the resultant narcissism is not personal, it is cultural. If one continues to seek to overpower that reality or to blame oneself for these failed connections, one is doomed—as Glück's poems dramatize—to repetition and diminishment.

For many writers, high modernism put to rest the mystical and idealist clams of romanticism. While they never gave up coherence, they resisted the subjective "I" as a vehicle for redemption or meaning. "The Modernist work of art proceeded not out of a conviction of organic continuity or even correlation with nature," Gelpi says, "but instead out of a conviction of the discontinuity between subject and object, and the consequent fragmentation of self and experience required the tight construction of the art object from the fragments. The Modernist artwork stood as an often desperate insistence on coherence, heroic considering the odds, amidst and against the ravages of time: the instability of nature, the unreliability of perception, and the tragedy of human history."[5]

But postmodernism's skepticism about organic form, about the separation of high and low culture, and about the ideology of any conceptual framework has left us with the stress of the entropic universe and no cultural institution to turn to, no *a priori* value that gives us as sense of scale and relation. What we pay for the failure of romanticism is too high a price for hard-hearted survival. Or as Glück aptly says in the rescue dream, "Seizure," "It was never focus that was missing. / It was meaning."

Glück's work, then, really marks the end of an age, though a number of other poets, male and female, most who don't write quite as skillfully as

Glück (Stanley Plumly; Stephen Dobyns, in his romance with the "dark self"; Jane Kenyon; and Mary Oliver come to mind), rely on this same set of values. Romantic transcendence, which began as a nostalgic act trying to recapture a relationship with nature and to escape the powerful machinery of the emerging Industrial Revolution—when the pastoral landscape was still available to them as grounding—failed Keats and Shelley even back then. As Gelpi notes, "On the one hand, its [romanticism's] high valuation of the self results in a commitment to radical subjectivity that cannot be subsumed under any general category; on the other, the ideal of intellectual judgment requires it treat all human actions as if they were subject to exhaustive third-person descriptions, which necessarily undermine the status of self-reflexive individuality."[6]

Glück's work has attached itself to a difficult historical moment: she has led her readers to a cultural crisis point for herself and many other women. Sexual liberation, which sanctions desire, underscores for women in this culture a new kind of selflessness: while sex in a consumerist culture remains a weapon, it offers only repressive power. If a woman seeks the mystical romantic ideal, selflessness, disillusionment, and brittle cynicism result. Her splintered and damaged self becomes more and more difficult to decipher because as cultural pressures intensify they also tend to become more diffuse, less visible, and thereby more abstract: it becomes more and more difficult to pinpoint an origin, a source for these unresolved feelings. Psychologist Kenneth Gergen, in *The Saturated Self*, reflects how certain aspects of the postmodern world provide a rush of stimuli that we cannot connect to any meaningful whole.[7] Recent sociological studies also reflect how media's assault on popular culture now interjects itself into our discourse with an intensity and speed never seen before (and we as individuals have diminishing power to recognize and influence the effects of those spheres). In matters of literary commerce, corporate takeovers of trade publishers and bookstores have intensified a celebrity culture in poetry: since fewer and fewer poets publish with trade publishers or—beyond a small circle of other writers—have access to a general reading public, those who feel they have been chosen feel like exceptions, special cases. It is inconceivable that public events, as well as the technological transformation of the industrial revolution, would not deeply affect a poet's relationship to his or her audience or sense of him- or herself. Who are we talking to, beyond ourselves? How can we, as individual artists, dream of transforming a culture that has deprived us of a sense of relation and placed us on its very margins with neither a discourse nor a community to work to resolve it? No wonder Glück positions herself as a mythic goddess as a way to reify her alienation and emptiness. It is no mystery that many American artists, spurred on by the ethos and promises of individualism, find so many ways to resist powerlessness by transcendence or, conversely, as with Louise Glück, when those strategies lead them to exile, ironically resign themselves to that powerlessness.

7.

....

TRAFFICKING IN THE RADIANT

The Spiritualizing of American Poetry

It's not possible to be sated with the world. I'm still insatiable. At my age, I'm still looking for a form, for a language to express the world.

—CZESŁAW MIŁOSZ

I cannot conceive of a personal God who would directly influence the actions of individuals, or would directly sit in judgment on creatures of his own creation. . . . My religiosity consists in a humble admiration of the infinitely superior spirit that reveals itself in the little that we, with our weak and transitory understanding, can comprehend of reality.

—ALBERT EINSTEIN

UNTIL RECENTLY, thanks to New Criticism and faith in the invincibility of the canon, modern American poets might have more comfortably felt they were exempt from, or could at least transcend, the pressures of their age. Poetry, in its loftiest purpose, was considered an expression of the spirit of the autonomous individual, the product of an eternal, timeless truth. But a combination of political, philosophical, literary, and scientific inquiries have all undermined these absolutes: the concept of the self, as I have discussed in the opening chapters, has been problematized, subjected to any number of contingencies, many culturally induced. In literature, both hierarchical judgments concerning harmony, paradox, and closure and the fixed notion of masterworks have come to be seen as ideological assertions that effaced social context and cultural differences.

If lingering in romanticism and writing in received forms provide contemporary American poets some retreat from these instabilities, recent preoccupations with both religiosity and spirituality also defend against them. These inward-turning quests for "ultimate truths" (to use Paul

Tillich's term) reflect a similar longing for signposts that will hold true for an individual and at the same time subject this "self" to law, ethical standards, or a faith in a higher power.[1] When mass culture penetrates and erodes our romantic notions of self and individuality, though, evidence of the effects of commerce and cheapened spirituality further challenge our faith in truth and absolutes. What appear to be inner revelations may just as often be reflections of the unselfconscious absorption of cultural clichés of the age; in fact, thanks to the entanglement of commerce and faith, the debased language of spirituality has contaminated all our discourses, including poetry.

The rise and decline of religious discourse has always reflected, albeit obliquely (just like the rise and fall of poets' reputations), a historical component: why would the critical vocabulary of contemporary poetry be exempt from these shifting pressures? My contention is that the recent rise of religiosity and the concurrent discourse of spirituality have diminished human agency and effaced many of the social causes of our anxieties. Those who use religion as a metaphorical expression of their powerlessness, or those who heighten various spiritual strategies often in their longing for private salvation, turn from the material world. Moreover, in the Judeo-Christian tradition, the belief in absolutes (as with many other religious traditions) creates a kind of hegemony over other belief systems. In poetry this issue often surfaces in problems of representation, the way the speaker universalizes particular experiences that often lead to legislation. Poets who feel obliged to tell the truth often subject their readers to the poet as spokesperson, a flawed concept most clearly articulated by Emerson's essay on poetry.

Furthermore, the resultant spirit-body dualism often has the effect of devaluing the body and the temporal in relation to the spirit: in other words, the desire of the individual to transcend materiality often leads to a private flight from both the social and sexual. Finally, the assault of imagery we see in the public sphere corrupts what we think of as the spiritual discourse; in this culture spirituality has currency: spirituality sells. And the language of spirituality is entangled, either crudely or subtly, with the economic, either directly or in the selling of the self for ego gratification.

It does not take long to uncover this entanglement in the culture at large. In a recent issue of *The New Yorker*, Nicholas Lehman writes about one way commerce corrupts our news reporting:

Most mainstream-media organizations, worried at being culturally and politically out of synch with many Americans, are making an effort to reach out—I frequently heard a promise to cover religion more seriously and sympathetically. For many, that's a business imperative, an attempt to broaden the audience, especially among conservatives. Neil Shapiro, the President of NBC News . . . said of NBC News' new anchor, Brian Williams, "He's a great journalist, a great reporter. Having said that, he's a huge NASCAR fan, has been since his father took him to the track when he was a kid. He cares a lot about his faith. . . . Brian does get it."[2]

It is no surprise that faith has been ascendant these last several years. According to the American Religion Data Archive, though there has been a slight decline in traditional Protestant sects, there has been an 8.8 percent increase in religious adherents since 1990.[3] And as Richard Marin notes, "What's more, belief in God may be getting stronger. In 1987, a Gallup poll found that 60 percent of those interviewed 'completely agreed' with the statement, 'I never doubt the existence of God.' Last October, the proportion expressing a similarly strong belief in God had grown to 69 percent, according to a poll conducted by Princeton Survey Research. Americans who say they have no religious preference are expressing greater belief in the hereafter—63 percent today, compared with 44 percent three decades ago. Overall, the proportion of Americans who believe in life after death rose from 77 percent in 1973 to 82 percent in 1998."[4]

This recent movement toward faith only tells a small part of the story. Self-help books offering spiritual advice abound. Oprah Winfrey has become something of a spirituality industry: she has managed to market several self-help spirituality experts, most notably Gary Zukav, who writes a column for her magazine. Her endorsement helped make his *In the Seat of the Soul* a best-seller for nearly three years. Zukav offers a New Age discourse. "On 'About Spirit' on the Oprah web page read, 'Your Spirit is at the core of who you truly are. We often forget to connect to this part of ourselves because of our busy schedules and full lives. But it is important to take the time to Remember Your Spirit to keep yourself centered and open to all the possibilities and joy you can bring into your life. . . . How Do You Remember Your Spirit? Everyone has an activity or process that they do to restore their sense of spirit, peace and well-being. And often, it's something simple that may not take a lot of time.'"[5] Well, thank goodness it doesn't require a lot of time, and aye, there's the rub.

Even more crudely, self-help books have adopted the language of spirituality, further contaminating the meaning of the word. In 2005, Dawn Ritchie and Kathryn Robyn's *The Emotional House* became a best-seller because it directly marketed this nexus between spirituality and commerce. The book promises to "guide you in taking action to transform your home into a dynamic living space that enlivens your spirit, supports your dreams, helps heal your broken relationships, and motivates your future."[6]

Coauthor Kathryn Robyn's credentials include being a "healing coach and Reiki Master in private practice. Ms. Robyn has led transformational workshops and support groups for over fifteen years, working with organizations such as Child Help USA, The Alcoholism Center for Women, The Healing Light Center and Alive and Well." The introduction to the book further claims: "By simply following the twelve easy steps, anyone can make changes in their home environment that will revitalize their dwelling and their lifestyle, beautify their space, organize family finances, impact family dynamics, and move them towards greater personal fulfillment. This program truly is therapy for your home!"[7]

This book might be dismissed as easy satire were spirituality not such common parlance in our culture: the twelve-step higher power discourse once reserved for alcoholics now includes living room suites; a weekend walk in the woods is now very spiritual; romances often are spoken of as having spiritual connections. Healing, once the province of twice-born ministers, is now applied to psychological discourses to describe any number of social traumas, from childhood history to the aftermath of a bad relationship. In other words, what we once thought of as private realms are pressurized by both the values and cultural usage: we absorb spirituality as part of our current idiom. And just as our ideas about truth and beauty have transformed by the force of history the assault of imagery in the social world (compare body images and aspirations in the 1950s to the emaciated models in our magazines now), so have our ideas about what constitutes spirituality. It is difficult not to be skeptical about the popular assertion among poets and others that any spiritual urge goes *deeper* than the political and social. More than ever, our autonomy is entangled with social forces: those romantic beliefs exempting the individual from the pressures of culture seem archaic and, in the case of some of our poets, sophistic.

Even resistance, such as attempts to insulate the individual from the public sphere, whether taking flight in suburbia to protect the nuclear family or adapting Eastern spiritual practices, cannot avoid the culturally specific: Western/Eastern spiritual practice differs greatly from one immersed, say, in Buddhist practice in Tibet. Our attitudes about desire and asceticism, compassion and love, cannot be segregated from the culture in which we have learned the signifiers for those terms.

Surely there are degrees and significant differences among current spiritual practices, and much of what I take up in terms of religiosity in this chapter is directed toward the spirit-body dualism of Judeo-Christian traditions. But the privatization of the spirit, the longing for a personal salvation free from the worldly, appealing as it might seem, is often haunted by the specter of the social, what is consequentially repressed.

While this resurgent quest for absolutes obviously affects the public sphere (the war in Iraq is in part a perverted product of those beliefs), the retreat from materiality (from valuing the body and the sufficiency of this world) also saturates our poetics. Many have written about the narcissism in our poetry as a sign of indulging in privatism; but since redemption or salvation is primarily individual (and increasingly removed from culture), spiritual salvation also attenuates that privatism. Elaine Scarry draws this parallel when she takes "the case of a God" in *The Body in Pain*: "The imagined image, or believed-in belief, may itself be capable of taking a future self-substantiating form . . . [but] at the moment when the made thing is only an idea or image or belief [with no verbal or material extension], insofar as it has any reality at all, it will only have reality in the mind of the embodied imaginer. . . . It will have no reality for anyone outside the boundaries of the believer's body."[8]

One hears many explanations for this recent recurrence of religiosity and easy spirituality into mainstream culture: the constantly promoted but failed promise of materialism to satisfy our inner lives, well-organized fundamentalist communities (modeled and advanced by social policies of the Bush administration, including cynical faith-based initiatives), the increasing conservatism of the media (not only in radio talk shows but also in the clinical gaze of therapeutic testimonials from the ilk of Dr. Phil and Dr. Laura), the perceived threat to Western culture by other religious sects, the threat to decency by secular humanism and the pornography of American culture. It is not an ahistorical accident that we more often look to a higher power to help cope with feelings of powerlessness: our society now reflects no shortage of irrational darkness; our current government represents the economic interests of a very few and moreover seems committed to hegemony over other religions and cultures; lobbying dollars decide more and more of our foreign and domestic policies, rendering "one person, one vote" the myth of democracy; the very core of our faith in individuality increasingly seems like an endangered species.

There is no question that contemporary poets mirror the culture's heightened attention to matters spiritual and religious. Recent collections—some more and some less authentically—by Jorie Graham, Cal Bedient, Olena Kalytiak Davis, Li Young Lee, Franz Wright, W. S. Di Piero, Michael Ryan, Jane Hirshfield, Mary Oliver, Grace Schulman, Mark Jarman, and Timothy Steele (whose "Toward the Winter Solstice" I discussed in the last chapter for its hegemonic assumptions about religiosity), just to name a few, accentuate our contemporary poets' attention to the spiritual. Neoformalist critic Christian Wiman has rightly chastised secular poets—I would have to include myself among them—for the frequency with which they have addressed God in their poems, even as metaphor. Even a cursory glance at the current sites of authority in poetry—that is to say, who chooses book prizes, who anthologizes, who awards grants (signs that reflect the values of the dominant culture)—also illustrates these changing values. This shift reverberates generationally, most importantly in the way younger artists naturally model their work after their accomplished teachers (most graduate writing programs *market* their programs by listing their most successful students). Our poetic icons have also changed: in the past three decades, Rainer Maria Rilke has replaced Pablo Neruda as one of our most influential poets (Neruda's sensual and political work saw prominence during the New Internationalism of the 1960s and 1970s). T. S. Eliot, whose status has fluctuated ever since he dominated generations of writers through the mid-1950s, is again garnering heightened attention. My point here is that this spiritual discourse is historically specific and is much more than an expression of individual longing: it is part of our current zeitgeist. In our art and in our lives we value the spiritual more in this age, for example, than we did in the 1960s and 1970s.

A cursory look at the Poetry Daily Web site shows plenty of spiritually centered poems: one of the most interesting includes Brad Leithauser's,

Dana Gioia's, and Mary Jo Salter's selection of Richard Wilbur's poems, each of which explicitly traffics in the radiant impalpable (my tone derides the ideological agenda in their choices, but readers can judge this excerpt for themselves).

> Though the unseen may vanish, though insight fails
> And doubter and downcast saint
> Join in the same complaint,
> What holy things were ever frightened off
> By a fly's buzz, or itches, or a cough?[9]

I am more interested in examining the current choice of this poem as a model for the art than I am in judging the poem itself (which was interestingly published in 1956); but who would have thought thirty-five years ago, when Philip Larkin was waxing nostalgically about the death of the Empire (in ironic poems like "Homage to a Government") and of God ("No God any more, or sweating in the dark; // About hell and that, or having to hide / What you think of the priest"), we would be highlighting the upbeat impalpable in lines like these or considering seriously W. S. Di Piero's poem "The Kiss," in his 2004 collection *Brother Fire*?

> The mossy transom light, odors of cabbage
> and ancient papers, while Father Feeney
> polishes an apple on his tunic.
> I tell him I want the life priests have,
> not how the night sky's millions
> of departing stars, erased by city lights,
> terrify me toward God. . . .
>
> Where am I, Father, when I visit a life
> inside or outside the one I'm in?
> In our wronged world I see things
> accidentally good . . .
>
> Tell what you know now
> of dreadful freshness and want,
> our stunned world peopled
> by shadows solidly flesh,

a silted fountain of prayer
rising in our throat.

The worldly dissatisfactions in this sincere poem include being a specta-
tor to racial injustice and the Cuban Missile Crisis; the author humanely
comes to believe "the wall's / filthy cracks . . . / held stories I'd find / and
tell." Thus, the speaker decides he will give voice to the voiceless. But this
poem's New Critical paradoxes, its mythic reference to the fall, its yearning for the life of the priest, and the description of worldly decay in the
"silted fountain" (all strategies seemingly influenced by late Eliot) still end
in an ambivalent desire to defer to the priest's authority and to "make our
prayers heard." The religious impulse in this poem authorizes the lyric
speaker's mission and morality: he has little self-consciousness about taking dominion over other people's stories, risking moral and verbal superiority. The poem sells its humility at the same time it appropriates other
people's stories. The British poet Douglas Dunn, in an early poem titled
"I am a Cameraman" (the camera as a metaphor for writing), suggests the
dangers of such spectatorship and representation:

They suffer, and I catch only the surface.
The rest is inexpressible, beyond
What can be recorded. You can't be them.
If they'd talk to you, you might guess
What pain is like though they might spit on you.

Di Piero's poem suggests the difficulty in the lyric poet's spiritual position-
ing: while the speaker presents himself with humility, his assertion that
he can represent others suggests a more complicated self-aggrandizement.
The gap between an artist's presentation self and his or her own complicated and uninterrogated worldly drives (here, self-justification of narrative for social action authorized by religiosity authority) complicates the
spiritual declaration in art.

Bonifacio Veronese's 1540s painting, *Il Ricco Epulone*, also known as
Dives and Lazarus, in Venice's Galleria D'Academia, portrays the allegory
of Lazarus and the beggar from Luke 16:19–31.[10] The stated subject is un-
christian behavior: a wealthy patron refuses the beggar. But here the beggar is banished to the lower right corner of the canvas; he is nowhere near
skeletal with hunger nor even shabbily dressed; his neutral fleshy colors,

far from the painting's center of interest, almost fade from view—even the dog that is supposed to be nipping at his clothes is apparently politely sniffing him. As in the Di Piero poem, poverty is viewed safely from afar. The center of the painting is reserved for the courtiers portraying luxurious and joyful Venetian life. Painted during the heyday of Venice's secular and mercantile dominance over its neighbors, *Il Ricco Epulone* celebrates the figures' colorful clothes and draperies of crimson and green. A noble, wooden, statuelike Moor child holds a musical score for the mandolin player. Our eye is drawn to the laughter, to dreamy sensual pleasure— one couple holding hands, another young man admiring the back of the lutenist's neck. The true subject of this historically transposed moment (from the age of Christ to the sixteenth century) is lushness and privilege: how lucky some of us are to be living in this cornucopia of luxury. The moment when Lazarus receives heaven's blessing temporally resides elsewhere and is not really Veronese's project here. The viewer can righteously leave the painting thinking well of himself for his sensitivity to the religious subject and at the same time receive all the titillating pleasures of commerce.

The invocation of piety and the invocation of the other-worldly while luxuriating and enacting material privilege reside uncomfortably together in the Veronese painting. Similarly, the sensitive lyric poet, usually insulated from poverty (in this case W. S. Di Piero, but I could have chosen any number of contemporary poets), humbly invokes his or her desire for spiritual revelation or pleads for Job-like justice, while under his or her work lies either ego display or the seduction of the fashionable; as with the Veronese painting, the art is an uninterrogated reflection of the dominant culture. I do not impugn the motives of any single poet, but I wish to underline that in a capitalist culture like ours, or like the mercantile culture of Veronese's time, the resurgence of these poems is entangled with the contradictory and corrupting fashions of commerce and culture. When the artist receives recognition for his spiritualizing vision, for consciously or unconsciously mirroring and promoting this intensifying cultural need for privatism and escape, the temptation to maintain cultural approval, to repeat those strategies, "auctions" that spirituality, to use Dickinson's diction. Furthermore, all the contradictions of bourgeois life—the desire to be seen as a good citizen, simultaneous with the infantile wish for safety and protection—reside in many of these poems. These poems long to tame the danger of living in this world.

Religiosity is far from monolithic: spirituality is not the exclusive concern of Christians, and there is a wide spectrum of Christian beliefs, from the nuns who served in Central America to Jerry Falwell and Pat Robertson; from the black church that played a leadership role to churches whose doctrines disdain the worldly altogether. Clearly, there are churches and individuals inside these institutions (like liberation theologists) who link worldly compassion, justice, and tolerance to redemption. One can turn, for example, to Emmanuel Levinas's post-Holocaust theology and its emphasis on the ethical responsibility to the here and now and the other. And some of our current poetry also reflects those concerns. But conventional Christian theologies emphasize the hierarchy of spirit over body; affirm salvation and truth as individual rather than collective; and depend upon the judgment, metaphorical or otherwise, of an other-worldly higher authority for guidance and forgiveness (as in the Di Piero poem).

No twentieth-century poet has better represented those Christian ideologies and the interest in religious salvation than T. S. Eliot. Eliot's work and aesthetics reflect many of the discomfiting outcomes of a retreat from valuing this world. He is also perhaps the most obvious example of an artist whose reputation has benefited from the shifting currency of religiosity. As recently as 1989, Cynthia Ozick wrote in *The New Yorker,*

> It's impossible nowadays to imagine such authority accruing to a poet. In his person, if not in his poetry, Eliot was false coinage. . . . certainly Eliot condemned the optimism of democratic American meliorism, he despised Unitarianism, centered less on personal salvation than on social good, & he had contempt for Jews as marginal, if not inimical to his concept of Christian community. In the 40s & 50s Eliot was absolute art: high art when art was its most serious & elitist. Eliot's aristocratic ideas which some might call Eurocentric & obscurantist no longer interest most literary intellectuals. . . . It is in the nature of fame to undergo revision: *Eliot appears now to be similarly receding into the parochial, even the sectarian.*[11]

Marjorie Perloff, though admiring Eliot's early experimentalism, responds to what she called Ozick's "harsh criticism" in the following way: "Who, in those post-sixties liberationist times could readily admire an overtly anti-Semitic, politically reactionary poet, who seemed to be obsessed with original sin, feared his own sexuality, and displayed an obvious contempt for women? 'Lord! spare us from any more Fisher Kings!,' quipped Frank O'Hara."[12]

Neither could have predicted the last decade's resurrection of Eliot (and the shift provides just one more example of how the idea of the canon is problematic as an eternal measure of great literature), but Eliot discussions are currently everywhere in our intellectual life, including new Web sites, new prizes, and an entire 2003 issue of *Modernism/Modernity*. One of the most recent tributes can be found in Mark Rudman's essay in *American Poetry Review*. Others have praised Eliot's quest for absolutes: Rudman concurs, saying he admires Eliot's "desire to touch something undeniable."[13] As with any claim for or aspiration to an ultimate truth, we are required to ask, *Whose truth is it, and who pays for that truth?* An absolute truth, specifically in Eliot's case the truth of Christianity, essentializes us; it authorizes *a priori* design and order, a hierarchy of soul over body, and it defends against subjectivity and the temporal. It not only assumes our own insufficiency as well as the insufficiency of the material world but ultimately takes dominion over others' visions.

Who pays for Eliot's quest for absolutes? The underbelly of his vision is the displacement of his fear of death and his externalizing that fear by demonizing the other: in his case the Jew. Much has been made of Eliot's anti-Semitism, especially since Anthony Julius's provocative 1995 book *T. S. Eliot: Anti-Semitism and Literary Form*; apologists like Craig Raine, in his 2007 biography *T. S. Eliot: Image, Text and Context*, claim these expressions as reflections of Eliot's speakers. And while one can justify any single piece of evidence, cumulatively Eliot's obsession with the Jew—having it both ways, expressing anti-Semitism while sometimes critiquing the speaker—makes it difficult to claim these comments as merely ironic representations of the speaker. In poems like "Gerontion" ("the jew squats on the window sill, the owner / Spawned in some estaminet of Antwerp / Blistered in Brussels, patched and peeled in London"), "Sweeney and the Nightingales," and "The Dirge," Eliot less frequently critiques the poems' speakers for their ethnic views; rather, he emphasizes their incapacity to transcend the corruption of materiality. In "Gerontion," for example, the ironies underline the speaker's willingness to dwell in this corrupt world, but the poem does not refute the Jew as an agent of this corruption. Additionally, in some of these expressions Eliot's irony is at the very least disputable, as in the following excerpt from "Burbank with a Baedeker: Bleistein with a Cigar":

But this or such was Bleistein's way:
    A saggy bending of the knees
And elbows, with the palms turned out,
    Chicago Semite Viennese.

A lustreless protrusive eye
    Stares from the protozoic slime
At a perspective of Canaletto.
    The smoky candle end of time

Declines. On the Rialto once.
    The rats are underneath the piles.
The jew is underneath the lot.
    Money in furs.

I am interested in the way Eliot's anti-Semitism contaminates his early and late work as well as his aesthetic and philosophical views (mirrored in his essays), not so much in and of itself, but in the way his spiritual views and his attitudes about Jews reflect his fear and hatred of the body. These ideas originate, I believe, in Eliot's conviction, first private and later articulated in *Christianity and culture: The Idea of a Christian Society and Notes towards the Definition of Culture*, that "the choice before us is between the formation of a new Christian culture, and the acceptance of a pagan one."[14]

These passages, consistent with his spiritual convictions, stem from his belief in absolutes. This conviction allows him to issue forth the famous sentence, "Reasons of race and religion combine to make any large number of free-thinking Jews undesirable."[15] The Jew frames his attitude toward the body, passion, and desire. In Eliot's anti-Semitism, the Jew becomes his threatening object of desire: his projective identification of Jews as representing the body, externalizing his feelings of guilt and shame onto the material body of the Jew, originates in his longing to transcend the body and the world, the implication of which is that the body is a source of debasement, sin, and decay. Given the source of this anti-Semitism, Eliot's stance becomes an explicable element in his longed-for vision of "purifying fire." What motored Eliot in *The Four Quartets* and what almost always motored him were lifetime fears, shame, sexual confusions, and disgust around the body; passion, housed in the transitory and irrational, is the main obstacle in his quest for fixity and permanence. He turns his obsessions, his fractured drives, into principles, principles that conflate economic, social, and metaphysical doctrines to create a fixed and consistently debased view of human culture. And if he wrestles with this vision of the body in "The Love Song of J. Alfred Prufrock" (here the "shallow" seductive woman's the object of desire), he accedes to it explicitly in *The Four Quartets*. To give in to passion and materiality in this poem is to be betrayed by a world fleeting, contaminated, and illusory, as deadly as the process of time itself. And to turn away from the passion-body-Jew nexus leads to dessication in this life. There's nothing left but to take flight.

Look at the closure of "East Coker," in *The Four Quartets*:

Our only health is the disease
If we obey the dying nurse
Whose constant care is not to please
But to remind of our, and Adam's curse,
And that, to be restored, our sickness must grow worse.

   The whole earth is our hospital
Endowed by the ruined millionaire,
Wherein, if we do well, we shall
Die of the absolute paternal care
That will not leave us, but prevents us everywhere.

Mark Rudman sees *The Four Quartets* as "infused with the torments of tenderness—a tenderness so immense it lacks no boundary."[16] That's not what I see in these lines, nor in much of the poem. Even if we allow for the devastating influence of World War I on his view of human possibility, this recasting of the fall is a life-hating vision: "The whole earth is our hospital" is a globalizing metaphor; it holds true only if every moment on earth is filled with and driven by the terror of death. Eliot is conscious of that view long before he composes the poem. His introduction to the April 1932 issue of *The Criterion* makes explicit his derision of humanism: "The mystical belief in herd-feeling, which has been elevated to a psuedo-science under such names as 'social psychology,' is one of the most disquieting superstitions of the day. . . . *It is a symptom of weakness, but the weakness is only in part pathological; for the rest it is just the essential feebleness and impotence of the individual man which Christianity has always recognized*."[17]

Later, in the same essay, he continues, "The religious habits of the race are still very strong, in all places, at all times, and for all people. There is no humanistic habit: humanism is, I think, merely the state of mind of a few persons in a few places at a few times. To exist at all, it is dependent upon some other attitude, for it is essentially critical—I would even say parasitical. It has been and can still be, of great value; but it will never provide showers of partridges or abundance of manna for the chosen peoples."[18]

This most dangerous advocacy of these absolutes is mirrored in our own current domestic and foreign policy. Since we possess the truth, whether it is the truth of Christianity or the truth of Democracy, we feel comfortable imposing those superior values on others. In his advocating a ruling aristocracy (implicit in "The Social Function of Poetry," but explicit in his later essays), Eliot works his way around the more fascist implications of values expressed obliquely in "Little Gidding," as Philp Yancey explains, in the following way:

> But how could Christian values be disseminated by a Christian upper class apart from some form of oppressive rule? The most practicable idea Eliot set forth on this score was what he called the Community of Christians. He noted the peril of specialization in modern culture, which tends to isolate religious thinkers from those in philosophy, art, politics and science. The Community of Christians would bring together the most fertile minds from various fields for the express purpose of defining Christian values for society at large. It would serve as a "Church within the Church." Eliot did not insist that all members of such a community be Christian believers, *only that the rulers accept the Christian faith as the system under which they were to govern.*[19]

Some of these same qualities can be seen in the implications of Timothy Steele's and W. S. Di Piero's poems. My purpose here is not to argue the greatness of Eliot's poetry, nor even to merely review evidence of what seems his obvious anti-Semitism, but to assert how the current wave of interest in spirituality meshes with and reauthorizes his vision. And, just as importantly, his poetry and prose demonstrate the potentially damaging effects of the quests for absolutes and the defensive fears that guide them. In *Totem and Taboo* and *Moses and Monotheism*, Sigmond Freud suggests that religion displaces our anxiety and fear of death; his writing provides some explanation for Eliot's vision, but it also helps explain some of the reasons for our current drift toward the spiritual. In contemporary American culture, rapid change threatens the stability of virtually every body of knowledge. Scientific and medical knowledge seem to change prescriptions for health and longevity on a daily basis; our understandings about the boundaries of gender and sexuality have blurred. We are much more susceptible to scientized explanations of our personality traits, our attractions, our disabilities, and our psychic dilemmas (such as depression). We currently assume that genetic and biological differences greatly determine our behaviors as well as our fates. This change in emphasis suggests that we have far less control over our own fates than we assumed in the 1960s, when we believed that changes in the environment would have an essential effect on the self and the culture. All these almost-volcanic shifts in belief systems mirror economic, political, and social disruptions that appear to threaten our country's economic and military dominance as well as our capacity to regulate ourselves as well as developing countries. If one were to believe the Bush administration's psychological branding of "the war on terror," these disruptions appear to threaten our values, civilization, and life itself.

In this context, Austin Cline perceptively summarizes Freud's belief that religious need (expressed in both *Future of an Illusion* and *Totem and Taboo*) sculpts a narrative to defend against such fluid worldly changes.

"A principle [*sic*] component for Freud was the feeling of helplessness, occurring in a number of different areas, namely external dangers, internal impulses, death, and society. As wish-fulfilling illusions, religious faith and gods had specific tasks: 'They must exorcize the terrors of nature, they must reconcile men to the cruelty of Fate, particularly as it is shown in death, and they must compensate them for the sufferings which a civilized life in common has imposed on them.'" [20]

Religious and transcendent spiritual belief both promise a release from the strictures of the contingent material world as well as from the reality principle; these defenses appear so much more necessary during times when we feel we cannot transform ourselves or our relationship to the world.

Freud believed "religion developed in response to human feelings of helplessness in the face of a world they cannot control. . . . Just as children have their earthly father to protect them from the common dangers of life Freud believed this need is often carried forward into adulthood and subsequently projected into the heavens creating a 'Heavenly Father' who also protects and cares for people. Alongside this, religious rituals were developed to protect the human ego from sexual impulses, thoughts and fantasies which had been repressed because the Church viewed such things as sinful. These rituals were a defence against these impulses ever finding expression in reality. To compensate this ritualistic 'castration' religion promises an after-life which will compensate the believer for the earthly pleasures they have given up."[21]

Freud brings me full circle to a different historical worldview, a view I believe provides one less bifurcated way to inhabit this world. Interestingly, statistics reveal a severe enrollment drop for seven mainline Protestant bodies during the decade 1965–75, a time of social protest and unrest; that drop contrasts both with their gains in the preceding ten years and with the continuing growth of selected conservative churches. The gap is more than 29 percentage points.[22] Those years registered wide-sweeping critiques of institutions, governmental and otherwise; during that time, we saw enormous growth in the civil rights movement, the antiwar movement, and the feminist movement. The scientific, philosophical, psychological, and metaphysical discoveries of modernity became a pervasive discourse in mainstream culture. Freud's theories, Einstein's theory of relativity, Heisenberg's uncertainty principle, Nietzsche's *Thus Spake Zarathustra*, Sartre's "Existentialism is a Humanism," and Derrida's and Foucault's skeptical interrogations of systems of knowledge all suggested a world without *a priori* design, a world where truth was relative and shifting. The movement toward acceptance of these values had a great effect on our poems and our lives. In poetry, respect for the irrational and materiality was expressed in the neosurrealist and realist poetry of the generation of Charles Simic, James Tate, James Wright, W. S. Merwin, Philip Levine, Adrienne Rich, Ethridge Knight, Allen Ginsberg, and others. There was an unprecedented interest in translation, in the international poetry of other cultures. Traditions counter to the canon, many overtly social and political and linguistic—from African American poetry's restoration of the oral tradition, to feminist poets addressing the social concerns of women, to postmodern poets challenging the aesthetics of modernism and representation—not only thrived but influenced the terms of our poetry during the years that followed. These poets' faith and doubts were tied to the social world and the here-and-now on earth. It's not that they lacked a faith in the impalpable but rather that the impalpable—love, for example—grew out of the material world and our imaginative associations with it.

This is not to idealize that poetry in relation to the poetry of our current age (many of the poems of the 1970s suffered from self-congratulation and willful, predictable rhetoric). I am not arguing so much the truth of these discoveries (although these values still form the basis of my own beliefs), but rather how this different view of experience illustrates a dialectical relationship between culture and art: one influences and drives the other. The studio of Charles Simic or James Wright differs from the studio of Jorie Graham or W. S. Di Piero. Change in cultural conventions influences not only our choice of iconic poets but also whose voices dominate the cultural airwaves. The social and metaphysical ideologies that underlie our poetry now both reflect *and* alter the terms and spectrum of our poetic arguments.

Few would question this effect of an ideological shift in the public sphere: to take an obvious example, when Bill Clinton was elected president, he was perceived as coming from the center-to-right wing of the Democratic Party. Years later, the author of welfare "reform," the promoter of balanced budgets, and the sponsor of the hypocritical "don't ask, don't tell" rules is presented and often demonized as the archetypal liberal. Howard Dean, not Stokely Carmichael, represents the radical fringe. The same shift holds true not only for our media but also for our poetry. This assertion about this shift has nothing to do with any reductive kind of political test for art: this does not mean that any poet who evokes the spiritual necessarily lacks authenticity or is socially or politically conservative. My central argument underlines how conventions, seeming expressions of individual need, grow out of specific social and historical moments; unexamined, these conventions can drive our poems. So it benefits our poems, as it benefits our poets and our lives, to examine those cultural and unconscious forces that shape whatever values surface in our poems.

This current commitment to the other-worldly does affect our commitment to *this* world. As Sartre said so eloquently in "Existentialism is a Humanism," in confronting the loss of absolute truths:

> when we speak of "abandonment" . . . we only mean to say that God does not exist, and that it is necessary to draw the consequences of his absence right to the end. . . . there disappears with Him all possibility of finding values in an intelligible heaven. There can no longer be any good *a priori*, since there is no infinite and perfect consciousness to think it. . . . Dostoevsky once wrote: "If God did not exist, everything would be permitted"; and that, for existentialism, is the starting point.

Everything is indeed permitted if God does not exist, and man is in consequence forlorn, for he cannot find anything to depend upon either within or outside himself. *He discovers forthwith, that he is without excuse.* For if indeed existence precedes essence, one will never be able to explain one's action by reference to a given and specific human nature; in other words, there is no determinism—*man is free, man is freedom. . . . That is what I mean when I say that man is condemned to be free. Condemned, because he did not create himself, yet is nevertheless at liberty, and from the moment that he is thrown into this world he is responsible for everything he does . . . .* As Ponge has written in a very fine article, "Man is the future of man."[23]

Sartre posits that *because* our lives are finite, every choice matters; we are without consolation or excuse. Those who believe this current readjustment, this shifting lens and movement toward spirituality, has served us well may feel more comfortable with this change than I do. But for those of us who identify with "free-thinking Jews" or who believe that the world on earth is effluvial, filled with goodness as well as darkness, sufficient beauty and difficulty, for whom contingency offers the pleasure of discovery as well as a threat to stability, we are "still insatiable . . . still looking for a form, for a language to express the world."

8.

CZESŁAW MIŁOSZ

The Late Style

EDWARD SAID'S RECENTLY PUBLISHED *On Late Style: Music and Literature against the Grain* supplies a contrarian view of the late work of great artists. Eschewing the "accepted notion of age and wisdom in some last works . . . reflect(ing) a special maturity, a new spirit of reconciliation and serenity [or] a miraculous transfiguration of common reality," Said asks, "What of artistic lateness not as harmony and resolution but as intransigence, difficulty, and unresolved contradiction?"[1] An artist's anxiety surrounding imminent knowledge of death often leads his or her late work to competing, fragmentary, and irresolvable truths. As Michael Wood culls from Said in his introduction, Beethoven, for example, "knew too much, from too many sources, for a unified culmination to have been possible."[2] Said, quoting his mentor Adorno on Beethoven, reflects, "His late work still remains process, but not as development; rather as a catching fire between extremes, which no longer allow for any secure middle ground or harmony or spontaneity."[3] Rembrandt's late self-portraits provide another artistic example of increasing complexity, self-doubt, difficulty, and fragmentation: the thickness of paint and the blank or underpainted sections of canvas exemplify resistance to harmony and completion. Said believes the outcome of the "artist fully in command of his medium nevertheless abandons communication with the established order of which he is a part and achieves a contradictory, alienated relationship with it. His late works constitute a form of exile."[4]

Czesław Miłosz's *Second Space*, written when the poet was in his early nineties and published posthumously a month after his death in 2004, would both fortify and complicate Said's argument. Miłosz is clearly a representational writer who rarely experiments with form *per se*: he is both socially and politically the most conservative poet under study here. Nevertheless, in his later work he makes himself available to contingency and uncertainty; remarkably, he wrestles with questions of faith and fixed truths; he unravels a lifelong religious conflict between spirit and body, between this world and the Christian heaven. In this last collection, Miłosz's faith in imagination as well as the spirit is often equivocal; simultaneously, his need for affirmation is more urgent and insistent. In the most lively and moving poems, he shows remarkable flexibility, shifting stances—from faith to doubt—within as well as among the poems. But these late works not only lead the author to exile (his literal exile from Poland is beside the point here, since that rupture occurred early in his writing career); while the poems exemplify "Adorno's fractured landscape [as] only one of the ways in which late works quarrel with time and manage to represent death in a refracted mode, as allegory," they also embrace a tragic but effluent human community.[5] In poem after poem, humans suffer injustice, uncertainty, grief and pity, humility and conceit; but in *Second Space*, these experiences lead Miłosz to humility and democratization, to a shared sense of suffering, anxiety, and incompletion.

Ultimately, the collection is filled with a passion for the earth, and it benefits from what appears to be—most evident in the culminating poem, "Orpheus and Euridice"—a great personal love. Further, this love radiates outward beyond the personal to the social world and to collective humanity. This earthly love also complicates Miłosz's spiritual beliefs and deepens his capacity for compassion; it enables him to pay tribute to human frailty and nobility, an expression of a reverence for life itself.

Take, for example, this section of the long poem "Treatise on Theology," packed with shifting and ambiguous stances:

Treat with understanding persons of weak faith.

Myself included. One day I believe, another I disbelieve.

Yet I feel warmth among people at prayer.
Since they believe, they help me to believe
in their existence, these incomprehensible beings.

I remember that they were made to be not much inferior to angels.

Under their ugliness, which is the stigma of their practical
    preoccupations,
they are pure, and when they sing, a vein of ecstasy pulsates in their
    throats.

Most intensely before a statue of Holy Mary,
as she appeared to the young girl in Lourdes.

Naturally, I am a skeptic. Yet I sing with them,
thus overcoming the contradiction
between my private religion and the religion of the rite.

The speaker claims "weak faith": his feelings change from day to day.
The lines "Since they believe, they help me to believe / in their existence,
these incomprehensible beings" are syntactically ambiguous: the line
break indicates their faith helps him to believe, but belief turns toward the
human with "in their existence" and is further undercut by "these incomprehensible beings." That phrase ambiguously connects both the heavenly
spirits and the believers. Miłosz uses memory—what he was taught as
opposed to what he believes—to try to place the faithful, but he suggests
they are supposed to be "slightly" inferior to angels. And in the stanza
about the statue of Mary, true faith seems to belong to an innocent child.
Even though the speaker simultaneously claims to be a skeptic and to embrace by a leap of faith the contradiction between his "private faith" and
"the religion of rite," the impetus for this complicated shift is the following
couplet: "Under their ugliness, which is the stigma of their practical preoccupations, / they are pure, and when they sing, a vein of ecstasy pulsates in
their throats." Humans restore his spiritual faith, but it is evidenced in an
earthly faith in both song and the sensual "vein of ecstasy" (the sublime)
pulsating in their throats. Throughout the collection, divinity embodied
in the earthly combats the implied ugliness and injustice of both history
and an abandoning god; it provides the scaffolding for Miłosz's faith, a
faith that faces death both with the courage of skeptical investigation and
with a lament for the passing of earthly pleasures.

Many of the poems explore Miłosz's doubts; others lament the death
of omniscience or valiantly attempt to refute the exclusively secular. If his
"Orpheus and Euridice" has the last word on the matter (the poem relies

on the myth mostly as a trigger), he settles on faith over doubt; but whether there is a god or life after death or not, Miłosz affirms human love.

Miłosz has always been an ambitious poet, even read in translation (Robert Hass deserves much credit for making many of the poems read so well in English). A look at the earlier poems, especially the first translations published by Seabury Press in the late 1970s, reveals a more didactic, cerebral, guilty, and ironic Miłosz (though in the anthology *Postwar Polish Poetry* he scolds his contemporary and lifetime competitor Zbigniew Herbert, who remained in Poland, for some of those traits).

Here is an excerpt from the scathingly ironic poem, "Incantation":

Human reason is beautiful and invincible.
No bars, no barbed wire, no pulping of books,
No sentence of banishment can prevail against it.
It establishes the universal ideas in language,
And guides our hand so we write Truth and Justice
With capital letters, lie and oppression with small.
It puts what should be above things as they are,
Is an enemy of despair and a friend of hope.
It does not know Jew from Greek or slave from master,
Giving us the estate of the world to manage.
It saves austere and transparent phrases
From the filthy discord of tortured words.
It says that everything is new under the sun,
Opens the congealed fist of the past.
Beautiful and very young are Philo-Sophia
And poetry, her ally in the service of the good.
As late as yesterday Nature celebrated their birth,
The news was brought to the mountains by a unicorn and an echo.
Their friendship will be glorious, their time has no limit.
Their enemies have delivered themselves to destruction.

This poem hardly relies on either lyric or narrative strategies: it is highly rhetorical, virtually devoid of the particular and sensory. Though smart and wrathful, its didacticism is well defended. Compared to the late work, its overwhelming intellect makes the poem a little arid.

Perhaps his most famous "Dedication"— a more particularized and stronger poem—would serve as a better example of the earlier work. The poem begins with a plea: "You whom I could not save, / Listen to me." It moves toward its closure with:

> What is poetry which does not save
> Nations or people?
> A connivance with official lies,
> A song of drunkards whose throats will be cut in a moment,
> Readings for sophomore girls.
> That I wanted good poetry without knowing it,
> That I discovered, late, its salutary aim . . .

Here the irony is maintained, but this *ars poetica*, couched in terms of self-aggrandizement and small-mindedness, laments the diminishing power of poetry (his own as well as others) to transform humanity.

Compare these poems with the incredibly moving "Late Ripeness"—although it is the most faith-affirming poem in *Second Space*, it still reflects Miłosz's changing views of self and flux and the material world. The poem is charged with humility: the entire movement of the poem is earthward, from the general to the particular and intimate, from the large to the small, from the agency of the individual to the democratic:

> Not soon, as late as the approach of my ninetieth year,
> I felt a door opening in me and I entered
> the clarity of early morning.
>
> One after another my former lives were departing,
> like ships, together with their sorrow.
>
> And the countries, cities, gardens, the bays of seas
> assigned to my brush came closer,
> ready now to be described better than they were before.
>
> I was not separated from people,
> grief and pity joined us.
> We forget—I kept saying—that we are all children of the King.
>
> For where we come from there is no division
> into Yes and No, into is, was, and will be.

We were miserable, we used no more than a hundredth part
of the gift we received for our long journey.

Moments from yesterday and from centuries ago—
a sword blow, the painting of eyelashes before a mirror
of polished metal, a lethal musket shot, a caravel
staving its hull against a reef—they dwell in us,
waiting for a fulfillment.

I knew, always, that I would be a worker in the vineyard,
as are all men and women living at the same time,
whether they are aware of it or not.

Here everything is in motion and flux: his ninetieth year is "approach-ing," his former selves are "departing," and he sees himself as a painter, his job to describe *the world* better (note the comparative here). The se-rial details move from the large ("countries") to the small ("gardens" and "bays of seas"—although here the garden has mythic proportions). His job as an artist has been assigned to him: there is no greatness about it. He "descended" to the human community, attached by pity and grief and our inability to use even a small percentage of our gifts. He invokes the democratic, first in religious terms ("as children of the King"), but the affir-mation becomes more diffusely defined in "where we came from." The de-tails in the penultimate stanza, parallel to the images in stanza 3, enact the timeless—in Whitmanian fashion, reminiscent of a passage in "The Sleep-ers" when the hero is bashed against the rocks—by alternating the inti-mate with the historical and metaphorical world of the ship.

The final metaphor, although paraphrasing the biblical Matthew 20:8, concentrates on the earthly and democratic: we are all "workers in the vineyard"; we do not rise up: we experience simultaneity independent of the hierarchies of consciousness ("all men and women living at the same time"—the tense "would be a worker" creating an indefinite and ever-present temporality). The temporal elements of the poem in the penulti-mate stanza both gather up and prepare for that modest labor: it is as if all human wishes (small and large, partial and unfulfilled, the challenging as well as the ordinary) dwell in each of us and need be released in and for the human community. Implied in the end of that stanza is that osmotic process (Whitman often works this way) that brings the dreams of others inside us while we are still on earth: that is as close to a working definition of love as a reader will find in *Second Space*.

In the title poem, heaven serves as much as a metaphor as a literal space; the speaker's imagination brings him there in the opening stanza. Oddly enough, in the "hanging gardens," he imagines a prefall paradise, not a site of virtue and sin. The stanza ends with a sublime moment, one where pleasure and pain are fused: the soul "tears," the body "soars." Only memory (as opposed to imagination or vision) brings him back to the up and down of traditional Christian belief.

> How spacious the heavenly halls are!
> Approach them on aerial stairs.
> Above white clouds, there are the hanging gardens of paradise.
>
> A soul tears itself from the body and soars.
> It remembers that there is an up.
> And there is a down.
>
> Have we really lost faith in that other space?
> Have they vanished forever, both Heaven and Hell?
>
> Without unearthly meadows how to meet salvation?
> And where will the damned find suitable quarters?
>
> Let us weep, lament the enormity of the loss.
> Let us smear our faces with coal, loosen our hair.
>
> Let us implore that it be returned to us,
> That second space.

The middle of the poem performs an amazing series of leaps: after his conviction about ascension, the speaker begins to question a loss of faith, and then the concepts of heaven and hell seem to have vanished: finally, the speaker sees salvation as entwined with the pastoral meadow (a reflection of those hanging gardens). The consequence of that loss disorients the speaker: things are no longer in their proper place. The speaker provides an image of the earthly in smearing the faces with coal, but also demands ritual. Ultimately, the poem's lamenting closure suggests that this "second space," whether it is imaginative space (without which the impalpable is unrecognizable) or a more literal heavenly space, was stolen from the earth. The tragic appeal, the plea, the supplication implied in "implore," reflects at least a sense of powerlessness to retrieve the afterlife and salvation.

In a much slighter poem, this acknowledgment of the secular is made explicit in a witty and ironic rhetorical flourish. Responding to Dostoyevsky's quotation from *The Brothers Karamazov* (quoted by Sartre in the previous chapter), even acknowledging the death of God, Miłosz suggests that our duty—a product of our shared frailties and grief dramatized in other poems—remains to the human community.

> If there is no God,
> Not everything is permitted to man.
> He is still his brother's keeper
> And he is not permitted to sadden his brother,
> By saying there is no God.

In "Werki," a poem grounded in a small town in Miłosz's Lithuanian past, space, memory, and the temporal again become sites of conflict. The poem opens with a pastoral scene, where the manmade music blends with the natural. In this seemingly timeless idyllic place, we find "a large view" of the moving river.

> An English horn, a drum, a viola making music
> In a house on a hill amidst the forests in autumn.
> A large view from there onto bends of the river.

But in the second stanza, the idealistic speaker is disturbed by the uncorrectable: he desires to save those who have already died (most likely in the Second World War), but the memory also leads him to wonder about what's become of them. They reside in an "unknown country."

> I still want to correct this world,
> Yet I think mostly of them, and they have all died.
> Also about their unknown country.
> Its geography, says Swedenborg, cannot be transferred to maps.
> For there, as one has been, so one sees.

And is it possible even there to make mistakes; for instance, to wander
about
Without realizing you are already on the other side.

With Swedenborg, the poem reenters the timeless and the spaceless—that
which material truths cannot explain—but we must also remember that
Swedenborg was a body mystic. Further, we understand that the speaker
has not yet *experienced* the other-worldly ("For there, as one has been, so
one sees"); he must therefore call on his imagination to conjure a version
of it. The speaker's imagination lets him wander, again in that osmotic
fashion, between the palpable and impalpable world of the "other side."

As I, perhaps, just dream those rusty-golden forests,
The glitter of the river in which I swam in my youth,
The October from my poems with its air like wine.

The priests taught us about salvation and damnation.
Now I have not the slightest notion of these things.
I have felt on my shoulder the hand of my Guide,
Yet he didn't mention punishment, didn't promise a reward.

In the speaker's imaginative dreams, where the spiritual resides, time is
rusty-golden: the autumnal image turns the speaker's air above the river
to wine. The miracle resides in dream and imagination: the pastoral pleasures of childhood. If we have any doubt about the secularization of the
spirit here (or at least its deinstitutionalization), the last stanza refuses
the church's notion of salvation and damnation: whether it's the muse
or the forces of conscience, of the unconscious or a God, the guide is left
ambiguous.

Miłosz offers a still more ambiguous vision of imagination in "Eyes,"
a poem that is in many ways transcendent, suggesting primarily a Words-
worthian understanding of "the world is too much with us." In his inner vision, he is able to conjure an illuminating vision of the many
"similarities" of humans without effacing their small—and unspecified—
dissimilarity.

My most honorable eyes, you are not in the best of shape.
I receive from you an image that is less than sharp,

And if a color, then it's dimmed.
And you were a pack of royal greyhounds once,
With whom I would set out in the early mornings.
My wondrous quick eyes, you saw many things,
Lands and cities, islands and oceans.
Together we greeted immense sunrises
When the fresh air set us running on the trails
Where the dew had just begun to dry.

Tonally, there are a number of distressing elements in the world of this poem, especially in the adjectives "dim" and "less than sharp." No longer can Miłosz compare his eyes to "a pack of royal greyhounds," no longer do they create "wondrous" spaces.

His being sick of the loud surfaces of the metaphorical circus of the world brings him to his similitudes. And if his gaze is pointed toward a single brightness, which is spiritual redemption, it comes at a great cost: the pleasures of human community (as other poems affirm, much of what he missed earlier in his life), painted with the metaphor of the circus, must be dismissed.

I am slowly moving away from the fairgrounds of the world
And I notice in myself a distaste
For the monkeyish dress, the screams and the drumbeats.
What a relief. To be alone with my meditation
On the basic similarity in humans
And their tiny grain of dissimilarity.
Without eyes, my gaze is fixed on one bright point,
That grows large and takes me in.

One can see the closure as an acceptance of the inevitability of death (his embracing or being embraced by it), or one can see—because his loss is so great—a less reliable and exiled narrator, forced to withdraw from sensory pleasures, in denial.

In other poems Miłosz views the imagination in a much more skeptical light, as in "Advantage." Reflecting on his embattled past and his illusory sense of power and certainty, he looks critically at his past need for recognition, competition, and revenge. Here his imagination serves as a vehicle of misguided power: only in his mind and poem might he "direct" or "orchestrate" the characters from his past—or at least so he thinks at the beginning of the poem.

> It's not difficult to have them at a disadvantage,
> Since they are no longer alive.
> I sit with them at a table. It's summer, before the war.
> The whole pension: I can do with them
> Whatever I want, even make them memorable.

Retrospectively, he recognizes himself as a smug young man, "arrogant out of misery and shyness"; his pretentious moral superiority, based on the theories of Schopenhauer, must in the present tense acknowledge those who had experiential knowledge of the dark "disreputable zone," a place, it seems, where we are most human but also capable, as in the case of the speaker, of great cruelty.

> What a perverse game, from a sixteen-year-old kid
> Arrogant out of misery and shyness,
> Who just keeps silent and smiles stupidly—
> Since a conversation about Schopenhauer was obviously not
> For the likes of them. They suspect that he is not normal,
> And in these matters they are usually competent,
> Since they "know life"; that is, the disreputable zone
> Underneath the polite prattle.
> And now I have you in my power, you wretches.
> One might say I am a chaplain of shadows.
> Here, no more gossip, no more amorous touching
> While you half-listen to my bitter talk.

Then this speaker, this "chaplain of shadows," allows for none of the transcendent longing of other poems in the collection. Instead of mocking the ordinary, as he did as a vain young man (wanting himself to be immortal through poetry and individual genius), he diminishes the importance of his judgments or his reputation after death. The redeeming closure of the poem, a half-revelation of negation, suggests that it is neither power nor authority he sought; rather, as his acknowledgment of Ed and Nina's relationship reveals, his desire for continuance was connected to love, a begrudging respect for the ordinary human community, and perhaps even those dark spaces (fantasy in the Platonic sense, but also connected—by the disreputable zone—to the conjugal pleasures of the body).

> I often envied you, Nina, Ed.
> Had you been able to guess bits of my destiny,
> Perhaps you would bear your mediocrity with more ease.
> With me here is the memory of a great illusion.
> Not proud. I was lower than was your circle
> Of mortal monads, servants of the flesh.
> So what if I won't perish entirely,
> If I leave an oeuvre, since the balance
> Is uncertain. I don't know. Perhaps I was right,
> Yet in truth this isn't what I wanted.

Here memory serves as superego and revision: ringing at the end of the poem is the half-bitterness of "So what if I won't perish entirely" (if the soul ascends) or "If I leave an oeuvre, since the balance / Is uncertain."

Miłosz explores that uncertain balance throughout most of the poems in *Second Space*, and if he uses irony it is often self-effacing, a reflective confession, an acknowledged mistake: he does not so much accuse others or dispense wisdom. In the touching and witty poem "Non Adaptation," he begins feigning helplessness, being fated; in the third stanza, though, he begins to question his agency, his hypersensitivity to his own pain, his dedication to an imagination based on flight and a desire to pin down a descriptive truth:

> I was not made to live anywhere except in Paradise.
>
> Such, simply, was my genetic inadaptation.
>
> Here on earth every prick of a rose-thorn changed into a wound.
> Whenever the sun hid behind a cloud, I grieved.
>
> I pretended to work like others from morning to evening,
> but I was absent, dedicated to invisible countries.

> For solace I escaped to city parks, there to observe
> and faithfully describe flowers and trees, but they changed,
> under my hand, into gardens of Paradise.

At the end of the poem, Miłosz resists closure: his regret is in absenting himself from the sensory world of the present, his displacement of love, projecting onto other women his desire to right the wronged past of his sister. What is even more complex is the final couplet, his acknowledging that his respect for religion was tied to grief, loss, and the need for reconciliation. In the past tense, it serves as an emblem of regret: dwelling in grief and loss, it offers neither transformation nor earthly love.

> I have not loved a woman with my five senses.
> I only wanted from her my sister, from before the banishment.
>
> And I respected religion, for on this earth of pain
> it was a funereal and a propitiatory song.

That longing for the earthly love of the senses, its urgency and vitality, had been replaced by use and a longing to return to innocence, to undo the past. What is most complicating in this couplet is his use of "respected" in the past tense. On the one hand it honors a postfallen world of grief and pain; but on the other hand, the past-tense phrase also implies he may no longer respect this reverence for the funereal. This regret is heightened— and religion contributes to it—because when his lover dies he has lost the possibility of loving a woman with his five senses.

In the final poem of the collection, "Orpheus and Euridice," many of the contesting truths of the collection come to light and are reconfigured in the aforementioned radiating love. Initially, one might think of Wallace Stevens's "The World as Meditation" as a source for the poem, but Miłosz is less interested in fidelity to ideas than he is an idea about fidelity: his faith and commitments are to the earthly.

The allegorical poem suggests Adorno's "fractured landscape" wrestling with death "in a refracted mode as allegory" in terms of his will to survive unbearable loss.[6] But unlike Glück's mythical poem—where in her first-person persona poems the poet as goddess elevates the lyric speaker—this lyrical poet's interest in myth, as one sees from the very first line, resonates primarily as triggering metaphor. "Standing on flagstones of the sidewalk at the entrance to Hades" reminds one of Charles Simic's ironic personifications, but this poem, filled with dedication and struggle, serves rather as elegy and ode.

> He remembered her words: "You are a good man."
> He did not quite believe it. Lyric poets
> Usually have—as he knew—cold hearts.
> It is like a medical condition. Perfection in art
> Is given in exchange for such an affliction.

> Only her love warmed him, humanized him.
> When he was not with her, he thought differently about himself.
> He could not fail her now, when she was dead.

These straightforward lines (excepting the ironic "like a medical condition") bring the conflict into action: how to retain that humanizing love in the face of the loss of its embodiment. Not only does the speaker partake of the sublime with "her," but the reflected lover here acts as conscience as well as a source of passion and transforming identity. In the interim, he is lost on earth, an earth he no longer recognizes. And like a modern Dante, he moves through a personal hell, but in this case confronting his own lingering and useless guilt:

> He pushed open the door and found himself walking in a labyrinth,
> Corridors, elevators. The livid light was not light but the dark of the
>   earth.
> . . . .
> He felt strongly his life with its guilt
> And he was afraid to meet those to whom he had done harm.
> But they had lost the ability to remember
> And gave him only a glance, indifferent to all that.

The quatrain beginning "He felt strongly his life with its guilt" foreshadows Orpheus's labor to shed that guilt. His shame neither corrects nor moves anyone else; it merely hinders his own capacity to embrace experience itself. From this point on the speaker wavers, confronted with new difficulties, the acknowledgment of earthly pleasure, and the urgency of all his failing senses. Armed with his lyre, he is able to defend against the abyss of nothingness:

> He sang the brightness of mornings and green rivers,
> He sang of smoking water in the rose-colored daybreaks,
> Of colors: cinnabar, carmine, burnt sienna, blue,
> Of the delight of swimming in the sea under marble cliffs,
> Of feasting on a terrace above the tumult of a fishing port,
> Of the tastes of wine, olive oil, almonds, mustard, salt.
> Of the flight of the swallow, the falcon,
> Of a dignified flock of pelicans above a bay,
> Of the scent of an armful of lilacs in summer rain,
> Of his having composed his words always against death
> And of having made no rhyme in praise of nothingness.

Confronted with the question of whether or not he really loved Euridice, the speaker is forced to inhabit the fact of her death, which ultimately shakes his faith:

> Under his faith a doubt sprang up
> And entwined him like cold bindweed.
> Unable to weep, he wept at the loss
> Of the human hope for the resurrection of the dead,
> Because he was, now, like every other mortal.
> His lyre was silent, yet he dreamed, defenseless.
> He knew he must have faith and he could not have faith.
> And so he would persist for a very long time,
> Counting his steps in a half-wakeful torpor.

Here Miłosz reaffirms the discovery made by many of the poems in the collection: his desire to be privileged and immortal, to be exempted from the human, had been costly to himself and to others. In his dreamlife, his unconscious, the will to power and selfhood drops away. To be defenseless, then, without the armor of identity or the special artist, to understand experientially we are all going to die and we have lost the hope for resurrection (here it serves as an illusion), allows him to live with his heart full but still without his love. Faith and doubt occur in equal doses in this poem, and the last stanza provides no culminating wisdom. Instead, the speaker acknowledges "How will I live without you" at the same time his senses are fully awakened (reminiscent of the paradox of Keats's speaker toward the end of "Ode to a Nightingale").

> Day was breaking. Shapes of rock loomed up
> Under the luminous eye of the exit from underground.
> It happened as he expected. He turned his head
> And behind him on the path there was no one.

> Sun. And sky. And in the sky white clouds
> Only now everything cried to him: Eurydice!
> How will I live without you, my consoling one!
> But there was a fragrant scent of herbs, the low humming of bees,
> And he fell asleep with his cheek on the sun-warmed earth.

In that modest final couplet, he recognizes that his redeeming love made it possible for him to love the earth. He acknowledges all the shattering vulnerability it provides as well as the grief and pain of the earthly ("everything cried to him"); then in that final couplet he retrieves some sensory pleasure from the "sun-warmed earth." The sun-warmed earth seemingly becomes a perfect emblem, a blending of the spiritual and the sensual, the earthly and the transcendent. That this tentative redemption takes place on earth also affirms the materiality of love. The import of sleep here, though, is ambiguous, suggesting multiple readings: not only embracing the earth but also confronting death. It affirms his exhaustion after reenacting the trauma of his lost loved one. But it also reflects a lament, a "hanging on," a reluctance to let go of the earth. For the earth is not only sun-warmed but also the burial site for his love, and that ultimately tore into and exhausted him. For him to live without that love in the world embodies both the frailty of his redemption and the terms of his exile.

The poem "A Conversation with Jeanne" (a friend and philosophy professor at the University of Geneva), from the late collection *Provinces* (1991), foreshadows Miłosz's wrestling with the very concept of lateness. Refusing or deprived of harmony and salvation, he "accepts" the "things of this world," merely "because they exist," because of their material and sensual pleasures. He does not doubt that "this poor earth was not enough," but he is also liberated by that insufficiency. Rather than ending up exiled, as Said suggests for poets for whom the late style leaves unreconciled,

Miłosz comes down from the mountain of wisdom and grows "small . . . and more free."

> You are right, Jeanne, I don't know how to care about the salvation of
>   my soul.
> Some are called, others manage as well as they can.
> I accept it, what has befallen me is just.
> I don't pretend to the dignity of a wise old age.
> Untranslatable into words, I chose my home in what is now,
> In things of this world, which exist and, for that reason, delight us:
> Nakedness of women on the beach, coppery cones of their breasts,
> Hibiscus, alamanda, a red lily, devouring
> With my eyes, lips, tongue, the guava juice, the juice of la prune de
>   Cythère,
> Rum with ice and syrup, lianas-orchids
> In a rain forest, where trees stand on the stilts of their roots.
>
> Death, you say, mine and yours, closer and closer,
> We suffered and this poor earth was not enough.
> The purple-black earth of vegetable gardens
> Will be here, either looked at or not.
> The sea, as today, will breathe from its depths.
> Growing small, I disappear in the immense, more and more free.

Nothing in this chapter suggests that Miłosz was a secular thinker; Said's premise framed the discussion because the tension and humanity of Miłosz's late work embodied in his confusion, in his unresolved wavering between faith and doubt. That he decries institutional religiosity in *Second Space* is, I think, inarguable. That he longs to sustain his deep faith I don't doubt; that he succeeds in that affirmation in some poems I also believe is true. But readers will also find in *Second Space* tentative and skeptical sentiments too, sentiments that not only lean toward the humane and the earthly but also acknowledge genuine doubt: a lifelong Catholic with a love-hate relationship with the church, Miłosz often had difficulty reconciling his guiding spirit with the irrational brutality of history.

Miłosz was a man of great appetites and great conscience. That he could not integrate these qualities, that in the later work he gave competing truths free reign, enabled him to embrace those disharmonies as a sign of the fullness of his and our humanity. This is the nature of his adventurousness. An earlier poem, "Confession," begins, "My lord, I loved strawberry jam." Virtually all the above-mentioned tensions between the material and spiritual, the sensuous and the superego, coexist in that line. In *A year of the Hunter*, he makes the remarkable clarifying statement: "Critics have sought an answer to the question: what is the source of all those contradictions in my poetry? In my prose, too, for that matter. I could enlighten them by referring to the several personalities who reside in me simultaneously, whom I have tried to suppress, generally without success. I didn't want to be so volatile, but what could I do? I hope that this diary . . . will be valued as one more attempt at demonstrating that I was conscious of the incompatibility of my various personalities."[7] And by the time Miłosz composes *Second Space*, no longer trying to suppress the multifaceted incongruities of self, accommodating himself the best he can to the irresolvable, in descending to the imperfections of the human, he produces his most moving, complex, humane work.

9.

....

STRATEGIC FICTIONS

The Mobile Architecture of Frank O'Hara's Poetry

"YOU DO NOT ALWAYS KNOW what I am feeling," begins Frank O'Hara's "For Grace after a Party." Implied in the richness of that rhetoric: a long-term closeness between the speaker and Grace, his peevishness about being misunderstood, and at the same time his disappointment that he can usually be "read" so easily. Like most of O'Hara's best work, the seamlessness of the statement, the charged conversational tone, might lead even a careful reader to believe in the lyric fiction of present-tense invention—the whimsical, spontaneous, even the random. But O'Hara's apparent spontaneity is a strategic fiction. I'm not speaking of O'Hara's intentions here, or of how many drafts his poems went through (Mozart held virtually entire scores inside his head), or of his writing methods (he was a notorious fictionalizer about his work: according to James Schuyler's letters, O'Hara never wrote his famous *Lunch Poems* during his lunch hour but rather when he came back to work after lunch). O'Hara's best work is intricately structured and foreshadowed; even the digressions serve as metaphorical parallels and contrasts for the poems' associative obsessions, which in poem after poem reveal O'Hara's irresolvable romantic quest for both constancy and surprise.

Frank O'Hara's influence, even fifty years after he wrote his most adventurous poems, is still abundant. You find traces of it in the work of John Ashbery, Kenneth Koch, the second-generation New York school poets, James Tate, Dean Young, Alice Notley, Arthur Vogelsang, David Lehman, many avant-garde younger poets, and a large cast of poets whose poems often seem so derivative that O'Hara's voice overwhelms theirs. The resulting work of such poets is often clever but slight: the poems lack individuation of voice (diction and tone), necessity, and shapeliness. For it is not an unmediated O'Hara we get in his poems: we get the full thrust of the passionate romantic (lover of Rachmaninoff), entangled with the cultured intelligence of the curator of MOMA who loved the way work was constructed in a modernist, often impersonal, and certainly not representational way. He was a modernist too in his faith in art's capacity to supplant the religious impulse, to create an internal aesthetic order that would offer its own self-enclosed harmonies. Art wasn't necessarily in itself redemptive: O'Hara's redemption came through Eros, the linguistic and the lusty, as an adaptive strategy for a chaotic and irrational universe. (After all, in "On Personism" he disdained the moral impulse of poetry, proclaiming, "improve them for what, for death?") His romance with the irrational, his love of the dark ("you just let all the different bodies fall where they may, and they always do"), served as a primary trigger for his subjects.

For an ironic imagination like O'Hara's (whose stance often walks the thin line between playfulness and cleverness, sentimentality and posturing, openness and repression), tone drives the poems the way music and story drive the ironies of a more formal poet like Philip Larkin. But O'Hara's modernism and his connection with abstract expressionist painters and pop artists like Roy Lichtenstein (Marjorie Perloff's important early study of O'Hara, *Frank O'Hara: Poet among Painters*, explores this connection) gave him license to translate painterly problems into poetry. So action paintings became poems in perpetual motion (accomplished by enjambments and long, breathless sentences); tonal issues (dramatized by color in painting) were pursued with a broad range of dictions; and, like many postmodern texts and paintings that would follow him, O'Hara made use of Lichtenstein's comic book studies and Rothko's somber abstractions, blurring the lines between high and low culture. One O'Hara poem can include hamburgers and malteds and Genet and Verlaine. As he demonstrated ironically in "Why I am Not a Painter," he painted with words the way Mike Goldberg made words with paint. He enacted in his verbs the principles of action painting: "I go," time "goes by"; he dramatized and distorted the temporal (all action takes place in the eternal present, the same kind of space occupied in Pollock's paintings). Thanks to the rapid movement of O'Hara's poems—orchestrated by sound as well as line, sentences that refused to be interrupted—he was able to virtually "paint over" preceding lines on the way to the next associative perception. In the processes of coming and going, of foregoing intention and subject for associative freedoms, O'Hara found mirrors in modern poetry and modern art.

In his innovative use of enjambment and syntax, O'Hara prefigured the postmodernists by often making language performative: his line breaks often signified syntactical changes in meaning and fluidity of stance. Those critics who think of O'Hara as a poet of personality (if that term means anything, it reflects the diction and syntax of what some critics call voice) fall for his jejune self-mythologizing as a spontaneous poet (he makes clear in his letters the limits of surrealist techniques like automatic writing) who reports and types up whatever comes into his head.

In O'Hara's signature poem, "The Day Lady Died," the almost-breathless last four lines give the illusion that the reader and writer arrive at the closure at the same time. The poem ends with a flashback, though, so the present tense, insisted on from the first line, just like time itself, is a willful fiction. The speaker's passionate connection with Billie Holiday is ecstatic, transforming time and space while altering the self and the speaker's sense of identity. Art leaves us breathless: its intimate connections prove to be simultaneously exciting and dangerous. They not only bring us closer to feeling but also expose us to the danger of contingency and loss, expressed in the poem in terms of destabilizing time, space, and identity: intimacy touches *and* breaks the heart. The experience is both communal and isolating (consciousness attenuates and abstracts). All of these matters are foreshadowed in the speaker's restlessness: he thrives because of his friendships, his feeling for art and other artists. But the world of feeling is at odds with the counterdesire of the poem: the speaker's attempts to thwart and defer uncertainty and contingency keep him dislocated and existentially alone. His anxiety is expressed in his exactitude about time and date, in the specificity of book titles, and names. Every stanza begins with an assertion of these certainties (as it turns out, all evasions) and ends with those qualities effaced, diminished, or dissolved. The stanzas end in strangeness and isolation because, in O'Hara's view, temporal experience by nature is always shifting, constantly moving. O'Hara, in his typically anti-effete fashion, talked about his "I do this I do that" poems not only because he was interested in action and gesture but also because as a modernist, he was keenly aware of movement. He was drawn to painters like Pollock, Klee, and DeKooning because of their movement, color, and composition. In most poems he embraced that movement as energetic and vitalizing, but in "The Day Lady Died," the loss of love and art takes away his capacity for sheer lightness and acceptance.

It is 12:20 in New York a Friday
three days after Bastille day, yes
it is 1959 and I go get a shoeshine
because I will get off the 4:19 in Easthampton
at 7:15 and then go straight to dinner
and I don't know the people who will feed me

I walk up the muggy street beginning to sun
and have a hamburger and a malted and buy
an ugly NEW WORLD WRITING to see what the poets
in Ghana are doing these days.
                              I go on to the bank
and Miss Stillwagon (first name Linda I once heard)
doesn't even look up my balance for once in her life
and in the GOLDEN GRIFFIN I get a little Verlaine
for Patsy with drawings by Bonnard although I do
think of Hesiod, trans. Richmond Lattimore or
Brendan Behan's new play or *Le Balcon* or *Les Nègres*
of Genet, but I don't, I stick with Verlaine
after practically going to sleep with quandariness

and for Mike I just stroll into the PARK LANE
Liquor Store and ask for a bottle of Strega and
then I go back where I came from to 6th Avenue
and the tobacconist in the Ziegfeld Theatre and
casually ask for a carton of Gauloises and a carton
of Picayunes, and a NEW YORK POST with her face on it

and I am sweating a lot by now and thinking of
leaning on the john door in the 5 SPOT
while she whispered a song along the keyboard
to Mal Waldron and everyone and I stopped breathing

The poem begins with pronouncements about exact time and place. The
opening lines assert certainty, but by the end of line 2 the word "yes" on
the one hand suggests affirmation but on the other serves as self-assurance.
The gesture about Bastille Day, besides vaguely suggesting "independence,"

brings the relaxation of time—it is summer and the speaker is about to venture out to "the country"; the celebration of the French holiday also foreshadows references to the foreign, which in later stanzas stand in for movement away from consciousness and the here and now.

In the last line of the stanza—a formal strategy that is repeated in virtually every stanza—we come to understand the speaker's need for knowing where and when: he doesn't "know the people who will feed him." Lighthearted and casual as the voice in the poem begins, that line suggests loneliness and isolation: the speaker is a metaphorical orphan (dependent? hungry?) or at least a solitary wanderer. With that rhetorical and metaphorical flourish, the casual and seemingly superficial surfaces of the opening lines are transformed.

The second stanza uses the hunger association to feed the speaker, and perhaps there is a little cheer in the phrase "beginning to sun." Besides which, the speaker must move away from his anxiety, which he supplants with the distraction of distance and surface. His glib response, seemingly far from him and his vague dilemma, is to see what the poets of Ghana are doing. Later in the poem, that distance is transformed by art, art as gift, celebration, and sign of friendship.

Once again, though, when the speaker wants to turn away, the stiff and formal Miss Stillwagon suddenly trusts the speaker—miracle of miracles, a person momentarily supplants the pecuniary. So with the poets of Ghana on his mind, with the possibility of a human connection, the speaker chooses gifts to show friends his care for them and in some way to suggest his alienation at this moment from American culture. He chooses foreign artwork for his friends (Genet, Verlaine, and Behan—all proponents of the passionate and the irrational) and chooses foreign pleasures for smoking and drinking. But these strategies, as in the closure of other stanzas, also fail both to enliven and distance. So he "practically go[es] to sleep with quandariness," an odd, elevated, intellectualized diction. He is perplexed, uncertain, and he seems almost paralyzed and depressed by so many choices: he's alienated and helpless. O'Hara intensifies this helplessness during the present-tense climax of the poem, when the speaker sees the headlines about Billie Holiday's death. She becomes the emblem in the poem for the ecstatic: his love, his passion, the heart in art, in song.

All this repression and deferral fails (as the O'Hara of "An Image of Leda" understands all too well), because he must face Holiday's death on his own. Time is odd and ambiguous in the poem: one way of looking at the poem is in terms of the tension between surface action and feeling, which suddenly shifts at the end of the poem. In this interpretation, the speaker has been all avoidance, preoccupied with errands: he is aimless until he sees the headline and is cast back into the past, where the immediacy of art crowds out everything else. But it is also possible that narrative time deceives here and that from the beginning of the poem the speaker knows and feels lost and is withholding the knowledge of her death from himself as well as the reader. In either case, we retrospectively look at the details and narrative in this poem and find that the daily contains both the pleasures of experience and ritualized bureaucratic boredom. The poem also reaches out, though oddly during an attempt to both defeat and honor the daily: there is an osmotic relationship among friendships, human connections, and art. In the final stanza, time virtually stands still: the flashback is immediate and eternal, bringing the past back into the present with more vitality than any of the previous apparent present-tense stanzas.

> and I am sweating a lot by now and thinking of
> leaning on the john door in the 5 SPOT
> while she whispered a song along the keyboard
> to Mal Waldron and everyone and I stopped breathing

The effect of this final stanza is breathtaking, but it also gathers up all the forces in the poem and intensifies them. The intimate connections are assonant ("whispered a song along"); the muggy sun motif is released in his sweating (but the sweating is also associated with his feelings of panic). Most of all, the tensions between the communal (earlier expressed as friendship) and alienation are accelerated and retain their ambiguity. So the syntax of the last line makes the speaker simultaneously part of and separate from the community of art ("everyone and I"). The effect of Billie Holiday's song (most certainly tragic in the mid-1950s when the poem is composed: her voice broken, but her interpretations so richly and heartbreakingly dark) is "breathtaking" in both senses of the word: ecstatic and deathlike. One thinks of Longinus's sublime, which involves an encounter with god and mastery: the sublime experience leaves one powerlessly transfixed with the need to reconstruct the self by returning to self-mastery. To live with such heightened emotional knowledge after such an encounter is impossible. The death of self implied in this poem makes one feel both more human and more alone—and most of all unavoidably conscious of our own deaths (metaphorical and otherwise).

It should be mentioned too how much here that transgressive impulses in the 1950s, artistic and otherwise, almost always articulated that existential "aloneness," that alienation from the "normal" and the corporate, the conforming vacuity of American culture. The O'Hara poem was written too in the midst of the threat of the Soviet Union, the cold war, and the atomic bomb, all of which suggested the possibility of instant annihilation. O'Hara's need for escape and fantasy is demonstrated in his romanticization of Europe, particularly France; at the same time, the heroic stance of the speaker, represented by his "leaning against the john door," James Dean style, is all American alienation, spectating rather than participating. That existential angst, that romantic feeling of loneliness, was a response to a dominant culture that found increasingly less room for either art or pleasure lovers; those feelings of exile must have been even more present for a smart gay man whose religion was art.

"A Step away from Them" is just as intricately structured and foreshadowed as the Billie Holiday poem. The poem is also obsessed with deferring knowledge of grief and loss and wrestles with art's capacity to transcend time set against the narrator's desire to live fully in the present tense. This concern is echoed in O'Hara's formal strategies throughout the poem. The ebullient present overflows with erotic energy, expressed in action, "hum-colored" synesthesia (often used by the poet as a vehicle of confusion, demonstrating the city's overload of sensation), lust, and the discomfiting—especially for readers now—exoticizing ethnicity. It should be noted, though, that in the gay community of the West Village and elsewhere during that time, racial intermixing signified rebellion against cultural segregating norms.

At first the speaker glorifies the city's contradictions: he likes the combination of its dirt and its playful shine: "dirty / glistening torsos" and "cats playing in sawdust." He loves the earthly "down the sidewalk." He likes the heavenly and the blending of the palpable and the impalpable: "The sun is hot, but the / cabs stir up the air." And of course he loves the sexuality, the "Negro" "languorously agitating" and the bodies exposed in summer. Beyond aesthetics, though, he is hardly conscious of danger or function on the sidewalk.

where laborers feed their dirty
glistening torsos sandwiches
and Coca-Cola, with yellow helmets
on. They protect them from falling
bricks, I guess. Then onto the
avenue where skirts are flipping
above heels and blow up over
grates.

And when "everything suddenly / honks," though he is conscious of time, he is completely immersed in the present tense: "it is 12:40 of / a Thursday." This consciousness of time represents a turning point in the poem; it provides a moment of transformation.

The next stanza moves from timeless pleasure in all this excess (lights in daylight) to the sensory and associative pleasure of eating that triggers memory. Juliet's hamburger stand reminds him of Giulietta Maina, and those lines are followed by his recognition of the unpleasantly absurd: a wealthy woman in furs taking her dog in a cab on a hot summer day. The speaker criticizes both the incongruous and ostentatious privilege and the woman's inability to take in the city's outdoor joys.

The moment is funny but also existentially absurd. Indeed, the whole question of function, which the speaker was casual about early on in the poem, begins to perplex. He tries to recover, noticing the Puerto Ricans who make the avenue "beautiful and warm." But the Puerto Ricans are strangers, unnamed, objets d'art; all this consciousness of time and beauty and warmth brings him inextricably to his lost artist friends. These artists are not only named but nicknamed ("Bunny"); they provide the speaker's intimate connections, and recollecting them shakes his confidence in the value of his impersonal pleasures. From this point on, all the preceding movements that served to give the speaker pleasure are problematized and developed further. "And one has eaten and one walks" is both impersonal and absurd: the meaning of one's life is no longer just the speaker's problem; the nudes then become associated with the dangers of bullfighting and finally with a torn-down Manhattan storage warehouse (ruined by time). The warehouse used to hold, the speaker thinks, the important Armory Show of 1913, the adventurous exhibition of modern painters that included American painters strongly influenced by contemporary European painters. Just as the world used to hold his artists, just as the speaker was formerly able to accept the dirt with the erotic play, the memory of that art work is perplexing or fading from view.

On the one hand, the ending of "A Step away from Them," revisits Keats's "Ode to a Nightingale": life is short, art is long. But on the other, the context of the poem complicates the metaphor. In a poem about displacement of feeling, having one's heart in one's pocket seems less romantic, more compartmentalized, outside the inhabited body, especially because that line is preceded by the casual "A glass of papaya juice / and back to work." Here the speaker cannot fully confront or inhabit the uncomfortable contradictions that the poem raises: does death of loved ones, does the loss of those connections, diminish life's fullness?

> First
> Bunny died, then John Latouche,
> then Jackson Pollock. But is the
> earth as full of life was full, of them?

The complex syntax of those lines, like the inquiry of the poem, cannot be unwound or resolved. The earth *seems* to be as full of life as it always was—absurd, romantic, full of danger and lust—but at the same time the speaker sees diminishment in the change (the buildings being torn down). At this moment in the poem, being focused on the here and now both mediates and takes flight from the wreckage of time and history. But the closure brings us back to the title and the speaker's indeterminate feelings about time and the daily in the face of those losses. "A Step away from Them" retrospectively asks the question, is he *just* one step from them (are they also in his metaphorical pocket), or is he *moving* a step away from them? If so, time as sequence ("First Bunny / died, then") creates distance, and the speaker is left with the fullness of his melancholy, which he can only defeat by going back to work.

Because O'Hara is historically situated at the beginning of an age critical of the conservatism of New Criticism—demonstrated in the resistance of Beat poets like Ginsberg—his biases are anti-intellectual and opposed to the snobbery of high culture. As Perloff underlines in her introduction to *Frank O'Hara: Poet among Painters*, quoting from "Personal Poem," "we don't like Lionel Trilling / we decide, we like Don Allen we don't like / Henry James so much we like Herman Melville." In this way, as Mark Tursi also suggests, O'Hara was also situated on the edge of the postmodern, where judgments about cultural currency were shifting.[1] Soon after O'Hara, Andy Warhol's Campbell's soup cans would arrive; but O'Hara was also titillated by hard hats, Hollywood gossip ("Lana Turner please get up"), nuts and bolts, and in "On Rachmaninoff's Birthday," "soup on the stove." What first appears to be a poem about madness turns out to be a romance with deflating earnestness.

Perhaps few O'Hara poems seem more spontaneous and clever than "On Rachmaninoff's Birthday." His ode to Rachmaninoff's music begins with the tumult of romantic music and the speaker poised (in the enjambment) between going and going off his "rocker." The poem's mock suicide mirrors the melodrama he loves in Rachmaninoff's music (as he loves James Dean in *East of Eden*, loving both the drama of the exaggerated romance while affectionately making fun of it). The poem then moves through a series of associative jokey transformations: the onset of the mad scene becomes a town in Massachusetts. The shadow of Newton, Massachusetts, becomes the "fig-newton / playing the horn." The absurd surrealism here is both demented (dissociative) and associatively imaginative. Most of all, every object transmutates. No thing can be held on to or stabilized. Everything, including the speaker, is on the edge, capable of "breaking into powder."

> Quick! a last poem before I go
> off my rocker. Oh Rachmaninoff!
> Onset, Massachusetts. Is it the fig-newton
> playing the horn? Thundering windows
> of hell, will your tubes ever break
> into powder? Oh my palace of oranges,
> junk shop, staples, umber, basalt;
> I'm a child again when I was really
> miserable, a grope pizzicato. My pocket
> of rhinestone, yoyo, carpenter's pencil,
> amethyst, hypo, campaign button,
> is the room full of smoke? Shit
> on the soup, let it burn. So it's back.
> You'll never be mentally sober.

The Russian tsars' palace becomes the speaker's random junk. The hinge lines of the poem are the surprising "I'm a child again when I was really / miserable." The powerless, disordered child ("grope pizzicato") is far from, for the speaker, inhabiting that idealized Eden (here again, time past and time present are simultaneous). In fact, the objects he finds in his pocket break through the temporal: a yo-yo is next to a hypo, a cheap stone next to a campaign button. Are these the pockets of the syntactically aforementioned child? And just when the room is about to go up in smoke he declares "shit," but he turns out not to be cursing the failure to order and control but to be abandoning it: the association with childhood has in fact freed the speaker to "let it burn." Because of the vague antecedents, "So it's back" doesn't easily unpack: "it" simultaneously hovers over the madness, childhood, and/or some semblance of acceptance.

The closure of the poem releases all those forces: the diction of "You'll never be mentally sober" at first suggests madness becomes a permanent condition; but the word is not mad, it's "sober," and furthermore it's not the "I" of the poem but the unnamed "you," which one assumes is the reader. In a modernist fashion, O'Hara has been able to—thanks to snapped-off perceptions and enjambments, a dreamlike translation of Rachmaninoff's music—evoke the romance with madness and entropy itself. Its effect, though, becomes absurd, not horrifying. It becomes impossible to take the drama of madness seriously, as O'Hara blurs the boundaries between madness and imagination, anxiety and play. The poem resolves neither ironically *nor* straightforwardly the dilemma of the speaker going off his rocker: he has dramatized what it feels like, and in the process he playfully lets go of his desire to control experience, resigning himself to the entropic irrational that seemed in the opening lines to drive him mad.

The poem points to why O'Hara's poems seem more playful than clever. As much as the subject of cleverness has been discussed, no definitions suffice. One person's cleverness is another person's vitalizing play or ironic/satiric revelation. The implication of the distinction suggests that cleverness is insubstantial, entertaining, a joke not to be returned to. O'Hara surely wrote, among his thousand-plus poems, a number of these kinds of poems (and what poet has not indulged him- or herself in word play or jokes, or less self-consciously an inadequate or shallow approach to a serious subject?). What makes O'Hara's work compelling is what makes the work of most poets compelling: an obsession, a poem written of personal necessity, tapping into the particulars of his age, coordinate with a tactile joy in the medium, the expression of that obsession. The way painters are in love with paint, O'Hara too is in love with his poetic materials. What this means is that he is capable both of surprising himself and the reader in midpoem, but he is conscious enough to seize on the lived history of the poem (the preceding lines) and narrative (the lines that surround the present tense of the poem) and use that history to shape and transform. For it is hard to imagine a poet being successful more than a few times accidentally: every poet I know and admire has a large dose of emotional intelligence and is attentive to the suggestion of gestures and the composition of experience. O'Hara is most attuned to the slippages of speech, the way words mean more than we intend them to mean. To the Freudian slip, to the half-conscious dialogue, to the gesture that demands more or less attention than a person may give it. That's why he is often an ironic poet, but not solely in the service of entertainment: his pleasure lies in bringing unconscious material up to the surface.

His more mobile love poems, like "Mary Desti's Ass" (surely one of the strangest persona/nonpersona poems ever written) and "Cornkind," rely on different strategies, though motion also becomes the vehicle of transformation in these poems. In the former poem, each stanza, each place, teaches the speaker something about repression and Eros. Repression for O'Hara is synthesized in figures of hierarchy: pleasure-haters, purifiers, bigots, bureaucrats, and the pretentious high culture mavens.

The poem opens by satirizing the flamboyant narcissistic display of name-dropping and one-upsmanship:

> In Bayreuth once
> we were very good friends of the Wagners
> and I stepped in once
> for Isadora so perfectly
> she would never allow me to dance again
> that's the way it was in Bayreuth
> . . . .
> it means something to exercise
> in Norfolk Virginia
> It means you've been to bed with a Nigra
> well it is exercise
> the only difference is it's better than Boston

Here the satirical elements conspire in an almost-polemical way to authorize desire both as in-the-moment lust and as love as an expression of that mobility, revealing his willingness to love (or lust) fully in the moment, William Blake style:

> He who binds to himself a joy
> Does the winged life destroy;
> But he who kisses the joy as it flies
> Lives in eternity's sun rise.

The closure of this O'Hara poem speaks to the unmediated pleasures and pains of living in an eternal present, and here he both honors and surprisingly abandons the ironies of the previous stanzas of the poem:

> and then in Harbin I knew
> how to behave it was glorious that
> was love sneaking up on me through the snow
> and I felt it was because of all
> the postcards and the smiles and kisses and the grunts
> that was love but I kept on traveling

Perhaps no O'Hara lines reflect the obsession that I underlined in the beginning of this essay: though he is tempted by the illuminated constancy of "an arrival point," he must leave what he loves; his restlessness and his pleasure in discovery (the real import of learning "how to behave") keep him moving.

"Cornkind" reflects both O'Hara's anxiety about choosing duration in love or passion in the moment; it is one of his more explicitly gay poems (although it also applies to childless heterosexuals). The rhetorical questions raised in the poem are "what of," meaning, what becomes of, or what do we care what others think and say? Why should we let worry and anxiety project ourselves into an unknowable future? Why should we believe the culminating justification for our sexuality is progeny? The poem moves through the speaker's anxieties about "deferred gratification," those advocating cultural clichés—which he considers alternately theatrical (Bette Davis), metaphorical (the seed of corn becoming the ear), absurd (Samuel Greenberg), homonymic (William Morris / Million Worries), all reflecting either adjacency, the temporal, or fantasy. In the line "what of 'what of,'" the *mise en abyme* becomes nounless and meaningless. The reso-

lution of the poem rejects idealized romantic love, desire that requires duration (in "On Personism," he says, "There's nothing metaphysical about
it. Unless, of course, you flatter yourself into thinking that what you're
experiencing is yearning"), and claims fusion as the joy of boundless animal present-tense sexuality:

what of "what of"

you are of me, that's what
and that's the meaning of fertility
hard and moist and moaning

William Morris, Bette Davis, and Samuel Greenberg all appearing in
one brief poem may fortify a reader's feelings about the "randomness" of
O'Hara's poems. Less sympathetic readers who feel excluded (either because they don't appreciate his tone or think his poems are filled with
name-dropping), may miss O'Hara's use of names as a fictive device.
Naming names often deflates artistic subjects and assumes intimacy: since
we're all acquaintances, the poem assumes we know who the speaker is
talking about. As characters recur in the work, they often create personal
myths: instead of Orpheus we have Mike Goldberg, who is a less literary,
more immediate signifier of a painter with whom O'Hara shares process.
Poems for Grace Hartigan (as in the ambitious "In Memory of My Feelings") are often more introspective and self-revelatory. Jane Freilicher becomes a painter who appreciates O'Hara's sense of romance, both personal
and artistic (as in "A Sonnet for Jane Freilicher" and "Jane Awake," where
he also projects onto her his own more feminine desires). Lytle Shaw asserts that O'Hara "uses the ambiguities of reference associated with the
names to invent a fluid and shifting kinship structure—one that opened
up the radical possibilities for a gay writer operating outside the structure
of the family," and this premise too makes sense.[2]

To return to "For Grace, after a Party," though the speaker claims, in
arch diction that underscores the ironic exaggeration of the statement,
that "it was love for you that set me / afire," in truth he is not only expressing his love but also pushing the absent Grace away. The speaker's need for
immediate gratification is betrayed by both his own unpredictable feelings
and the way in which "odd[ly]" his feeling defended and anonymous allows him to feel intensely.

            in rooms full of
    strangers my most tender feelings
            writhe and
    bear the fruit of screaming.

These lyric lines, though providing the most iambic meters of the poem, mediate the speaker's satisfactions with jagged, antipoetic line breaks and clotted syntax: fullness is followed by strangers, tender feelings "writhe" and only "bear the fruit" of screaming. No fruit at all. Rage and frustration: the occasion that has made feeling possible has also rendered action impossible. The speaker is both safe and unsatisfied (there is no evidence of the speaker being gay, but the emotional landscape of this poem would make an excellent cover). Grace doesn't know what he is feeling because his feelings are confused, surprising, and uncontrollable, and they are not always available to him when she is present. These lines allow him to pursue and advance the double edge of desire and domesticity or friendship and closeness. The action of the poem moves away from an other being familiar enough to be able to predict his needs in advance; but the speaker also feels that to be known is to be predictable, subject to dull repetition. A perfect double bind.

The unsatisfying closure of the poem moves further and further from Grace (Grace Hartigan the painter and the pun of grace itself). The warm spring air, which ironically brought forth a tirade instead of spring's usual promise of fruition, is transformed into warm weather "holding," implying stasis and the stale. Grace becomes "someone" and then disappears from the poem altogether. Under the guise of a love poem, O'Hara has written the poem as a defense of irrational surprise and his own unavailability, but it is a strategy in this poem that fails his speaker.

O'Hara's sensibility commands him to excess, as in the line "it was love for you that set me / afire," and he is fond of exclamation marks in many of his poems. Size and scope, of feelings and images, play a big role in O'Hara's discourse. Those excesses, feelings of grandiosity, his making master narratives of his momentary love affairs and mock manifestos, are mediated by his self-consciousness—his self-knowledge. So often in poems he will put forth those excessive sentiments and undermine them with irony, self-deprecation, or glibness. Although I described him as capable of the jejune, the open, boyish, sensitive soul O'Hara often appears in the voice of the self-consciousness naïf. It's most obvious in an early poem, pretentiously titled "Les Etiquettes Jaunes," one translation of which could be read as "Yellow Protocol":

Leaf! You are so big!
How can you change your
color, then just fall!

. . . .

Leaf! don't be neurotic
like the small chameleon.

Here he playfully attaches himself to the yellow leaf in a child's voice: he asks the innocent question, undermined by "you are so big"—how big could a leaf be? He leaves us with the suggestion that we're residing in the world of metaphor: what bad manners of a leaf to "change your / color"—the enjambment makes us wait to consider what else might be changing—and then "just fall!" O'Hara's speaker means this worry about mutability while he parodies the romantic identification with nature and its recurrent parallels. The joke in the closure, characteristic of O'Hara's jokes, is only half-joking. To think of a leaf as neurotic is absurd. But the chameleon, that's a figure—as someone who changes feelings frequently and unpredictably, experienced most obviously in his enjambments—the speaker knows well. The big leaf becomes the small chameleon. The big chameleon: who could that be?

Few poets arouse such extreme responses as devotion or disdain as O'Hara. A reader's attachment to O'Hara's sensibility depends to some extent on the pleasure of irony and playfulness with tone. He is, in every way, an urban poet. Neitzsche once said that a joke is "the epigram on the death of a feeling," but O'Hara teaches us otherwise.[3] O'Hara's humor and irony are meant to reveal, with the qualifying knowledge that openness can lead to earnestness, self-aggrandizement, and a vulnerability that must be turned away from to survive the world and the worldliness of the New York landscape. Irony, as a sequence of revealing then concealing, expresses both O'Hara's stance toward the unconscious and his romance with darkness, Eros, and the unknown. The "erotic zones" can only be seen reflected in others, as in "Poem" ("I don't know if I get what D. H. Lawrence is driving at"):

and I suppose
any part of us that can only be seen by others
is a dark part
I feel that about the small of my back, too and the nape of my neck
they are dark
they are erotic zones as in the tropics

One can see the tenderness expressed in those lines as well as in the closure of the poem; and here the naïve, unguarded voice of the speaker allows him to recognize both his own limited understanding of his own dark desires and the need for love and darkness to urge us on and into the light.

a coal miner has kind of a sexy occupation
though I'm sure it's painful down there
but so is lust
of light we can never have enough
but how would we find it
unless the dark urged us on and into it
and I am dark
except when now and then it all comes clear
and I can see myself
as others luckily sometimes see me
in a good light

The lighthearted pun at the end of the poem is not meant as a joke to entertain or make the reader laugh as in some comic poems. Here, as elsewhere, O'Hara manipulates tone, tries on voices, and structures the movement of his poems to organize a vision that transgresses the puritan impulse. In the process he provides the rich multiple and mobile suggestions of poetry. Perhaps he wrote "you do not always know what I am feeling" not only because feeling is private and defended but also because the many poetic strategies of Frank O'Hara allowed him to feel many, often conflicting, feelings at once. That's at least how we see him "in a good light."

C. K. WILLIAMS AND JOHN ASHBERY

On the Edge of Romanticism and Postmodernism

AT FIRST GLANCE JOHN ASHBERY and C. K. Williams seem like strange poetic bedfellows: Ashbery the playful, ironic, withholding, apparently aesthete avant-garde language experimentalist, Williams seemingly boundlessly emotional, the earnest social realist, the interior-minded secular Jew. They are both obsessive writers, although Ashbery's work is motored more by the dissociative id than superego and Williams is just the opposite. Williams is more influenced by Whitman in his convictions about the fragile transformations of personal and collective history, while Ashbery found correspondences with the flux and mobility of action painting. Along with more conservative poets of their generation, both poets may be drawn to the momentary coherence and erotic fusion of romanticism, but they also understand it as a fiction that can account for neither the slippery outcomes of subjectivity, a declining faith in the authority of the individual, nor the inevitable entropy of experience. While Williams retains more allegiance to representation, Ashbery's glance backward often takes a metaphorical cast: he works to find correspondences that momentarily approximate what "it feels like." Whereas more conventional poets like Louise Glück unapologetically view the world through the lens of the poem as illumination, attitudes privileging art and nature (nature providing metaphors of correspondence and continuance), both Williams and Ashbery require postmodern strategies to mediate and interrogate romantic values. Their poems gather tension and are enlivened by moments of fissure and the breakdown of those sought harmonies.

Williams and Ashbery navigate dilemmas of temporality and syntax using poetic strategies that defy chronos and efface plot, and they blur temporal knowledge by modifying or erasing insights with contradictory or ambivalent qualifications. In "Soonest Mended," Ashbery's speaker talks about "a kind of fence-sitting / Raised to the level of an esthetic ideal." While Ashbery relies more on layers and layers of displaced metaphors and multiple voicings to argue with the originating premises of his poems, Williams relies more on syntax and fractured narrative. Not only do these poets' narratives resist resolution, but they both employ diction that is simultaneously unstable and subjective, dense and at the edge of the decipherable. Their obsession with contingency and self-conscious removal not only unites them but also places them on the margins of the representational voice poem and the postmodern.

Williams's early published work was characterized by a jumpy kind of neosurrealism, employing the punctuationless lines and enjambments of W. S. Merwin and more familiar confessional writing. Later he makes more effective use of his interest in line and meditation, but only when he finds *his* Whitman. His Whitman is not the optimistic, visionary cataloguing poet: the poets live and reflect on different ages and stages of American empire. But Williams shares Whitman's anxieties about Eros and democracy, and he is drawn to the most complex, least rhetorical, and least egocentric Whitman—the dark and modern poet, the poet who honors flux and contingency without papering over it, who linguistically uses the coordinate clause to trouble chronology and pattern by blurring, intensifying, qualifying, and contradicting. Whitman's changes of mind inside the sentence, his use of line and syntax to mimetically create thought in action, serve as an antecedent of the postmodern. The following passage from "There Was a Child Went Forth" calls up frenetic movement, a willingness to probe murky difficulty and darker possibilities, leading us to understand how the child, like the sentence, goes forth, but movement and change provide his only certainty.

> The mother at home, quietly placing the dishes on the supper-table;
> The mother with mild words—clean her cap and gown, a wholesome
>   odor falling off her person and clothes as she walks by;
> The father, strong, self-sufficient, manly, mean, anger'd, unjust;
> The blow, the quick loud word, the tight bargain, the crafty lure

Beginning with the idealized portrait of the mother, the speaker moves from mildness to cleanliness, as if he is bleaching the page, preparing her palpable absence, until she becomes a "wholesome odor," a spirit and a spirit dissembling (the sense falling off her) in motion as she passes by. The description of the father is more volatile and transformative, as if it takes the speaker time to face the difficulty; when he does, that highly charged male authority, which we at first read as positive (especially following the description of the mother), slides into the abusive ("mean, anger'd, unjust"). Once his idea of the family crucible begins to fall from the ideal, the speaker's perception of reality and his connections with those who model his behavior begin to splinter: the father is then described as using language to cheat and seduce ("the crafty lure"); thereby, the poet's primary tool for deciphering the world is corrupted. The assured description of the mother is transformed into longing, a "yearning and swelling heart," but with no place to take it. A passage that begins as tribute ends up in doubt, with the recognition that one's sense of "reality" is fleeting, subjective, and illusory.

> The family usages, the language, the company, the furniture-the
>   yearning and swelling heart,
> Affection that will not be gainsay'd—the sense of what is real—the
>   thought if, after all, it should prove unreal,
> The doubts of day-time and the doubts of night-time—the curious
>   whether and how,
> Whether that which appears so is so, or is it all flashes and specks?

C. K. Williams's poem "My Mother's Lips," from *Tar*, is representational, but it takes a radial, provisional view of the speaker's relationship with his mother. As a romantic, Williams, like Whitman, begins his poem attempting to capture narrative moments in time. The poem serves as a lesson to speaker and reader about the failure of romantic illumination: we revise our past every time we conceptualize it; each arrival point is greeted with a concomitant "unraveling." Again like Whitman, moving through time as well as the syntax of the sentence, nothing remains fixed or certain. Each stanza recreates a different tone by using different rhythms, by using consonance and assonance to harden and soften, and by deploying wide-ranging diction to create an effect of directness and intimacy or to create distance and objectivity. In the speaker's confused, retrospective power struggle, he is caught between the desire for autonomy and the desire for connection and love. In "My Mother's Lips," the transformations are both self-conscious and strategic, because the poem simultaneously registers the price and pleasure of change, of words, and of self. And the closure of the poem brings us to its necessary irresolution: both subjectivity and the temporal rob him of the New Critical insight and leave him instead with the rich density of experience, which occurs simultaneously in the present, in memory, and in the imagination.

Wrestling with the power of speech to create a separate self, the poem's speaker moves from awe to rage at his mother's omnipotence, specifically her power over him: because she apparently takes away his words, he projects onto her a godly *prima causa*.

> Until I asked her to please stop doing it and was astonished to find
>   that she not only could
> but from the moment I asked her in fact would stop doing it, my
>   mother, all through my childhood,
> when I was saying something to her, something important, would
>   move her lips as I was speaking
> so that she seemed to be saying under her breath the very words I was
>   saying as I was saying them.
>
> Or, even more disconcertingly—wildly so now that my puberty had
>   erupted—*before* I said them.
> When I was smaller, I must just have assumed that she was omni-
>   scient. Why not?
> She knew everything else—when I was tired, or lying; she'd know I
>   was ill before I did.
> I may even have thought—how could it not have come into my
>   mind?—that she *caused* what I said.

And while he recreates the subjectivity of his feelings with great immediacy (so much so that they inhabit the present tense), even in retrospect the speaker cannot make these scenes cohere into a truth: she "seemed to be saying" and "I may even have thought." From that point on the poem seems to move developmentally, advancing toward equality ("It's endearing to watch us again in that long-ago dusk, facing each other, my mother and me. / I've just grown to her height, or just past it: there are our lips moving together") and then toward the suggestion of passion ("there are our lips moving together"), followed by the letting go. When the speaker moves out of his cocoon, he must live with feelings of wrenching loneliness, adult sensuality, and the confusion that comes with the first suggestions of autonomy.

> When I find one [a cocoon] again, it's that two o'clock in the morning, a grim hotel on a square,
> the impenetrable maze of an endless city, when, really alone for the first time in my life,
> I found myself leaning from the window, incanting in a tearing whisper what I thought were poems.

> I'd love to know what I raved that night to the night, what those innocent dithyrambs were,
> or to feel what so ecstatically drew me out of myself and beyond. . . .
> Nothing is there, though,
> only the solemn piazza beneath me, the riot of dim, tiled roofs and impassable alleys,
> my desolate bed behind me, and my voice, hoarse, and the sweet, alien air against me like a kiss.

As the speaker moves toward adulthood, the world and the word become less decipherable (an "impenetrable maze" and an "endless city"). And just as Whitman's speaker in "There Was a Child Went Forth" doubts his capacity to make the world cohere in poems, Williams's speaker's feelings are nothing more than a "tearing whisper" that he had once misread as poems.

In the last stanza, the speaker acknowledges both his longing and the impossibility of knowing what was said, what "drew him out of himself and beyond" (with all the doubleness of "out of himself"). "Nothing is there, though." The instability of the diction is almost vertiginous in its unraveling multiplicity. "The riot of dim," the "impassable alleys," "sweet," and "alien" all at first appearance create the New Critical paradox, uniting opposites; but the desolate bed is *behind* him (in the past or the narrative present?), and it is against him (in proximity, or in his way?) like a kiss: an affectionate kiss, a kiss that seals his attachment, that makes it impossible for him to find another partner? His look at the past in his attempt to understand his linguistic and experiential origins reveals "nothing" there. He is kept from his own past because he is constantly revising it, because the emptiness of nothing "there" cannot be articulated; and because one can never locate oneself in time and space, the poem's closure brings the speaker to mystery in its largest sense: whatever the effect of the past, whatever retrospective meaning we give to our histories, they are at best tentative impositions on the unknowable. This kind of Cézanne-like perspective acknowledges a longing for fixity, being able to recover and hold onto a moment, to locate a truth about a scene—here his mother's and his own tangled motives. But because they exist only in relationship and transform over time, the quest is endless, elusive, and the very stuff of his own song.

Many poems in *Tar* originate in this romantic desire to return to the past, to preserve it in amber, to hold and comprehend it, even though Williams's speakers' intuit or understand that experience is entropic. In "Still-Life," the speaker goes back to the initiation experience of holding hands with a girl, and as he desperately wants to bring that intensity and passion in the present tense, he understands

> not, after all, even the objective place, those shifting paths I can't re-
> ally follow now
> but only can compile from how many other ambles into other woods,
> other stoppings in a glade—
> (for a while we were lost, and frightened; night was just beyond the
> hills; we circled back)—
> even, too, her gaze, so darkly penetrating, then lifting idly past, is so
> much imagination,
> a portion of that figured veil we cast against oblivion, then try, with
> little hope, to tear away.

In "Neglect," the movement of the syntax transforms a scene using coordinate clauses even within a single sentence: "It was cold, but not enough to catch or clear your breath: uncertain clouds, unemphatic light. / Everything seemed dimmed and colorless, the sense of surfaces dissolving, like the Parthenon." Uncertain becomes unemphatic, the dimmed becomes colorless, and while until this point the landscape seems merely pale, the sentence moves on to dissolution. Mimetically, the language demonstrates the speaker's narrative experience in the poem: stopping in a town that has been raped by the coal companies in Pennsylvania and abandoned. Metaphorically, the past itself has been abandoned, history is an erasure, or in the horrifying final images of the poem, the speaker moves toward ritualized waste. "All that held now was that violated, looted country, the fraying fringes of the town, / those gutted hills, hills by rote, hills by permission, great, naked wastes of wrack and spill, / vivid and disconsolate, like genitalia shaved and disinfected for an operation."

In his most recent collection, *The Singing*, Williams's obsessions remain the same, but his approach edges closer to the premises of postmodernism: truth is, as Michel Foucault maintains, nothing but a power regime. The title poem brings together Williams's familiar romantic longing for connection with his self-conscious recognition of that indecipherable universe. The poem bespeaks cultural alienation and psychological drives over-running our knowledge of self or other. The impulse here, as in many of Williams's best poems, intertwines the personal and the social. While the narrator looks for signs of reciprocity between him and a black stranger he encounters on a walk, he is forced to acknowledge his tangled motives, a web of self-interest and self-deception. Williams recognizes that the desire to identify and be accepted is entwined with a narcissistic desire to be seen as a "good person." The poem ultimately satirizes the liberal humanist's blurring of difference (we are all one). Williams uses his signature syntactical strategy to qualify, contradict, and undermine the easy transcendence.

At the beginning of "The Singing," the speaker listens to the young man's "cadenced shouting / Most of which I couldn't catch I thought because the young man was black speaking black." To ease his own discomfort, the speaker tries to find kinship with the young black man by projecting onto him: "It didn't matter I could tell he was making his song up which pleased me he was nice-looking." For a moment, the speaker's frenetic desire to be included leads him to believe the young man is addressing him with "song": "We went along in the same direction then he noticed me there almost beside him and 'Big' / He shouted-sang 'Big' and I thought how droll to have my height incorporated in his song."

The polyphony of voices, the elevated diction of "droll," set against the "black talk," helps us understand why the speaker cannot decipher the song: the poem is encoded with class and racial misunderstandings that mirror, incidentally, recent American history between Jews and blacks in this country. Many liberal Jews (such as those portrayed stereotypically in Alice Walker's *Meridian*) want to be liked, want to assuage the guilt of privilege at the same time they want to be considered special individuals. After the narrator hears the young black man say "I'm not a nice person" (even though he is "nice-looking," it turns out he is not bourgeois), the narrator must ultimately reject the romantic "lyrical spilling over." The cadenced shouting is indecipherable, the speaker catches a fragment or two (which he first assumes is spoken to him) but comes to understand "That if my smile implied I conceived of anything like concord between us I should forget it. . . . // nothing else happened his song became indecipherable to me again." The final meditation of the poem tentatively eulogizes the separation between our need to be heard and attended to by some spiritualizing song: "Sometimes it feels even when no one is there that someone something is watching and listening / Someone to rectify redo remake this time again though no one saw nor heard no one was there."

Williams's desire to imagine a world that is sanctified by language or expression is undermined not only by racial projection but also by estranged and irrational urban life: in other words, by history. Expression fails to render him individual, nor can it make the world cohere by signification. Williams uses verbs that continually blur and qualify to show that self-deception corrupts our longings for concordance, correspondence, equality, and our faith in imagination or a designing higher power. It may *feel* as if "someone is there" (the black man, god, an open, welcoming human being), but nothing can redo or rectify history.

In the surprising poem "Gravel," the speaker also looks for signification but the world will not provide it.

> It's not, "Look what I found!" but the gravel itself,
> which is what puzzles adults, that nothing's there,
>
> even beneath, but it's just what Catherine most likes,
> that there's no purpose to it, no meaning.

But this innocent play (reminiscent of figures in Blake's *Songs of Innocence*) becomes complicated and darkened when a stranger spits at Catherine in the subway. The speaker cannot account for, justify, or give meaning to this "crook, the creep, the slime." But as he had told the story from a distance (again the narrator has only the words), he is speechless—he can only shudder:

> as I,
> now, not in a park or playground, not watching a child
>
> sift through her shining fingers those bits of shattered
> granite which might be our lives, shudder again.

In "The Clause," the desire to pursue an integrated self, to create meaning and order by consciousness, acts of mind, ironically generates a self-perpetuating labyrinth of instability and uncertainty:

This entity I call my mind, this hive of restlessness,
this wedge of want my mind calls self,
this self which doubts so much and which keeps reaching,
keeps referring, keeps aspiring, longing, towards some state
from which ambiguity would be banished, uncertainty expunged;

this implement my mind and self imagine they might make together,
which would have everything accessible to it,
all our doings and undoings all at once before it,
so it would have at last the right to bless, or blame,
for without everything before you, all at once, how bless, how blame?

In the closing stanza of "The World," the speaker also chides his desire to signify, to judge and create symbol, thereby taking flight from inhabiting the material world.

Each sprig of lavender lifting jauntily as its sated butterfly departs,
Catherine beneath the beech tree with her father and sisters, me
      watching,
everything and everyone might stand for something else, *be* something else.
Though in truth I can't imagine what; reality has put itself so solidly
      before me
there's little need for mystery. . . . Except for us, for how we take the
      world
to us, and make it more, more than we are, more even than itself.

On the one hand, Williams's secular materialism critiques the project of making more of the world, for trying to find fictive correspondence (metaphor in art), spiritual meaning, and coherence, because the interjection distorts reality, the actual material world. On the other hand, as the artist is driven to express, to communicate, to transform consciousness, to seek justice, Williams conversely worries that utterance has lost its power to communicate. In one of the darkest historical poems in *The Singing*, "In the Forest," the voices of civilization, the alleged voices of reason, only veil self-interest and helplessness. Again, the Enlightenment project is a mere regime of truth:

> They'd been speaking of their absurd sentences, and of the cruelty of
> so-called civilization,
> and the listeners imagine the old man is going to share his innocent
> rapture,
> but No, he says, No, the trees and their seeds and flowers are at war
> just as we are,
> each species of tree relentlessly seeks its own ends;
>
> . . . .
>
> Does it matter what words are spoken? That the evidence proves one
> thing or another?
> Isn't the ultimate hope just that we'll still be addressed, and I know
> others are, too,
> that meanings will still be devised and evidence offered of lives having
> been lived?
> "In the North, the trees . . ." and the wretched page turns, and we
> listen, and listen.

Lost in a world that lacks a moral center but nevertheless requires continuous choice and judgment, Williams's poems thrive on the need to investigate difficulty. Their concentration on the dark bespeaks the desire to account for the irrational, the unjust. The cost of these stirrings for Williams is his acknowledged blindness to the world *as it is* and his "insane collision" with the dark; for we live in a world not plaited with meaning but one that arouses us and our senses (reinforced by the image of the child in the passage below) but that does not cohere. This collision lacks an antecedent, but we can assume it as simultaneously the speaker's desire for omnipotence and a description of an unjust world lacking in truth.

> But why, even in dreams, must I dwell on the dark,
> in the dire, in the *drek*? A foal in a dappling field,
> I might have dreamed, a child trailing after with a rope,

But no, the sense, the scent nearly, the dream-scent,
was wild frustration; not pity but some insane collision
with greed, and power, and credulity, above all.

John Ashbery also wants to posit the self in the world and wants art to account for it; he also finds it impossible to both inhabit experience and extract its meaning. In "Robin Hood's Barn," his speaker says, "To be there is not to know it"; in other poems he struggles with his longing. "Is anything central? / Are place names central?" Or, "Are we never to make a statement?"

John Hartmann's useful essay on Nietzsche's unpublished "On Truth and Lies in a Nonmoral Sense" could have been written with Ashbery in mind. "In this essay, Nietzsche describes all the truths of man as being illusory, or, better still, metaphoric. 'Truths are illusions which we have forgotten are illusions . . . metaphors that have become worn out and have been drained of sensual force.'"[1]

In Ashbery's poems, not only do concepts function as metaphors, but metaphors function as illusions, partial explanations that are displaced and shattered by the next set of metaphors. His speakers are perpetually caught in the gaps between the need to order experience by naming and knowing and a willingness to accede to the more vulnerable flux of feeling and experiencing. Naming becomes a way to hold onto or to pin down experience, but it also acts as a distancing device, primarily through self-conscious removal. In Nietzsche's essay, he considers that "all conceptualizing is metaphoric, meaning a lie: 'we believe that we know something about the things themselves when we talk of trees, colors, snow, and flowers; and yet we possess nothing but metaphors for things—metaphors which correspond in no way to the original entities.'"[2]

Formally, Ashbery reverses this process: he uses metaphors in his attempt to approximate and communicate his experience, but each failed, incomplete, inaccurate, or disassociative metaphor blurs and obstructs that experience, addles or confounds it, so he is forced to change the lens for his vision, his way of viewing that experience. He perpetually remains the outsider, joining others only in their confusions: either those who are tormented by the absurd and whimsical fictional conventions that regulate experience or those who are living out the chaotic consequences of refusing or failing to keep up with them.

Beginning with his first mature work, *Double Dream of Spring* (and

I concentrate on the middle work in this chapter because although the late work offers many formal experiments, his obsessions and strategies remain primarily unchanged), Ashbery uses quickly changing and inadequate metaphors as a formal expression of the ineffable and the slippery fiction of truth. This collection uses traces of narrative, representation, and meditation, all in the service of trying to come to terms with the instability of this linguistic and experiential universe. His justly praised signature poem, "Soonest Mended," employs and abandons several kinds of metaphors to describe the ambivalent experience of either wanting "to be small and clear and free" or to be "holding on to the hard earth so as not to get thrown off." He begins with a tonally straightforward artistic simile that soon collapses. "On the brink of destruction, / Like heroines in *Orlando Furioso*" becomes the comic Angelica in the Ingres painting "considering / The colorful but small monster near her toe"; a few lines later the artistic metaphors mutate to the comic strip character Happy Hooligan (a textbook example of the collapse of distinctions between high and low culture), who "Came plowing down the course" (introducing a new metaphoric landscape, not yet specified; the "course" will later be transformed into an athletic event, complete with stadium). Moving from the illustrative field of visual art, Ashbery shifts to "book learnin'": "only by that time we were in another chapter and confused." The vague references of that sentence do not make clear whether the speaker is a character in a book or whether he is reading some kind of instruction manual on how to live. Or, more literally, he remains undecided "About how to receive this latest piece of information," even doubting that what he received was information. He worries about his capacity to figure his individual place in the scheme of things. "Weren't we rather acting this out / For someone else's benefit." In any case, confusion, the snagging and shifting of these linguistic approximations, only leaves the speaker further away from himself. As Nietzsche claimed, these concepts, these faulty and inconsistent metaphors, lead to anxiety and falling behind. The poem begins, after all, "barely tolerated, living on the margin / In our technological society."

Making use of the pun "To reduce all this to a small variant," the speaker begins to explore metaphors of scope and scale, "thoughts in a mind / With room enough and to spare for our little problems." To escape by being "miniscule on the gigantic plateau." Later, the metaphors pile up as landscapes, details from a farm, games, the flickering sky as universe, and so on. This moving on from one illusory approximation to the next (the chapter metaphor places us inside the artifice of the work of art) drama-tizes, in praxis, that he has moved "past truth / The being of our sentences." He makes explicit there the gap between language and expression and life as it is experienced—which is Nietzsche's point exactly, one pursued later by French deconstructionists.

One of the metaphors, in an attempt to decipher the palpable chaos, acknowledges "we are all talkers . . . but underneath the talk lies/" (a wonderful enjambment there emphasizes the consequence of conceptual-izing experience) "The moving and not wanting to be moved, the loose / Meaning, untidy and simple like a threshing floor." Having moved to the agrarian for another attempt at meaning, he finds signifiers for fragmenta-tion: it's all detritus. Two secondary meanings of threshing reinforce the association with intellection: to thresh it out, which is to examine repeat-edly, or to beat severely or thrash. This attention to disparate and multiple meanings has always created the richness and density of poetry, but for Ashbery these dizzying differences (evident in his attention to dispersed diction in virtually all of his poems) lead to the fragmentary meanings of the "threshing floor."

One of the primary causes of fragmentation in this faulty landscape is the temporal: Ashbery is obsessed with how time moving forward alters every moment that preceded it. When he says, "Tomorrow would alter the sense of what had already been learned," the temporal complicates and undermines this process of understanding one's relationship to the world. History and change destabilize fixed knowledge and stable relationships.

Although unstable metaphors provide one way to dramatize performa-tively Ashbery's irresolvable vision, asymmetrical and unresolved conflicts in his diction provide another. Ashbery is fascinated by the objective and the clinical as distancing devices, just as he is interested in the imprecision of slang and jargon. His poems create a stew of these disparate levels of diction: his choice of words often provides cues for the reader for shifts in tone, for creating conflicting stances that he lays down on the page like layers of paint.

In "Mixed Feelings" from *Self-Portait in a Convex Mirror*, he bifurcates the speaker's voice into the sensory and the intellectual, alternately inhab-iting a moment and conceptualizing it. The narrative trigger for the poem is a faded photograph of what the speaker construes as young women pos-ing in front of a World War II airplane. The photograph makes a resonant trope for a work of art, for memory, as well as for the vagaries of pop culture. But the very first line introduces the sensory, which interestingly attacks the sense, preparing us for the way in which our senses and our sense do not match up.

> A pleasant smell of frying sausages
> Attack the sense, along with an old, mostly invisible
> Photograph of what seems to be girls lounging around
> An old fighter bomber, circa 1942 vintage.
> How to explain to these girls, if indeed that's what they are

Ashbery cleverly uses vintage names ("Ruths, Lindas, Pats and Sheilas") to create a counter to the speaker's abstract intelligence. Feigning intellectual superiority, this unreliable narrator sees his dilemma as explaining "the vast change that's taken place / In the fabric of our society." Using formal, professorial diction, the speaker has a job to decipher meaning. But the figures for the work of art, the daily everyday "girls" who are "creatures . . . / Of my imagination," cannot retain one fact: "Maybe they were lying but more likely their / Tiny intelligences cannot retain much information. / Not even one fact, perhaps." It is not the imagination's job to synthesize or conceptualize. And Ashbery's parodic voice underlines the pretense of attempting to create a unitary vision about the meaning of change. So the girls respond with the deflating "Aw nerts . . . / This guy's too much for me."

Throughout the poem, the speaker deludes himself into thinking the intellect is superior to the sensual and sensory. He thinks he has these "creatures . . . / Of my imagination" figured out.

> I am not offended that these creatures (that's the word)
> Of my imagination seem to hold me in such light esteem,
> Pay so little heed to me. It's part of a complicated
> Flirtation routine, anyhow, no doubt.

Not surprisingly, in the more surreal moments of the poem, the intellectual speaker confuses time and place: the intellect is locationless, the senses inarticulate. Nevertheless, he is drawn to them at the same time he is dismissive, and as in the rest of the poem, he is filled with "changes of mind" because looking, feeling, and acting do not lend themselves to fixity, coherence, or closure.

I like the way
They look and act and feel. I wonder
How they got that way, but am not going to
Waste any more time thinking about them.
I have already forgotten them
Until some day in the not too distant future

In a poem where the desire for harmony—the union of intelligence and the senses—fails, the world of art and experience exemplifies density, flux, and disappearance. However, in his imagination, which is not subject to the vagaries of time, the speaker thinks he can conjure these girls and they can all "babble . . . about the forests of change."

In many other poems, Ashbery struggles with trying to fix and know the world, to join signifier and referent: "Is anything central? / Are place names central?" Or, "Are we never to make a statement?" In "Worsening Situation," he says, "Everyone is along for the ride, / It seems. Besides, what else is there?" In "No Way of Knowing," he acknowledges difficulties surrounding the performative: "But I was trying to tell you about a strange thing / That happened to me, but this is no way to tell about it, / By making it happen. It drifts away in fragments."

The above lines gloss Ashbery's postmodern strategies: in other places, where Ashbery is enacting rather than summarizing, creating dramatic tension out of the language, diction, and unfolding syntax, the reader experiences the dislocation in the diction rather than in reporting the subject matter of the poem. In "Ode to Bill," a poem whose project is to account for his way of writing, the poem archly moves through surprise after surprise, not only revealing the mind in motion as it works to decipher, changing its mind from clause to clause, as Whitman often did, but also never landing on an explanation:

I am coming out of one way to behave
Into a plowed cornfield. On my left, gulls,
On an inland vacation. They seem to mind the way I write.

Or, to take another example: last month
I vowed to write more. What is writing?
Well, in my case, it's getting down on paper
Not thoughts, exactly, but ideas, maybe:

Ideas about thoughts. Thoughts is too grand a word.
Ideas is better, though not exactly what I mean.
Someday I'll explain. Not today though.

Moving from the abstract metaphor ("one way to behave"), the gulls hunt for the detritus: that trope often becomes the material for an Ashbery poem (reminiscent of another one of Ashbery's influences, Wallace Stevens's "The Man on the Dump"). Then he projects onto them, as they hover, their disapproval. This mysterious deminarrative, it turns out, serves as an example of writing. Working with the aftermath of what has been cleared, the speaker/writer dwells in a moment of romanticism: if Whitman can translate bird songs, Ashbery can interpret the gulls' motives. But in the twentieth century, the moment is ironized, patently absurd. While at first reading we might be disarmed by the cleverness, the coy mysteriousness, Ashbery does mean what he says. To live and write in the moment, an artist doesn't explain.

The next stanza borrows from Elizabeth Bishop's strategy in "Poem" ("About the size of a dollar bill"), when Bishop's speaker says, "our visions coincided / no, visions is too grand a word"). In each poem the writer has it both ways: what is crossed out and what is revised both appear, but in Ashbery's case the acknowledgment that he can't pin an experience down, his willingness not to fall into the romantic epiphany, leads him again to metaphor, to gather correspondence in another example.

I feel as though someone had made me a vest
Which I was wearing out of doors into the countryside
Out of loyalty to the person, although
There is no one to see, except me
With my inner vision of what I look like.

He cannot settle on the inner vision of what he looks like—to dramatize the mind in motion—because his motives, his understanding of his own mind, are so provisional; but it does describe one of Ashbery's aspirations. Only at the end of the poem, a closure that resembles so many of his closures in this middle period, do the romantic and postmodern sensibilities meet. Talking about a horse in this plowed field, the speaker metaphorizes his melancholy, his nostalgia for the moment gone: he invents correspondences that disappear before our eyes "for we must, we must be moving on."

He moves away slowly,
Looks up and pumps the sky, a lingering
Question. Him too we can sacrifice
To the end, progress, for we must, we must be moving on.

The masterpiece poem from *Self-Portrait in a Convex Mirror* is "Grand
Galop," itself a kind of action painting, moving through the pop-art-like
quotidian to the broadly philosophical and back. The poem dramatizes, in
both disparate narrative and lyric passages, the gaps between the conceptual and the sensory data of experience. We experience performatively the
randomness of experience as well as our frustration and desire to organize
experience. This dramatic process produces a rainbow of tones, a variety
of stances, all different approaches to solving the conflict or letting it go.
In the following passage, Ashbery considers experience and the language
used to describe it as constantly unfolding, each moment altered by what
preceded and what followed it. What makes this poem modern, written
in twentieth-century America instead of some more general philosophical
or rhetorical claim, is the assault of sensory data, the speed of modern life
itself:

It's getting out of hand.
As long as one has some sense that each thing knows its place
All is well, but with the arrival and departure
Of each new one overlapping in the semi-darkness
It's a bit mad. Too bad, I mean, that getting to know each just for a
    fleeting second
Must be replaced by imperfect knowledge of the featureless whole,
Like pocket history of the world, so general
As to constitute a sob or a wail unrelated
To any attempt at definition.

This temporal mobility alters so much of modern life, including the difficulty of getting to know someone, the anxiety concerning what's next,
especially when one does not have a moral order, an ideology, to filter the
experience.

Frank Lepkowski does an excellent job of summarizing past criticism of
"Grand Galop." But he also makes the following claim and then relies on
a witticism by John Hollander to reinforce it: "The poem proceeds from

stems of language to an invocation of spring and its display in shrubs and flowers, followed hard by the banal realm of everyday life. Its representation by entries from the school cafeteria menu is 'not an ecstatic Whitmanian catalogue,' in Hollander's felicitous formulation, but more like a recital by W. C. Fields, trying to incapacitate further an already nauseated bank examiner."[3]

Certainly, one can find a playful, almost infantile element to parts of the poem (Ashbery's use of slang to deflate the predominance of the elevated diction of intellect), but Hollander reduces Whitman's ecstatic catalogues; many of them offer discrete transformations and reversals, not as strategies for entire poems, as Ashbery does, but as strategies that reverberate within any number of sentences. In this famous passage from "Crossing Brooklyn Ferry," what begins as cataloguing the dark side of the speaker turns out to complicate and romanticize it; ultimately, his greatest sin had been not expressing his passions to those passersby:

> The wolf, the snake, the hog, not wanting in me,
> The cheating look, the frivolous word, the adulterous wish, not wanting,
> Refusals, hates, postponements, meanness, laziness, none of these wanting,
> Was one with the rest, the days and haps of the rest,
> Was call'd by my nighest name by clear loud voices of young men as they saw me approaching or passing,
> Felt their arms on my neck as I stood, or the negligent leaning of their flesh against me as I sat,
> Saw many I loved in the street or ferry-boat or public assembly, yet never told them a word

In this remarkably modern passage, the association with the animal and the metaphorical signs we associate with them syntactically transform at every moment. He equates the "cheating look, the frivolous word, [and] the adulterous wish," thereby democratizing the Judeo-Christian hierarchies. From there he slowly moves away from the deadly sins to the daily, then being called by young men; as it turns out, it is not the adulterous wish that takes moral precedence, but repression. "Saw many I loved in the street or ferry-boat or public assembly, yet never told them a word," turning the early part of the sentence, thought in motion, on its head.

Ashbery's leaps, his version of these reversals and changes of mind, are much wider, but they are not so different in kind. Again, from "Grand Galop":

> So this tangle of impossible resolutions and irresolutions:
> The desire to have fun, to make noise, and so to
> Add to the already all-but-illegible scrub forest of graffiti on the shit-
> house wall.
> Someone is coming to get you:
> The mailman, or a butler enters with a letter on a tray
> Whose message is to change everything, but in the meantime . . .

In typical Ashbery fashion, he provides a longing and a motive for a fictive order (the closest he gets to modernism's romance with art's coherence as compensatory for a chaotic universe). But fun transmutes to noise and then to graffiti: the movement veers toward the indecipherable and the grotesquely daily. The surprises cannot be located in decay: the paranoid moment of someone "coming to get you" becomes smaller, then larger, and always unpredictable, which enacts the Heisenberg principle applied to change. So what can Ashbery do but darken the word stage? He ends without an ending, without resolution, but rather with a metaphorical moment that approximates the irresolvable dilemma. "But now we are at Cape Fear and the overland trail / Is impassable, and a dense curtain of mist hangs over the sea." We are left with anxiety, and the whole poem exploits it: anxiety, in the existential sense, is authorized by uncertainty, not knowing where to go, what comes next.

> I cannot decide in which direction to walk
> But this doesn't matter to me, and I might as well
> Decide to climb a mountain (it looks almost flat)
> As decide to go home

These choices are followed by other random choices in "these pauses that are supposed to be life," and they brush, for a moment, against the entropic before retreating to the passage of diaries, which shows that consciousness does not change us—desire changes us, the world that acts on us changes us: "It is this / That takes us back into what really is, it seems, history— / The lackluster, disorganized kind without dates."

"Ut Pictura Poesis" sums up Ashbery's obsessions best and offers his understanding about not only how history and time have altered the function of art but also how the modern human is left with a Sisyphian task; unlike Camus' Sisyphus (who must embrace process), though, Ashbery will not settle on matters of value, thereby commodifying experience. It is not so much that he embraces flux but that he finds it inescapable. That is the postmodern dilemma: that we live in history, history as syntax, always unfolding with the next thing: as Ashbery writes in "Mixed Feelings," "the vast change that's taken place / In the fabric of our society, altering the texture / Of all things in it." The closure of "Ut Pictura Poesis" again settles on Ashbery's irresolvable obsession: the speaker's desire to discover is entangled with the romantic longing to decipher. The very nature of consciousness mediates against their simultaneity: they are always at war with one another, always repositioning themselves.

> You when you write poetry:
> The extreme austerity of an almost empty mind
> Colliding with the lush, Rousseau-like foliage of its desire to
>   communicate
> Something between breaths, if only for the sake
> Of others and their desire to understand you and desert you
> For other centers of communication, so that understanding
> May begin, and in doing so be undone.

OLENA KALYTIAK DAVIS

Revising Tradition—The Retro-New

ONE OF THE MANY MEASURES of ambition in poetry is the extension of the medium. One thinks of how Charlie Parker's and Dizzy Gillespie's use of chord progressions expanded and transformed jazz improvisation, how Cézanne's landscapes altered composition and representation, or how Caravaggio's live working-class models reconfigured both painting and religious mythology. These artists were not alone in creating those techniques, nor were they naïve about artistic precedent: clearly they absorbed conventions of their own and past ages. But with an inner urgency, drawing from the world they already knew, they stumbled on some discovery (from their art or elsewhere) that triggered an innovation and, on rare occasions, extraordinary change. You can hear Haydn and Mozart in Beethoven, but you wouldn't find sufficient precedent for the Ninth Symphony or his late quartets. Sometimes those changes, as in confessional poetry or superrealism in painting, provide more modest extensions of their art. By extension in poetry I mean making use of literary antecedents but bringing one's formal gifts, obsessions, and, most of all, imaginative faculties to occasion change. Some of these poets discussed in earlier chapters of this book include Lyn Hejinian, Claudia Rankine, Diane Williams, Harryette Mullen, and John Ashbery. We call these artists innovators, a term as fraught with complication as originality, but some of the recent work of Olena Kalytiak Davis demonstrates an inventiveness, a freshness, and a vitality that make her work recognizable and in some ways singular. One of Davis's projects is her use of sampling or covers, quotations and interpretations from others' poems inside her own, much the way bebop musicians quoted "I Got Rhythm," or the way hip-hop arts sample Motown songs to create a dialogue or an argument or to parody one of those historic romantic voices. Her objective is to emphasize literature's experiential function: to enlarge consciousness, to make literature emotionally and intellectually applicable to both artist and audience. The work is smart, alternately witty, disagreeable, and moving; the resultant poems seem entirely intimate, but they also gather the concerns of the age while employing a variety of poetic modes and linguistic practices. Her work admits crossings out, Freudian slips, instant messaging–type talk, and archaic diction. Words and their function clearly excite her. Above all, innovation aside, her poems bristle with a love of texture and the exploratory, substantive implications of language as emotional expression.

Davis's approach to intimate writing is intriguing but also artful. She presents the reader with seemingly unmediated and uncensored, almost diary-like details of daily life side by side with the willful theater of a presentation self: the poet writing, the poet constructing and choosing what she wants us to see. Thus, the "I" (which she recently placed in quotation marks) is always at stake and on view; at the same time, she acknowledges that identity as a necessary socially and artistically constructed fiction. These complex and conflicting notions of self (*I'm spontaneously making myself available, I'm making this up,* and *I'm figuring this out in the act of writing*) are inextricably entangled: the poet and the person, the public and the private, are impossible to stabilize. Negotiating these overlapping arenas—what's literally true, what's metaphorically true, what's imagined—has always been one of poetry's many tasks, but Davis's poems implicitly and explicitly bring to the forefront both the function of writing and wide-ranging emotional exploration. Her poems ask questions: Who do we write for? How do we represent ourselves authentically given what words can and cannot provide, when self-knowledge is incomplete, transient, driven by mystery, desire and need, repression and wish-fulfillment fantasy?

One of Davis's strategies is engaging and manipulating the reader's discomfort: she is simultaneously "confessional" and "postmodern." Romantically drawn to the self at the same time proposing it as elusive and fragile, she brings the reader closer to the lyric voice of the poet; at the same time, we can't locate exactly what is true, who is addressed, or whose truth it is. At a time when the culture is in a tizzy about fact and memoir, when everyone is confessing everything, Davis's vulnerability draws the reader into the empathic, while at the same time she employs and satirizes the voyeuristic pleasures of the poet "exposing" herself. So her interrogation of those truths becomes both her own obsession and one hot-button signpost of our age.

One way Davis extends the medium is by postmodernist collapsing of high and popular culture (in a variety of tones, dictions, and voices); but she also borrows forms from popular culture. The original literary sources, from William James to Emily Dickinson, become reconfigured as competing or reinforcing voices. She appropriates, reveres, converses with, and finds correspondence in all these voices, often inside a single poem. A version of Dickinson's "I cannot live with You" will appear side by side in a poem full of contemporary slang. She can quote from Catullus (or use a Lowell-like "version") and use "IZ" in the same poem. While knowing the source of the literary quotations enlarges the context for the reader, the content of the material is almost always available in the poem itself. The function of knowledge, literary or otherwise, in Davis's work is always acknowledging integration or fissure, probing the gap between words and experience, between perception and reality. Her desperate identity quest, then, is tempered by other voices reminding the poem of the blurry limits of self.

Her recent blog on *Poetry* magazine's Web site illustrates the sampling that speaks to her imagination. Here she uses, more baldly, some of the same strategies that enliven her poems:

02.03.06
the day everybody (everybody? anybody?) 's been waiting for: and on
    the fifth day they had
SEX!

you wanna know what i'm wearing?

well, first there was the inky cloak, then i changed into my antic dis-
    position: my doublet all unbraced, my stockings fouled, ungart'red
    and down-gyved to my ankles, and then, of course, my traveler's
    sea gown, scarfed about me.

and now . . .

now i'm wearing nothing

but the art between us

and long underwear and jeans and wilco t-shirt and hoodie and puffy
parka and pink-yellow-blue woolen cap and handmade muffler
and mittens and big boots. (and dark circles under my eyes) (this
blog and the eye cream are not doing dick!) hey, it's alaska!and you
try paying for the heat on a blogger's salary. (this ain't no *poetry*
magazine!)

so, yes, you gotta create your own.[1]

She begins by simultaneously seducing the reader and satirizing her relationship to the reader; the "sex" here emanates from the sensuousness of
language: she lets Shakespeare's *Hamlet* speak for her so she can approach
the ambiguous "now I'm wearing nothing / but the art between us" (the
everybody/anybody dualism foreshadows the narcissistic display and inse-
curity about her aloneness). After the address from *Hamlet*, and once that
love of the Eros of language drops away, she introduces the prosaic diary
entry: she talks street talk, she almost measures the distance in longing between the beauteous and archaic language of high literature and her own
life. At first we're convinced the art has been dropped: she's just reporting.
But in fact, the melancholy Hamlet has turned into a solitary blogger, the
"unbraced doublet" becomes the "wilco t-shirt" and failed cosmetic; the
humor is sparked by the postmodern collapsing of the two voices. Which
moves us more: the mad melancholy and chaos that originates in Hamlet
or the disorganized diction and poverty of the blogger? The reader requires
the harmonies of the first world to heighten the connections and distance
between literature and experience. Those strategies, finding in literature
some correspondence to self and sampling it, then apparently dropping
the literary mask, brings that past into the present. But it also bespeaks
an imagination that inhabits literature and not just quotes from it. At
every turn, the writer attempts to incorporate the texture of the word into
the self in a search for truthfulness. A close look at her prose description
lets the reader know too she has created—in her selection of details—a
presentation self, an image of herself as shivering, as poor, as a sucker for
commerce as she is aging. When I say Davis's poems speak to the age, not
only is she speaking to our voyeuristic urges, but she is also speaking to
the hierarchy of art and *Poetry* magazine. *Poetry*—reflecting social status
and class (she refers to the big donation *Poetry* magazine got from the Lily

Foundation)—doesn't dole out the money to its working poets. When Davis bites the hand that feeds her, enjoying the forum as a mild protest, the reader allies him- or herself with the poor artist; of course, that is the unmediated image she projects for us. But when we combine "nothing but the art between us" and "so we gotta create our own," the reader is left with the ambiguity in the final statement: create out own art, our own financial security, or—I believe—uncover the nexus between the two.

Davis's use of sampling echoes, extends, and alters parallel strategies employed in many of the arts. There have been many direct references to other works of art all through the history of literature: painters often paint their versions of other historic paintings inside their canvases; sampling occurs in hip-hop and R & B, in jazz, and most frequently in be-bop. Dexter Gordon, Johnnie Griffin, and Charlie Parker were masters of quoting a melody, phrasing, motifs, riffs, and diatonic and chromatic playing, all improvised and accomplished without breaking faith with the given chord-change progression. The parallel to Davis's work occurs when she borrows literary texts because they speak to her; she listens, and then she weaves them into her other voices in a poem (even when she recognizes that using someone else's language puts her under the "anxiety of influence," distorting the content of the other authors' poem).

There are a few obvious dangers to this kind of poetic experiment: most obviously cleverness and literary name-dropping. While it is true that her poems occasionally suffer from coyness, moments of solipsism, and overly clever puns or midair line breaks, Davis joins a small number of poets whose respect for (and knowledge of) literature competes with her desire to express, as originally and contemporaneously as she can, a fully engaged self. Implicit in her use of sampling is acknowledging that poems create their own discrete experiences: poems move us like any other experience. Other writers who also redesign, revere, and undermine the literary include experimental writers Susan Wheeler (who samples Chaucer in *Ledger*), Harryette Mullen, Stephanie Strickland (in *WaveSon.nets*), and, a more traditional lyric poet, D. A. Powell, who simultaneously invokes and parodies received forms. Davis's own second book is titled *Shattered Sonnets, Love Cards, and Other Off and Back Handed Importunities*. All these poets partake, in their revisionist ways, of what I call—to acknowledge the role of the past in shaping our future—the retro-new.

In one of the most moving shattered sonnets, "the unbosoming," Davis simultaneously reveres, appropriates, and argues with her literary antecedents' addresses to the Lord (Hopkins, Berryman, and Rilke in his *Sonnets to Orpheus*). She uses one Berryman quotation, "Heavy bored," from *77 Dream Songs*, to balance his late poetic prayers. She also quotes a phrase from an early Heather McHugh poem, "Housewifery." McHugh is something of an influence, sometimes felicitous, sometimes not (as when Davis overly depends on the idiomatic cliché, or breaks lines in midword to hyperemphasize part of a word). Davis's poems are much more interiorized and less philosophical. While McHugh makes language a primary *subject* of her poetic inquiries, Davis uses language more kinetically, to enact, to create movement: it is one medium of change.

I have been a day boarder, Lord. I have preferred the table to the Bed.
I have proffered, Lord, and I have profited, Lord, but little, but not. I
    was Bored,
Lord, I was heavy, Lord. Heavy bored. Hopeless, Lord, hideous, Lord.
    Sexless.
I was in love, Lord, but not with you. The nine malic moulds, Lord.
The butcher, the baker, the under-taker. Lord, I was taken under. I
    Repeat
Myself, Lord. I re-peat myself as the way back, the way back to Myself,
Lord. I have trembled. His face, Lord, and Yours. I am unlovely, Lord,
    I Nam
Not precious, Lord. Spy better, Love, and You will see: Inamnothing.
    I have Seen
How lovely, Lord, how lovely You are, Lord, but I refused to kneel. I
    Refuse
To knell Your loveliness. I refuse to kiss. And I refuse to tell. I am
    unwilling, Love.
I am unwell. Unkempt. My hideous loins, Love. My body, which is all
    Wrack
And screw, Love. All slack and crewel. At Your beck and call, Love, at
    His Beck
And call. Crestfallen, Love. Of the fallen breast. Un-clean of eye.
    Loose of Thigh.
Ridiculous, Love. Most serious, Love. Unshod. Unshriven. In vain
    and in Rain,

Love. I Live and I Wire. I Wive, Lord, but I Fathom Not.

The poem's title points the reader toward a rejection of the feminine, the motherly, and the sexual, as well as the social Dickinsonian "wife." Lord becomes a masculine principle as well as God. The lyric speaker is filled with self-loathing and regret; but even though she confesses, she will not submit to the Lord's authority. After a transforming love, the central anxiety of the poem, she is looking for a way back to herself, a journey that becomes a quest for authenticity and autonomy. The reference to Samuel Beckett's *Murphy* and the malic moulds offers readers a clue (that can be found elsewhere in the poem): leaving the malic moulds, his uniform, Murphy becomes impalpable "love gas." More importantly, he becomes nothing within nothing, which is the lyric speaker's great fear. Her dependence on love (what Adrienne Rich calls "women's sinecure") and men (every type of them), have stripped away her identity. But as Lord linguistically transforms to Love, something else happens: a witty counterforce—linguistic transmutation—offers resistance. After she is "nothing," she says "how lovely" and refuses to knell or kneel. She refused it in the past (a clue to her suffering in love as well perhaps), and she refuses it in the present. At first she refuses to "kiss," rejecting Eros, but then she turns it into the idiomatic "kiss and tell." She is being coy with the Lord. She is unwilling either to love or to submit. The effect of this resistance is far from revelatory. Being traditionally feminine gives her few resources: her body is all "wrack and screw," as in the McHugh poem she quotes from. They are both "slave(s) of love," but unlike for McHugh, the fetish brings Davis no erotic pleasure. Undefended, she must be "un"—all negation. The last line is simultaneously playful (as "live wire") but taken separately, as in her separate state, she lives and she "wires": language, the "word" that she and her poetic ancestors had depended upon for revelation, provides only a medium for distance and confusion.

In the long "poem convincing you to leave your wife," Davis reverses Dickinson's stance in "I cannot live with You." For Davis, as a modern woman, choosing not to live with someone becomes a rejection of convention and commitment: the lover does not interject between the speaker and Christ, but neither can he satisfy her restlessness nor her ambivalence nor save her from her own emptiness: "i have decided that we do not want other people's (wives') husbands / as we do not want our own."

The poem's "we" is reflexive, at once directed to the lover and herself (a strategy Davis uses often, blurring the addressee to imply the difficulty of separating what desires originate in an other as opposed to our own needs or projections). What love offers here is simultaneously self-referential and submissive, but it honors risk.

> (i cannot live with you becuz
> that would be
> IZ life!)

> . . . . . .
> so, i will do as i am told:
> love your neighbor as yourself
> and put your cup up on your shelf
> ask the kindly sexton for some kinky sex
> on the slide and on the sly on the fence
> (if you're brave enough to try)

She corrects Dickinson's romantic longings with the realization of what "IZ" life, separating the real from the ideal. This philosophical pragmatism allows her to find poetry in a more intellectual, clinical, and scientized philosophical diction: from William James's "The Will to Believe." These quotations deflate both the morality and insufficiency of her circumstances, giving expression to the repressed wish of Dickinson's poem.

> *FOR* (listen up!) *no concrete test of what is really true has ever been*
> *agreed upon.*

> *FOR SOME make the criterion external to the moment of perception,*
> . . . .

> *OTHERS make the perceptive moment its own test:*
> *use common sense* (à la reid)
> *use synthetic judgment a priori* (kant not cunt)
> *the inconceivability of the opposite* (but i was never into that)
> *the capacity to be verified by sense* (now, now, now that!)
> *the possession of complete organic unity*
> *or self-relation* (realized when a thing is its own other)

> o brother!
> i long to be realized like that!

Here the lyric speaker wrestles with her need for her lover, while also long-ing for "realization"—in poetic terms, "organic unity." She wants to inhabit her own body (the capacity to be verified by senses). The parenthetical asides represent personal and contemporary responses to the philosophical assertions in the manner of call and response; these phrases long for ro-mantic fusion—the will to believe—at the same time that subjectivity, the multiple possibilities of truth, her own inadequacy to love, to live in the present, and her inability to be her "own other" make the wish impossible to achieve or embrace.

Thus, the satiric and straightforward elements in the poem intermingle freely. The assertion "to be realized" in the passive voice accounts for her de-pendence on others (love) for self-affirmation, but it also playfully incorpo-rates the onanistic element in "realized when a thing is its own other." The rhyme of "o brother" with "other" serves to dismiss the Jamesian prescrip-tion (the slang of the postmodern signaling the satiric); at the same time, she cannot let go of her quest for the romantic ideal of completion in love.

The poem closes by echoing two of Davis's mentors; she alludes to Dickinson's famous "wife" and Sylvia Plath's "Lady Lazarus" ("neverthe-less / nevertheless," echoing "nevertheless I'm the same identical woman") and "The Applicant" (where the self is replaceable and useable). Using some of Plath's kind of homonyms and rhymes and self-abnegation, she adds Stein-like syntactical associations at the same time she employs a jagged but heavy end-stopped rhyme. These associations are far from dis-sociative: they address and intensify the notes—emptiness, lack of self, and multiple role playing—sounded earlier in the poem:

> my heart is cool
> and black
>
> is fool and blank
>
> nevertheless
> nevertheless
>
> i remain,
> the wife that staid and the wife that left
> the wife that laughed and
> the wife that slayed

riffs miffs thoughts knives . . .

what exists and
what, alas, does not

what i wast
and what i art

not

word is and
word was (unheard
of!) rauschenberg has painted
a new painting, i dare not
(meet me there)
go!

Finally, the speaker attempts to divert her—and our—attention to a
painting by Rauschenberg, but ultimately the poem turns on her admoni-
tion not to "go" (and desire to "meet me there") addressed to lover and
reader ("word" is the subject of the poem as well as the colloquial "common knowledge" of the idiom). This complex closure fills the reader with
conflicting instructions: having been told that she is a zero, a darkness,
Davis's speaker decides to "remain" playing, not merely the binary that
Plath uses (Siren/victim) but all the parts. She can settle on no single vision, can settle on being no one person in time and place, but she establishes dramatic motive and causality: she is limited both by being—or
being seen as—the wife and by her conflicting feelings of not caring what
others think of her versus being a slave to the word "is." In this poem,
besides evoking the more eternal tragedy of lost love, Davis also strikes an
important chord that speaks to our age. In an unstable culture that sells
titillation and freedom while rhetorically valuing an often-stifling commitment to permanence, the individual becomes anchorless: the meanings
of love and self have been stripped of artifice and a sense of relation.

Using her gifts of association in "the lais of lost long days . . . " ("lais" punning on "lays" as well as French for poetry), Davis connects memory, love,
and poetry. Spurred on by her inability to put in the past a past love or to
fully inhabit that vulnerability so that she can transform the trauma by re-

living or rewriting it, she connects these figures by the way they each contribute to her dilemma. All the metaphors refer, with great simultaneity, to the three above subjects, centered on "how I can attend to so little for so long." Obsessed with her failure to master either art or love, she dramatizes the claustrophobic effect of living her interior life. The windows are closed. Her indecisiveness, her self-consciousness, and most of all her fear of inauthenticity (expressed as a lack of "great art" or being a mere forgery or type) all account for her sense of failure. As she says, "I'm sure somebody has already lived this life, this wife, for me." When it comes to poetry, the associations regress from the natural hummingbird, to the more hopeful window out on the world, to just plain poems. Later, Davis's speaker feels "isn't great art," not only because of her feelings of inadequacy, but also because of her desire to control and fix a simile "under glass." Again, the italicized lines from Dickinson's "I cannot live with You," provide a subtext for the poem. The lost love is momentarily recaptured ("under glass") with a clip she replays. But replaying also leads to self-derision and stasis, to "repeating" herself, because there's no one else there.

> Today I used my new little hummingbird of a poem to get a big hum
>   mingbird of
> A bug out the only open, able, window. All my poems are humming
>   birds, are windows,
> Are poems, mostly painted shut. Mostly, suffocate and smile. But, hey,
>   I know a good
> Simile when I trap it, under glass. *Like a cup. Discarded. Sordid. YOU
>   COULD*
> *NOT.* The visitors come from all over to see how I can attend to so
>   little for so long. So
> Long so sweet! I said that in one of my latest poems. (One of my last.)
>   I have finally got-
> Ten permission to repeat myself! Myself, never was one to relive the
>   past, but now
> I've seen that one clip many many times. *Because your Face would put
>   out*
> *Jesus'.* Still enjoy it. *That new Grace.* Still think I'm sitting too far
>   back. *Pale. Home-*
> *Sick. Eye.* Still realize it isn't great art. Nothing is. Wire sculpture that.
>   I know, I know,

It's been done. As I am sure somebody has already lived this life, this
    wife, for me. Poor
Fuck. Sick Fish. Lately, I want, (o!), I wish, all my poems to end in, to
    end with,
Spring. The word, I mean. *AND I, COULD I?* Lately, I head steadily
    for,
Tread slowly toward, Abelard. Froward, I mean. I mean, Aberdeen.

Words, her love of them, and her failure to live up to them (and to
Dickinson's) are what she has. She would like her poems to end in spring
as a sign of hope and renewal, a return to nature and the out-of-doors.
Davis makes use of space metaphors, but she finds herself conflicted about
how much space or distance she requires. While the inside is sealed up,
"painted shut," her lyric speaker's interest in the words of others creates
distance from her own feelings, even as it expresses and replaces them
for her (what is she without Dickinson in this poem?). After quoting the
poem, she decides she is "sitting too far back" because there is no direct,
immediate engagement. So instead of going forward she goes "froward,"
contrarily, toward love as tragedy. Interestingly, her repetition of "I mean"
signals to the reader that she means more than one thing at once, that she
either qualifies what she means or changes her mind, and that she doesn't
know what she means. Or, defined by love, she questions what meaning
she has. The very last word in the progression belongs to Aberdeen, the site
of Shakespeare's tragedy. Aurally, the progression, typical of Davis's movement in a poem, makes sense: the reference to *MacBeth* does cast a light on
the tragedy of ambition in art. It calls back her desire to stop writing ("One
of my last"), her desire for largeness of scale (not the small hummingbirds,
which seem insufficient to "great art"), as well as her confusion about lo-
cating who she is in time and space.

    It would inadequately serve this poem to consider Davis's poetry the
intellectualized dilemma of a literary person (an impatient reader might
ask, *Why don't you just drop the literature and learn to love?*) Language and
poetry for Davis signify both the possibility of freedom (that window) and
correspondence (someone else has "captured" what I feel). Poems are also
"so long" (also as in goodbye) and "so sweet" *and* her work: she labors over
words, the small. But she has neither sufficient words nor faith, so by the
end of the poem, having tried to capture (or decipher) what has already
happened, she has no idea where her future will take her. This poem ex-

emplifies how a work can incorporate literary antecedents directly and emotionally. The references to literature are signposts, muses, priests, or therapists: she tries to learn about experience from them, as we as readers who love poetry also inevitably do.

In "may be you are like me: scared and awake," Davis makes use of the depressions of Dickinson and Plath. Using the archaic diction of "lain" set against the Plath-like jagged rhyming speech of "I'm of that type that's mostly / Hype," she hopes desperately that she is not alone in being a shell of a person, "all pose." All this in an effort, as in Frost's "Come In," to "be let in," to be "heard," to be "called."

A wreath of violets lain where my brain used to be. Matutinal,
frantic. The usual. Scalded and cold. I descend. I work like a bird.
I hear spring coming from a long mile off. A distant jungle-meadow.
It comes, it sings. Says: To be heard you must be let, be in. To be
    heard
It is best to hum, like water. It's true, I am barnacled and black.
    The un-
Derbelly, the sternum, the prow.

                        Was, I used to confess the nuns.
Was, the prettier they were the less they said. Week after week
    whispered
The one I loved like a secret: "I must avow. I'm of that type that's
    mostly
Hype." I let Him forgive her merely on the strength of her brow.
    Sister,
Says I, wear it like a wife. Then I'd go wash my hands in mint and
    rose.
May be, you are like me: all pose.

                        May be, you are cutting each word harder
And harder, to listen, I'mall *watchandwile,waitingtobe Called*.
    Lordy-lordy-lord,
When I asked to be left alone, I didn't mean, like, now, like, this.
    Full-deep:
All solace and solecism. Un-sail-able. Un-vale-able. To spring, to light,
    to sleep.

The last stanza of this poem I find miraculous: trapped in her passivity and confusion, aware of her status as a doubter and an outsider, she feels "unnaturally" stuck and abandoned, by both god and love. In the beautiful and risky couplet "When I asked to be left alone, I didn't mean, like, now, like, this. Full-deep: / All solace and solecism. Un-sail-able. Un-vale-able. To spring, to light, to sleep," morning has been transformed to mourning; spring, being a long way off, makes her "un-vale-able," unavailable. This wit is on the edge of clever (she sees her own cleverness as failing her in terms of her "wile," which also connotes manipulation), but tonally it is full and heartfelt. There is a thin line between Shakespearean wit and the narcissistic display of self-conscious wordplay: for this reader she successfully walks that line. The love of language in fact becomes her act of faith: language play becomes both a form of Eros and a displacement of it. In this final transformation, she knows that outside of this "depression"— and she can only name it, like an incantation—there is spring, light, and sleep. This line evokes, in tenor and substance, the end of Plath's "Tulips," which ends with "a country far away as health."

Recently, Davis has received considerable attention, having been labeled a "postconfessional" poet. The imprecise term doesn't really suit her work, and it seems to have different meanings for everyone who uses it. James Rother refers to the movement simply as a new generation of confessional writers (Rich, Olds, and Forché). Ellen Davis, in a review of a Rebecca Wolff collection, identifies it as "Confessional writing using experimental technique," which could very well describe Lowell's and Plath's poetry in the late 1950s, when both poets abandoned their more traditional subjects and styles to make public what was formerly private, to say "what happened" in colloquial diction.[2] Davis's entertaining the reader's voyeuristic pleasure (while meeting it with her own often self-conscious narcissistic display) might tempt some to emphasize the unorganized autobiographical details in her work; but as she says in her blog, "my kids, avgustyn 6 (augie, gobi, gogobee, goose, deck) and olyana 41/2 (lyana, lyalya, lyalyabee, little bean, lulu, lyali, lollipop) yes, hi! i really **am** a mother, (and/ but/so IS NOTHING SACRED TO YOU? IS EVERYTHING BLOG-ABLE????)"[3] Davis, like Lowell and Plath before her, sculpts these details, structurally and otherwise, for her art. In the above passage, as in many passages in her poems, she has it both ways: she transgresses socially acceptable boundaries for her art. Is she exempt from the capitalist urge for acquisition? Is she willing to use herself as an example of the consequential damage that appropriating experience does to oneself and others? As discomfiting as the above passage may be, and as much as a reader may judge it, the answer is yes: Olena Kalytiak Davis self-consciously uses experience to make her art; it's the danger and pleasure of confession, heightened in an age where confession has so much currency, from TV talk shows to celebrity blogs to magazines at the supermarket checkout to poets who confess in *Poetry* magazine that they've become practicing Catholics. One difference between Davis and a number of other confessional writers is that she also critiques the practice, making her use of the personal (and to quote Alice Notley, "who knows what's really true?") illuminating, elusive, and disconcerting all at once.[4] It implicates the reader in the corruption. We ask, who's the author? Who's the person? Why are we seduced into the latter when it is the interchange between the two that makes the artist's work live? Isn't there an element of appropriation in all art, and where does one draw the line about what can be used and what can't?

In some of her most recent work, including "The Lyric 'I' Drives to Pick Up Her Children from School: A Poem in the Postconfessional Mode," which appeared in *Fence*, Davis parodies the postmodern tenet that the "I" is socially constructed, that there is no identity or writing self; at the same time, she employs modernist and postmodernist strategies to expose process, including Freudian slips and crossings out, to include notes for the poem. She creates wide-ranging dictions both to satirize and appropriate high art. In responding to a comment that poet Cate Marvin made about her work, Davis writes on her *Poetry* blog, "which leads me to cate's remark about everyone having to have 'a' tradition, and thinking my work based on not really being able to find a one. . . . but maybe, the anxiety of influence, that there must be a profound and complex act of misreading (but does it have to be of poetry texts?) and that 'that reading is likely to be idiosyncratic and it is almost certain to be AMBIVALENT.'"[5] Her declaration, finding an ambivalent place in relation to any tradition, is crucial because it leads her to parse strategies from a variety of sources and movements, while never—even in a single poem—forming an allegiance to one. Her ambivalence seems less an expression of exile than one of fragmentation and—in Freudian terms—the infantile oral desire to absorb the world and not differentiate between self and other. So while she finds correspondences with the self everywhere and nowhere, her ambivalence also underlines the dilemma of the value and limit of history and traditions (other people's stories) in instructing us how to live.

Later in "the lyric 'i,'" using dada techniques, aping the random, she glosses the poem's conflict at the same time she enacts it. The "i"—in quotation marks because the lyric speaker experiences no unity but a set of contradictions—seeks to plait meanings for her sexuality, her intellect versus her intuition, her love of language as a vehicle of exploration and distraction. While the confessional poem appears to detail many experiences, the speaker also points out to us that the "autobiographical poem" "mythologizes the poet's life in accordance with the conventions of this time. It relates not what has occurred but what should have occurred, presenting an idealized image of the poet as representative of his literary school."

> *i lost my sex / poem!*
> *how did it go?*
> *i know it was called*

> SEX

> *something about my bosky acres,*
> *my unshrubb'd down*
> *'bout all being tight and yare*
> *'bout all being tight and yare*

> *(bring in tiresias?)*
> *did you say soothe?*
> *tiresias, who ~~lies~~ fucking more?*
> *whoops.*

> *who likes fucking more?*

> *("bring in / / the old thought / / (allen grossman doing yeats)*
> *that life prepares us for / / what never happens")*

She interrupts the middle of the poem, declaring a dailiness that might or might not be true: picking up her kids from school, being looked at by men in a truck, looking at a mountain range fantasizing about her ambivalent relationship to her own sexuality and gender (sometimes female identified, sometimes male identified).

"i" also likes "human drama".

"i" really enjoyed "i ♥ huckabees".

"i" thought sex was overrated for a long time, then not for a year and a half, and now, again.

"i" gives, well, has given, good head.

"i" takes it like a man.

. . . .

"i" remembers that "as long ago as 1925, boris tomashevsky, a leading Russian formalist critic, observed that the 'autobiographical poem' is one that mythologizes the poet's life in accordance with the conventions of this time. it relates not what has occurred but what should have occurred, presenting an idealized image of the poet as representative of his literary school".

"i" wants to be a man like Marjorie perloff, helen hennessy vendler, boris tomashevsky.

"i" thinks, on the other hand, "i mean i like in art when the artist doesn't know what he knows in general; he only knows what he knows specifically".

"i" thinks: "that mantel piece is clean enough or my name isn't bob rauschenberg".

"i" just wishes "i" could talk more smarter theory, no

"i" just wishes "i" could write more smarter poems, no

"i" thinks "WHY I AM A POET AND NOT A . . ."

"i" thinks "KALYTIAK DAVIS PAINTS A PICTURE".

"i" wants to include the word 'coruscate' in it, and, possibly, a quote from Rudolf Steiner.

"i" wishes she could remember abram's definition of the structure of the greater romantic lyric, but that it presents "a determinate speaker in a particularized, and usually localized outdoor set-ting, whom we overhear as he carries on, in a fluent vernacular which rises easily to a more formal speech, a sustained colloquy, sometimes with himself or with the outer scene, but more fre-quently with a silent human auditor, present or absent," and that "the speaker begins with a description of landscape;" and that "an aspect or change of aspect in the landscape evokes a varied but integral process of memory, thought anticipation, and feeling which remains closely involved with the outer scene," and that "in the course of this mediation the lyric speaker achieves an insight, faces up to a tragic loss, comes to a moral decision or resolves an emotional problem," and that "often the poem rounds upon itself to end where it began, at the outer scene, but with an altered mood and deepened understanding which is the result of the intervening mediation" evades her.

All this is heady stuff, but it is funny too, making use of techniques made famous by Ashbery, registering the mind in action. And while one might see limits to these stylistic devices, both in terms of effacing the social world and repeating a particular poetic strategy, Davis's poems are not intended to be merely clever. She is deadly serious in her inquiries and in her desire to authentically express the full range of her convictions, qualifications, contradictions, failures, and desires. In the process, while she structures her poems associatively, she almost always accounts for the structure for a poem and rarely loses sight of a central conflict. Her work is often dizzying, even breathtaking, all the more so because of her self-effacing playfulness, her conversational change of expressions, and her probing emotional intelligence; and in the mode of Frank O'Hara's poems, she is frankly sometimes a laugh riot.

Toward the end of "the lyric 'i'" all the threads return: the plot, picking up her daughter from school, her gender and sexuality worries, her parallel search for correspondence (including a quote from Bob Dylan), her wrestling with what is knowable about the self and other:

"i" loves "everything passes, everything changes, just do what you
    think you should do".
"i" thinks Dylan is singing to "i".
"i" thinks he means now, and now, and now; daily.
"i" is almost there.
"i" wonders if "i's" mediation is too long, has gotten away from "i".
"i" thinks it should take precisely as long as the ride: 15 minutes tops;
    well, 30 in a snowstorm.
"i" knows it is not snowing.
"i" wonders if "i" should at this point even refer to "i's" mediation.
"i" thinks "man can embody truth but he cannot know it".

"i" thinks "especially under stress of psychological crisis".

"i" thinks of the diaphragm still inside her.

"i" shutters at the audacity of her sex.

Just as the reader might shudder at the audacity of her poems. "I" is almost there, but always arriving.

Though this final chapter began by asserting that one measure of ambition in poetry is extension of the medium, it is not an endorsement of innovation *per se* as an aesthetic stance. As Dana Levin smartly implies in a recent *American Poetry Review* essay, experimentation for its own sake (i.e., dissociated from necessity) can become mere exercise. In current usage, Pound's "make it new" (the meaning of which varies from user to user) often suggests a naïve liberal view of poetry as making progress. Practically speaking, "making it new" often replicates what is current (notice the many books of poems that now carry their own "legitimizing" footnotes, or the plethora of so many numbingly impersonal end-stopped surreal poems). Levin is rightly skeptical of our "New World" romance with the new, and Levin tempers that newness by demonstrating how Pound looked back to the past to see and learn from what has been done. To echo Levin's last sentence, which also sheds light on one plausible justification for Davis's explicit use of covers in poetry, "Wherever innovation may take us, whatever closed region it may open, what Pound reminds us is this: to be original is not to be sourceless."[6]

There is also a counterdanger to innovation: stasis. Many poets are still writing Elizabeth Bishop's poems; many more poets write the same poems over and over again, using the same strategies and aesthetic principles they learned early in their writing careers. A capacity for formal change, then, assuming it is relational (i.e., triggered by some tangle of innerdrive, what we read, as well as experience in the world), helps poets mirror corresponding changes in experience, reflecting the growth of their own lives in their work. How can we use ritualized language to describe experience that alters what we already know?

On her blog Davis alludes to this concern and consciously grapples with it. She ungenerously speaks of her own first collection, which, on its own terms, is very good: "my first book was written completely in response to my contemporaries (not that i ever call or called them that), and especially my mentors. my mentors are few, are, like, four: mostly the poets i worked with when getting my mfa. i wrote most of the poems in that book while working with them, in reaction to the stuff they made me read (which was by and large contemporary) (which was, come to think of it, by and large by their friends)."[7] So it took courage to find her own way without abandoning her love of literature: she dug in and looked backward for ways to move her art ahead.

Davis's work requires a hybrid of traditions and their extensions to honor a world where language and experience are constantly shifting but have the power to teach and wound. As a lyric poet, Davis possesses an essential gift of using associative writing not to dissociate feeling from intellection but rather to make lyric connections *syntactically*, from word to word and sentence to sentence, eschewing the more linear powers of narrative. Implicit in her lyric vision, then, is a mistrust of causality, the fixing of trauma or pleasure to a locatable event (the signature virtue of plot). In the process, Davis's poems deflate a stock criticism of postmodern poetry: that representational poems have heart, while postmodern poems are all head. This kind of dualistic thinking is far too glib and defensive: it places consciousness and emotion as directly oppositional forces. One accesses and articulates feeling with an act of mind, and any poetry conscious of making choices engages in abstraction and intellection. Moreover, I have heard many a naïve student (and a few practicing poets who should know better) make similar criticisms of more traditional poets: they consider Stevens or Bishop poets similarly cerebral and short of feeling. The claim demonstrates, for one thing, an insensitivity to temperament (in Bishop's and Stevens's case, reticence is far from feelinglessness); a careless reader will miss Stevens's playfulness, his passion for embodiment and the sensual in poems like "The Snowman" or "Floral Decorations with Bananas," or his fears in poems like "Domination of Black." Temperament certainly plays a part in Davis's frenetic voicings, as does her discomfort in adhering to any particular tradition rather than creating an amalgam of ancestral voices combined with her own stylistic tics and concerns.

Davis's love of her medium and her desire to be inclusive, her willingness to take in the heartfelt wisdom of the past to address questions of identity and her relationship to others in the present, give urgency to her vision. At one point in "the lyric 'i'" poem, she says, "'i' wants to include the word 'coruscate'" in it and, "possibly, a quote from Rudolf Steiner." Her love of words, the impulse and import behind them, and her desire to make linkages argue for her love of poetry as a way to make discoveries and to sometimes avoid "trap[ping] under glass" the wondrous meanings they supply. Her apparent compulsion to sacrifice anything and everything for her art makes visible complicated poetic secrets and moral concerns in a quest for what Paul Tillich once called "higher meaning."[8] And there lies the true meaning of transcendence: not leaving the body, but dwelling in the world of language and the language of the world not only to recreate experience but also to create it.

NOTES

INTRODUCTION

1. Ralph Waldo Emerson, "The Poet," Essays: Second Series (1844), http://www.emersoncentral.com/poet.htm.

2. Lyn Hejinian, "The Rejection of Closure," *The Language of Inquiry* (Berkeley: Univ. of California Press, 2000), 47.

1. ON THE MARGINS: *Verse Poems*

1. Robert Lowell, "Epilogue," *Day by Day* (New York: Farrar, Strauss, & Giroux, 1977).

2. ON THE MARGINS: *Prose Poems*

1. Michael Benedikt, introduction to *Twenty Prose Poems* (San Francisco: City Lights, 1988), iv.

2. Harryette Mullen, in an interview with Cynthia Hogue, has called it "the mongrel text." "Mullen's idea of this kind of hybrid poetry is that there are different registers of language, cultures—high and low—spliced and interlaced together textually. For example, in her book, *Muse & Drudge* . . . we noticed the use of the Greek poet Callimachus (c310–c240 BC) next to Sapphire (Sapphire Stevens, a figure from the popular radio and television show 'Amos & Andy,' 1928–1956) as well as uses of the Greek poet Sappho. And we noticed the movement in and out of languages and registers of discourse, like the blues." Mullen, quoted in Hogue, "Three Conversations with Mei-mei Berssenbrugge," *Jacket Magazine* 27, http://jacketmagazine.com/27/hint-bers.html.

3. David Mason, *The Hudson Review* 58, no. 2 (2005): 321.

4. Conversation with Elvin Jones, May 1976, Cincinnati, Ohio.

5. Laura Bardwell, "Anne Waldman's 'Both Both,'" *Jacket Magazine* 27, jacketmagazine.com/27/w-bard.html.

6. Lyn Hejinian, "Two Auckland Talks," University of Auckland, March 21 and 23, 1995. www.nzepc.auckland.ac.nz/misc/hejinian1.asp.

7. *Colorado Review* 28, no. 2 (2001): 78. A revision of this piece, much preferred by the author, appears in her *Romance Erector* (Dalkey Archive Press, 2001).

3. MIXED MESSAGES: *Hearing Voices*

1. I. A. Richards, quoted in "Tone," by Fabian Gudus and T. V. F. Brogan, *New Princeton Encyclopedia of Poetry and Poetics* (Berkeley: University Presses of California, Columbia, and Princeton, 1993), 1293.

2. Ellen Voigt, *The Flexible Lyric: The Life of Poetry* (Athens: University of Georgia Press, 1999), 91.

3. Mikhail Bakhtin, *The Dialogic Imagination: Four Essays*, ed. Michael Holquist, trans. Caryl Emerson and Michael Holquist (Austin: University of Texas Press, 1981), 293.

4. Bakhtin, *The Dialogic Imagination*, 21.

5. Linda M. Park-Fuller, "Voices: Bakhtin's Heteroglossia and Polyphony, and the Performance of Narrative Literature," *Literature in Performance* 7 (1986): 1–12. http://www.csun.edu/~vcspc00g/604/voices-lpf.html.

6. Robert Motherwell, quoted in http://quote.robertgenn.com/auth _search.php?authid=67.

7. Christian Wiman, "The Sonnet: Fourteen Fragments in Lieu of a Review," *Sewanee Review* 109, no. 4 (2001): 843–47.

8. Liners notes to *Chopin and Mendelssohn Cello Sonatas*, Mercury Presence LP SR90320 (1956); Wiman, "The Sonnet," 647.

4. FORM: *Neoformalism Revisited*

1. My first essay on the subject appeared as "Neo-Formalism: A Dangerous Nostalgia," in *The Ira Sadoff Reader* (Middletown, CT: University of New England Press, 1991).

2. James Weldon Johnson, ed., preface to *The Book of American Negro Poetry: 1922.* http://www.bartleby.com/269/1000.html.

3. Langston Hughes, "The Negro Artist and the Racial Mountain," *The Nation,* June 23, 1926, 692–94; W. E. B. DuBois, "Criteria of Negro Art." DuBois initially spoke these words at a celebration for the recipient of the Twelfth Spingarn Medal, Carter Godwin Woodson. Reprinted in *The Crisis* (October 1926): 291.

4. David Mason, "The Poetry Circus," *The Hudson Review* 60, no. 1 (2007). http://www.hudsonreview.com/masonSp07.pdf., p.1.

5. PhilosophyArchive.com. http://www.philosophyarchive.com/concept. php?philosophy=Aesthetics.

6. Robert Wicks, *Stanford Encyclopaedia of Philosophy.* http://plato
.stanford.edu/entries/schopenhauer/.

7. David Mason, "A Prince in Motley," review of *Peeping Tom's Cabin: Comic Verse 1928–2008*, by X. J. Kennedy, *Contemporary Poetry Review* (2008). http://
www.cprw.com/Mason/Kennedy.htm.

8. Charles Harper Webb, "The Poem as Fitness Display," *AWP Chronicle*, March–April 2008. http://www.ryangvancleave.com/articles/webb_poem_
as_fitness.htm. Webb uses the term "elite" no fewer than ten times in the essay.

9. American Academy of Poets, Poets.Org. http://www.poets.org/view
media.php/prmMID/19294.

10. Gary Waserman, "Ragtime," in *Jazz: New Perspectives on the History of Jazz*, ed. Nat Hentoff and Albert J. McCarthy (New York: Rinehart, 1959), 44.

11. http://www.wcupa.edu/poetryconference/philmag.html.

12. The Original Hip-Hop Lyrics Archive http://www.ohhla.com/
anonymous/504_boyz/ballers/holla.504.txt.

13. I mention elsewhere that poems are culturally specific, so I don't include British and Irish poets here, since their traditions and histories differ from American literature. And while British literature generally seems weighed down by tradition, it is difficult to find British poets writing successfully in received forms: Douglass Dunn and Simon Armitage are possible exceptions who live up to the Larkin generation of British poets. Irish poets' resistance is still very much caught up in the formal, just as Mayakovsky's generation wrote formally in Russia to protest a repressive dominant culture.

14. John Rockwell, "Help for the Old and Safe, Neglect for the New and Challenging," *New York Times*, February 13, 2004. http://query.nytimes.com/
gst/fullpage.html?res=9D0CE2DF133AF930A25751C0A9629C8B63&sec=&
spon=&pagewanted=2.

5. HISTORY MATTERS: *A Minority Report*

1. Russell Banks, "Sarah Cole: A Type of Love Story," in *Success Stories* (New York: Harper Perennial, 1996), 160.

2. Pamela J. Annas, "The Self in the World: The Social Context of Sylvia Plath's Late Poems," *Women's Studies* 7, no. 1–2 (1980): 171; emphasis added.

3. Frantz Fanon, *Black Skin, White Masks,* trans. Charles Markmann (New York: Grove Press, 1967), 23.

4. Barbara Hardy, from Modern American Poetry Web site, quoted from *The Survival of Poetry: A Contemporary Survey* (London: Faber and Faber, 1970). http://www.english.uiuc.edu/Maps/poets/m_r/plath/tulips.htm.

5. Mao Tse-Tung, *Quotations from Chairman Mao*, first pocket ed., 1. http://www.art-bin.com/art/omao22.html.

6. LOUISE GLÜCK: *The Death of Romanticism*

1. Albert Gelpi, "The Genealogy of Postmodernism: Contemporary American Poetry," *Southern Review* 26, no 3 (Summer 1990): 517–18.

2. Charles Feidelson, introduction to *The Modern Tradition: Backgrounds of Modern Literature* (New York: Oxford Univ. Press, 1965). http://www.noteaccess.com/THEMES/SymbolismMT.htm.

3. Feidelson, introduction to *The Modern Tradition*.

4. Theodor Adorno, "Cultural Criticism and Society," in *Prisms*, trans. Samuel Weber and Shierry Weber (Cambridge, MA: MIT Press, 1967), 24.

5. Gelpi, "Genealogy of Postmodernism," 518.

6. Gelpi, "Genealogy of Postmodernism," 518.

7. Kenneth J. Gergen, *The Saturated Self* (New York: Basic Books, 1991), 184.

7. TRAFFICKING IN THE RADIANT: *The Spiritualizing of American Poetry*

1. Paul Tillich, *The New Being* (Omaha, NE: Bison Books), ch.8.

2. Nicholas Lehman, "Fear and Favor," *The New Yorker*, February 14–21, 2005, 176.

3. http://www.thearda.com/arda.asp.

4. Richard Morin, "Do Americans Believe in God?" *The Washington Post*, April 24, 2000. http://www.washingtonpost.com/wp-srv/politics/polls/wat/archive/wat042400.htm.

5. June Mears Driedger, "Spirituality According to Oprah," 43–44. http://www.mennovision.org/driedger.pdf.

6. Book description on Amazon Web site. http://www.amazon.com/Emotional-House-Redesigning-Your-Change/dp/1572244089.

7. Book description on Amazon Web site.

8. Elaine Scarry, *The Body in Pain: The Making and Unmaking of the World* (New York: Oxford University Press, 1987). http://www.ufobreakfast.com/archive/00000075.htm.

9. Poetry Daily Web site, http://www.poems.com/threewil.htm. It should be noted that Wilbur's poems employ wider-ranging strategies: I'm interested here in what elements of Wilbur's poems form the current celebration of his work.

10. An image of the painting can be found at http://www.wga.hu/frames–e.html?/html/b/bonifaci/index.html.

11. Cynthia Ozick, A Critic at Large, "T. S. ELIOT AT 101," *The New Yorker*, November 20, 1989, 119; emphasis added.

12. Marjorie Perloff, *21st Century Modernism: The "New" Poetics* (Boston: Wiley-Blackwell, 2002), 163.

13. Mark Rudman, "Reading T. S. Eliot at My Cousin's Farm in the Gatineau," *American Poetry Review* 33, no. 5 (2004): 55.

14. T. S. Eliot, *Christianity and Culture* (1948; rpt., San Diego: Harcourt, 1988), 10. The remark was made in 1938, at a time when it was known that Jews were—to put it mildly—exiled and exported from German culture.

15. T. S. Eliot, lecture at the University of Virginia, 1933; printed in *After Strange Gods* (1934); withdrawn after that.

16. Rudman, "Reading T. S. Eliot," 55.

17. T. S. Eliot, "Introduction," *The Criterion*, April, 1932.

18. Eliot, *Selected Essays* (London: Faber and Faber, 1952), 473.

19. Philip Yancey, "T. S. Eliot's Christian Society: Still Relevant Today?" *Christian Century*, November 19, 1986, 1031. http://www.religion-online.org/showarticle.asp?title=1076; emphasis added.

20. Austin Cline, "Agnosticism/Atheism." http://atheism.about.com/library/FAQs/religion/blrel_freud_helplessness.htm; quoting Sigmund Freud, *The Future of an Illusion*, vol. 21, *The Standard Edition of the Complete Psychological Works of Sigmund Freud*, trans. James Strachey (London: Hogarth Press, 1968), 146. http://www61.homepage.villanova.edu/kevin.hughes/documents/sigmund_freud.htm.

21. Freud, *Totem and Taboo.* http://www.faithnet.org.uk/Science/Psychology/freudreligion.htm.

22. Halvorson, Peter L., *Atlas of Religious Change in America, 1952–1990* (Atlanta, GA: Glenmary Research Center, 1994).

23. Jean Paul Sartre, "Existentialism is a Humanism." http://www.marxists.org/reference/archive/sartre/works/exist/sartre.htm.

8. CZESŁAW MIŁOSZ: *The Late Style*

1. Edward Said, *On Late Style: Music and Literature against the Grain* (New York: Pantheon, 2006), 7.

2. Michael Wood, introduction to Said, *On Late Style*, xii.

3. Said, *On Late Style*, 10.

4. Said, *On Late Style*, 8.

5. Wood, introduction to Said, *On Late Style*, xii.

6. Said, *On Late Style*, 12.

7. Czesław Miłosz, *A Year of the Hunter* (New York: Noonday, 1995), as quoted in the Internet Poetry Archive, "Biography: Czesław Miłosz." http://www.ibiblio.org/ipa/poems/milosz/biography.php.

9. STRATEGIC FICTIONS: *The Mobile Architecture of Frank O'Hara's Poetry*

1. Mark Tursi, "Interrogating Culture: Critical Hermeneutics in the Poetry of Frank O'Hara," *The Nieve Roja Review* 4. http://nieveroja.colostate.edu/issue4/ohara.htm.

2. Lytle Shaw, *Frank O'Hara: The Poetics Of Coterie* (Iowa City: Univer-

sity of Iowa Press, 2006). http://www.uipress.uiowa.edu/books/2006-spring/fraoh.htm.

3. Friedrich Nietzsche, *Human, All too Human*, trans. R. J. Hollingsdale, 2nd ed. (Cambridge: Cambridge Univ. Press, 1977), 261.

10. C. K. WILLIAMS AND JOHN ASHBERY: *On the Edge of Romanticism and Postmodernism*

1. John Hartmann, "Nietzsche's Use of Metaphor." http://www.geocities.com/Athens/1575/nmetafor.html.

2. Hartmann, "Nietzsche's Use of Metaphor."

3. Frank J. Lepkowski, "John Ashbery's Revision of the Post-Romantic Quest: Meaning, Evasion, and Allusion in 'Grand Galop.'" *Twentieth Century Literature* 39 (1993): 174.

11. OLENA KALYTIAK DAVIS: *Revising Tradition—the Retro-New*

1. Olena Kalytiak Davis Poetry Foundation Blog. http://www.poetryfoundation.org/dispatches/journals/2006.01.30.html.

2. James Rother, quoted by Ellen Davis, review of *Figment*, by Rebecca Wolff. http://hcl.harvard.edu/harvardreview/27/wolff_review.html.

3. Olena Kalytiak Davis Blog. http://www.poetryfoundation.org/dispatches/journals/2006.01.30.html.

4. Alice Notley, "Experience," in *The Mysteries of Small Houses* (New York: Penguin, 1988), 19.

5. Olena Kalytiak Davis Blog. http://www.poetryfoundation.org/dispatches/journals/2006.01.30html#Tuesday.

6. Dana Levin, "The Heroics of Style: A Study in Three Parts," *American Poetry Review* 35, no. 2 (March/April 2006): 47. http://www.aprweb.org/issues/mar06/levin.html.

7. Olena Kalytiak Davis Blog. http://www.poetryfoundation.org/dispatches/journals/2006.01.30.html, comments response.

8. Tillich, *The New Being*.

WORKS CITED

Adorno, Theodor W. *Prisms*. Translated. by Samuel Weber and Shierry Weber. Cambridge, MA: MIT Press 1967.

Annas, Pamela J. "The Self in the World: The Social Context of Sylvia Plath's Late Poems." *Women's Studies* 7, no. 1–2 (1980): 171–83.

Ashbery, John. *Selected Poems*. New York: Penguin, 1986.

Bakhtin, Mikhail. *The Dialogic Imagination: Four Essays*. Edited by Michael Holquist, translated by Caryl Emerson and Michael Holquist. Austin: University of Texas Press, 1981.

Banks, Russell. *Success Stories*. New York: Harper Perennial, 1996.

Bardwell, Laura "Anne Waldman's 'Both Both.'" *Jacket Magazine* 27. http://www.jacketmagazine.com/27/w-bard.html.

Benedikt, Michael. *Twenty Prose Poems*. San Francisco: City Lights, 1988.

Bhabha, Homi K. "The Other Question: Difference, Discrimination, and the Discourse of Colonialism." *Literature, Politics, and Theory: Papers from the Essex Conference, 1976–1984*. Edited by Francis Barker, Peter Hulme, Margaret Iverson, and Diana Loxley. London: Metheun, 1986. 148–72.

Brown, Norman O. *Life against Death*. Middletown, CT: Wesleyan, 1985.

Coltrane, John. *Ascension*. New York: Polygram CD, 1965.

———. *Fearless Leader*. Berkeley, CA: Prestige CD, 2006.

Davis, Ellen. Review of *Figment*, by Rebecca Wolff. http://hcl.harvard.edu/harvardreview/27/wolff_review.html.

Davis, Olena Kalytiak. "The Lyric 'I' Drives to Pick Up Her Children from School: A Poem in the Postconfessional Mode." *Fence* 8, no. 1–2 (2005): 99–104.

———. *Shattered Sonnets, Love Cards, and Other Off and Back Handed Importunities*. New York: Bloomsbury, 2003.

Day, Jean. *The Literal World*. Berkeley, CA: Atelos, 1998.

Di Piero, W. S. *Brother Fire*. New York: Knopf, 2004.

Dickinson, Emily. *Final Harvest*. Boston: Backbay Books, 1974.

Du Bois, W. E. B. "Criteria of Negro Art." *The Crisis* 32 (October 1926): 291.

Dukas, Helen, and Banesh Hoffman. *Albert Einstein: The Human Side.* Princeton, NJ: Princeton University Press, 1979.

Dunn, Douglas. *New and Selected Poems.* New York: Ecco, 1988.

Eliot, T. S. *Christianity and Culture: The Idea of a Christian Society and Notes Towards the Definition of Culture.* New York: Harcourt Brace, 1949.

———. *The Complete Poems, 1909–1962.* New York: Harcourt Brace Jovanovich, 1991.

Emerson, Ralph Waldo. "The Poet." *Essays: Second Series (1844).* http://www.emersoncentral.com/poet.htm.

Fanon, Frantz. *Black Skin, White Masks.* Translated by Charles Lam Markmann. New York: Grove Press, 1967.

Feidelson, Charles. *The Modern Tradition: Backgrounds of Modern Literature* New York: Oxford University Press, 1965.

Freud, Sigmund. *Civilization and Its Discontents.* New York: Norton, 1989.

———. The Future of an Illusion. Vol. 21, *The Standard Edition of the Complete Psychological Works of Sigmund Freud.* Translated by James Strachey. London: Hogarth Press, 1968.

———. *Moses and Monotheism.* New York: Vintage, 1955.

———. *Totem and Taboo.* New York: Norton, 1950.

Galvin, James. *Elements: Poems.* Port Townsend, WA: Copper Canyon Press, 1988.

Gelpi, Albert. "The Genealogy of Postmodernism: Contemporary American Poetry." *Southern Review* 26, no. 3 (1990): 517–41.

Gergen, Kenneth J. *The Saturated Self.* New York: Basic Books, 1991.

Glück, Louise. *Ararat.* New York: Ecco Press, 1992.

———. *Descending Figure.* New York: Ecco Press, 1980.

———. *Firstborn.* New York: New American Library, 1968.

———. *The First Four Books of Poems.* New York: Ecco Press, 1995.

———. *The House on Marshland.* New York: Ecco Press, 1975.

———. *Meadowlands.* New York: Ecco Press, 1996.

———. *The Seven Ages.* New York: Ecco Press, 2001.

———. *The Triumph of Achilles.* New York: Ecco Press, 1985.

———. *Vita Nova.* New York: Ecco Press, 1995.

———. *Wild Iris.* New York: Ecco Press, 1993.

Gregg, Linda. *Too Bright to See.* Port Townsend, WA: Graywolf Press, 1981.

Guest, Barbara. *Fair Realism.* San Diego: Sun and Moon, 1989.

Hall, Donald, Robert Pack, and Louis Simpson. *The New Poets of England and America.* 1957. New York: Meridian Books, 1974.

Halvorson, Peter L. *Atlas of Religious Change in America, 1952–1990.* Atlanta, GA: Glenmary Research Center, 1994.

Hartmann, John. "Nietzsche's Use of Metaphor." http://www.geocities.com/Athens/1575/nmetafor.html.

Haydn, Josef. *Symphony Number 22.* Adam Fischer, Austro-Hungarian Orchestra. Budapest: Naxos, 2001.

Hejinian, Lyn. *The Language of Inquiry.* Berkeley: University of California Press, 2000.

———. *My Life.* Los Angeles: Green Integer, 2002.

———. "Two Auckland Talks." Lectures, University of Auckland, March 21 and 23, 1995. http://www.nzepc.auckland.ac.nz/misc/hejinian1.asp.

Hughes, Langston. *The Collected Poems of Langston Hughes.* Edited by Arnold Rampersad. New York: Vintage Books, 1995.

Jameson, Frederic. *The Political Unconscious.* Ithaca, NY: Cornell University Press, 1982.

Johnson, James Weldon, ed. *The Book of American Negro Poetry.* 1922. http://www.bartleby.com/269/1000.html.

Julius, Anthony. *T. S. Eliot, Anti-Semitism, and Literary Form.* New York: Cambridge University Press, 1995.

Kaufmann, Walter. *Existentialism from Dostoyevsky to Sartre.* New York: Meridian, 1957.

Keats, John. *The Complete Poems.* New York: Modern Library, 1994.

Komunyakaa, Yusef. *Dien Cai Dao.* Middletown, CT: Wesleyan University Press, 1988.

Kristeva, Julia. *Revolution in Poetic Language.* 1974. Translated by Leon S. Roudiez and Margaret Waller. New York: Columbia University Press, 1984.

Kyger, Joanne. *As Ever: New and Selected Poems.* New York: Penguin, 2002.

Lepkowski, Frank J. "John Ashbery's Revision of the Post-Romantic Quest: Meaning, Evasion, and Allusion in 'Grand Galop.'" *Twentieth Century Literature* 39 (1993): 251–65.

Levin, Dana. "The Heroics of Style: A Study in Three Parts." *American Poetry Review* 35, no. 2 (2006): 45–48.

Loeffelholz, Mary. *Dickinson and the Boundaries of Feminist Theory.* Urbana: University of Illinois Press, 1991.

Lowell, Robert. *Day by Day.* New York: Farrar, Strauss, and Giroux, 1997.

Lyotard, Jean-François. *The Postmodern Condition: A Report on Knowledge.* Minneapolis: University of Minnesota Press, 1984.

Mao Tse-Tung. *Quotations from Chairman Mao.* First pocket ed. http://art-bin.com/art/oma022.html.

Mason, David. "Poetry Round-Up." *Hudson Review* 58, no. 2 (2005): 321.

———. "A Prince in Motley." Review of *Peeping Tom's Cabin,* by X. J. Kennedy. *Contemporary Poetry Review* (2008). http://www.cprw.com/Mason/Kennedy.htm.

Miłosz, Czesław. *Collected Poems.* New York: Ecco Press, 1990.

———. *Second Space.* New York: Harper Collins, 2004.

———, ed. *Postwar Polish Poetry.* New York: Doubleday, 1965.

———. *A Year of the Hunter.* New York: Noonday, 1995.

Mullen, Harryette. *Sleeping with the Dictionary.* Berkeley: University of California Press, 2002.

New Princeton Encyclopedia of Poetry and Poetics. Edited by Alex Preminger and T. V. F. Brogan. Berkeley, New York, and Princeton: University Presses of California, Columbia, and Princeton, 1993.

Nietzsche, Friedrich. *Basic Writings of Nietzsche.* New York: Modern Library, 2000.

———. *Human, All too Human.* 2nd ed. Translated by R. J. Hollingsdale. Cambridge: Cambridge Univ. Press, 1997.

Notley, Alice. *The Mystery of Small Houses.* New York: Penguin, 1998.

O'Hara, Frank. *The Collected Poems of Frank O'Hara.* Edited by Donald Allen. Berkeley: University of California Press, 1995.

Park-Fuller, Linda M. "Voices: Bakhtin's Heteroglossia and Polyphony, and the Performance of Narrative Literature." *Literature in Performance* 7 (1986): 1–12.

Perloff, Marjorie. *Frank O'Hara: Poet among Painters.* New York: George Braziller, 1977.

———. *21st Century Modernism: The "New" Poetics.* Boston: Wiley-Blackwell, 2002.

Plath, Sylvia. *Ariel.* New York: Harper and Row, 1965.

Pollak, Vivian. *The Anxiety of Gender.* Ithaca, NY: Cornell University Press, 1986.

Raine, Craig. *T. S. Eliot: Image, Text, and Context.* New York: Oxford, 2006.

Rankine, Claudia. *Don't Let Me Be Lonely.* Minneapolis: Graywolf, 2004.

Richman, Robert. *The Direction of Poetry.* Boston: Houghton Mifflin, 1990.

Ritchie, Dawn, and Kathryn Robyn. *The Emotional House: How Redesigning Your Home Can Change Your Life.* Oakland: New Harbinger, 2005.

Rudman, Mark. "Reading T. S. Eliot at My Cousin's Farm in the Gatineau." *American Poetry Review* 33, no. 5 (2004): 47–58.

Sadoff, Ira. *The Ira Sadoff Reader.* Middletown, CT: Univ. of New England Press, 1991.

Said, Edward. *On Late Style: Music and Literature against the Grain.* New York: Pantheon, 2006.

Scarry, Elaine. *The Body in Pain: The Making and Unmaking of the World.* New York: Oxford University Press, 1987.

Shaw, Lytle. *Frank O'Hara: The Poetics of Coterie.* Iowa City: University of Iowa Press, 2006.

Slater, Philip. *The Pursuit of Loneliness.* 3rd ed. Boston: Beacon Press.

Steele, Timothy. *Missing Measures: Modern Poetry and the Revolt against Meter.* Fayetteville: University of Arkansas Press, 1990.

———. *Toward the Winter Solstice: New Poems.* Denver: Swallow, 2006.

Stein, Gertrude. *Three Lives and Tender Buttons.* New York: Signet, 2003.

———. *What are Masterpieces?* New York: Pitman, 1970.

Taylor, Judith. *Curios.* Lexington, KY: Sarabande, 2000.

Tursi, Mark. "Interrogating Culture: Critical Hermeneutics in the Poetry of Frank O'Hara." *The Nieve Rioja Review* 4. http://nieverioja.colostate.edu/issue4/ohara.htm.

Vogelsang, Arthur. *Left Wing of a Bird*. Lexington, KY: Sarabande, 2003.

Voigt, Ellen. *The Flexible Lyric: The Life of Poetry*. Athens: University of Georgia Press, 1999.

Wagner, Linda. *Critical Essays on Sylvia Plath*. Boston: G. K. Hall, 1984.

Waldman, Anne. *Marriage: A Sentence*. New York: Penguin, 2000.

Waserman, Gary. "Ragtime." In *Jazz: New Perspectives on the History of Jazz*, edited by Nat Hentoff and Albert J. McCarthy, 44. New York: Rinehart, 1959.

Webb, Charles Harper. "The Poem as Fitness Display." *AWP Chronicle*, March–April 2008.

Whitman, Walt. *Leaves of Grass*. Edited by Sculley Bradley and Harold W. Blodgett. New York: Norton, 1973.

Wicks, Robert. *Standford Encyclopedia of Philosophy*. http://plato.stanford.edu/entries/schopenhauer/.

Williams, C. K. *Tar*. New York: Farrar, Strauss, and Giroux, 1983.

———. *The Singing*. New York: Farrar, Strauss, and Giroux, 2004.

Williams, Diane. "Dear Ears, Mouth, Eyes, and Hindquarters." *Colorado Review* 28, no. 2 (2001): 78.

Wiman, Christian, "The Sonnet: Fourteen Fragments in Lieu of a Review." *Sewanee Review* 109, no. 4 (2001): 643–47.

Wright, James. *Above the River*. New York: Farrar, Strauss, and Giroux, 1990.

Yancey, Philip. "T. S. Eliot's Christian Society: Still Relevant Today?" *Christian Century*, November 19, 1986. http://www.religion-online.org/showarticle.asp?title=1076.

Young, Dean. *Design with X*. Middletown, CT: Wesleyan University Press, 1988.